CLAMP

8

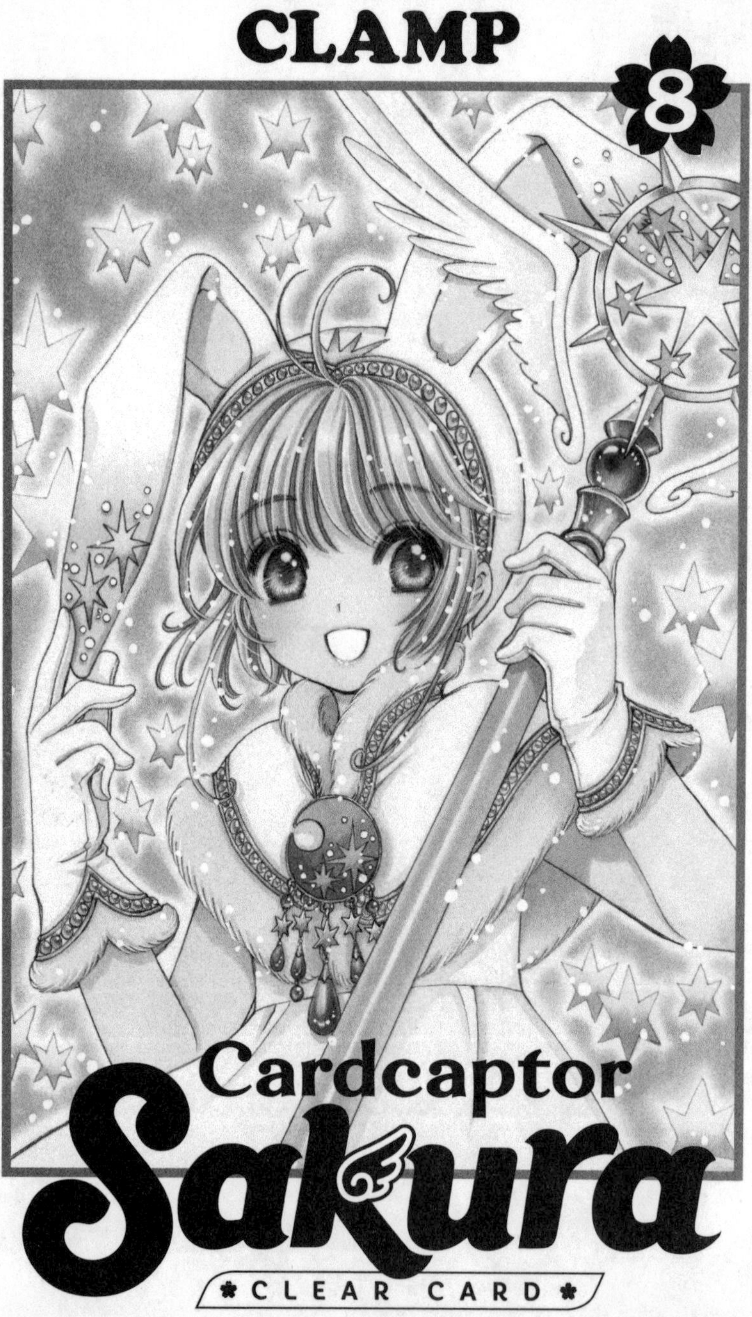

Cardcaptor Sakura

CLEAR CARD

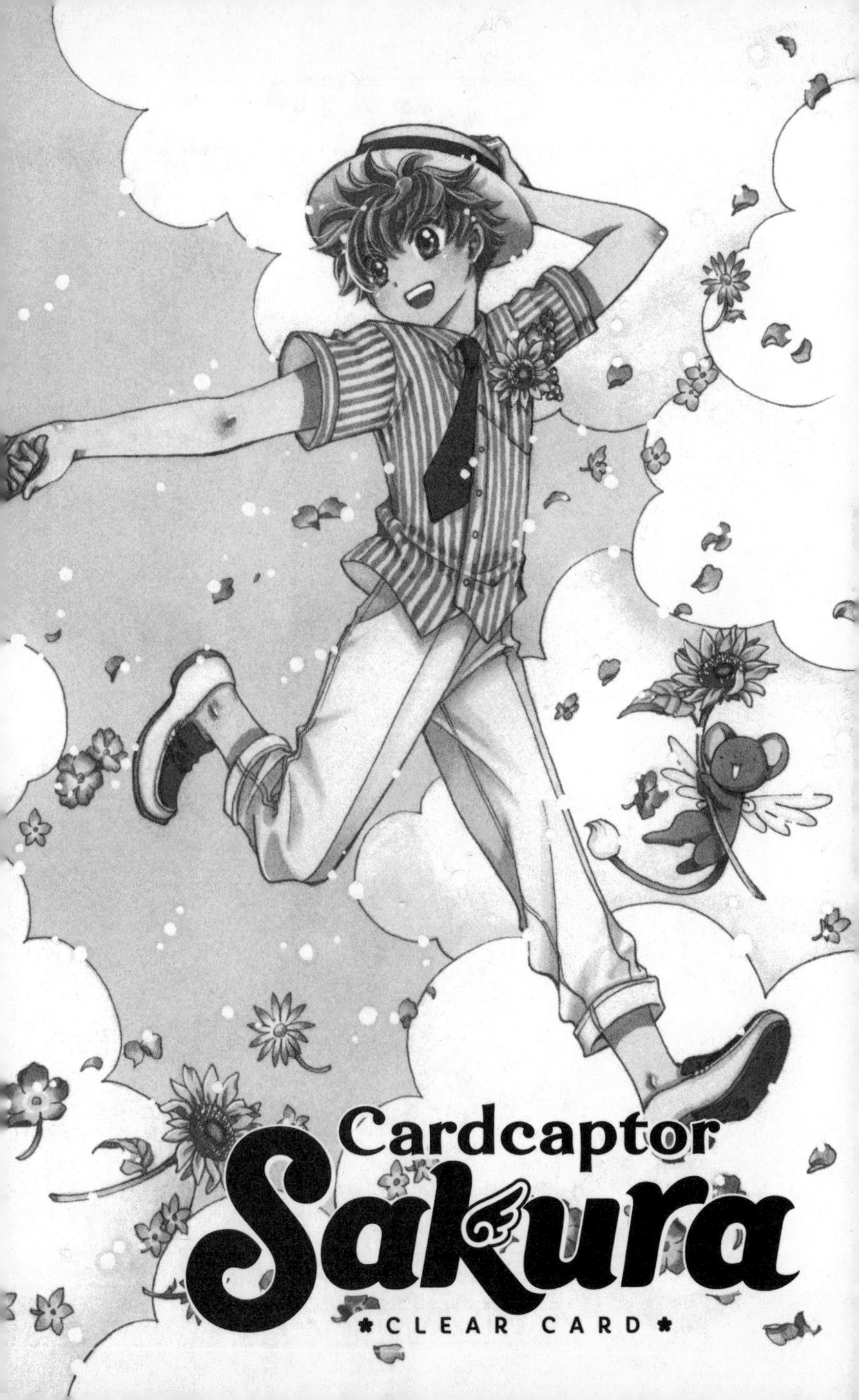
Cardcaptor
Sakura
CLEAR CARD

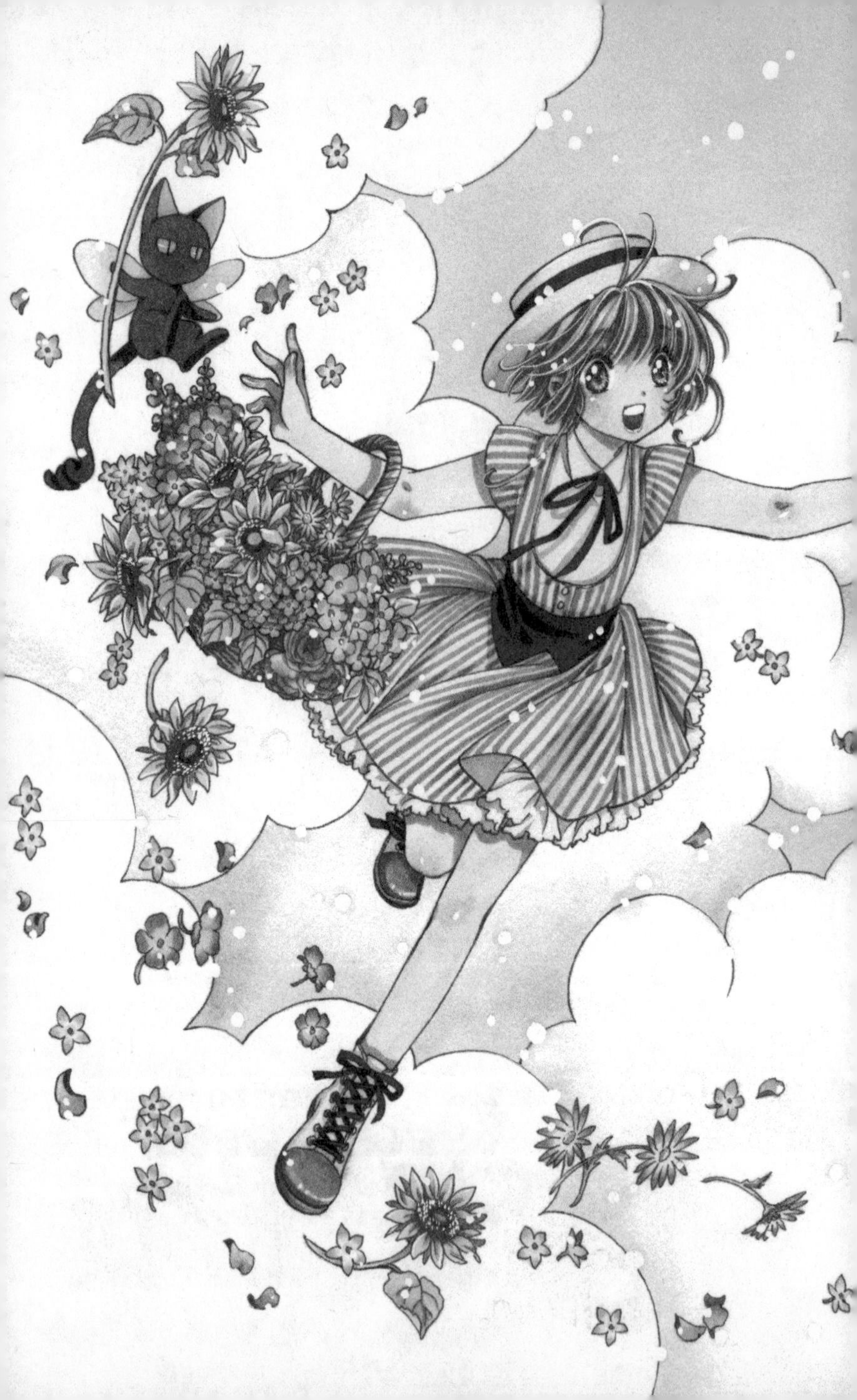

Cardcaptor Sakura

CLEAR CARD

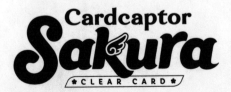

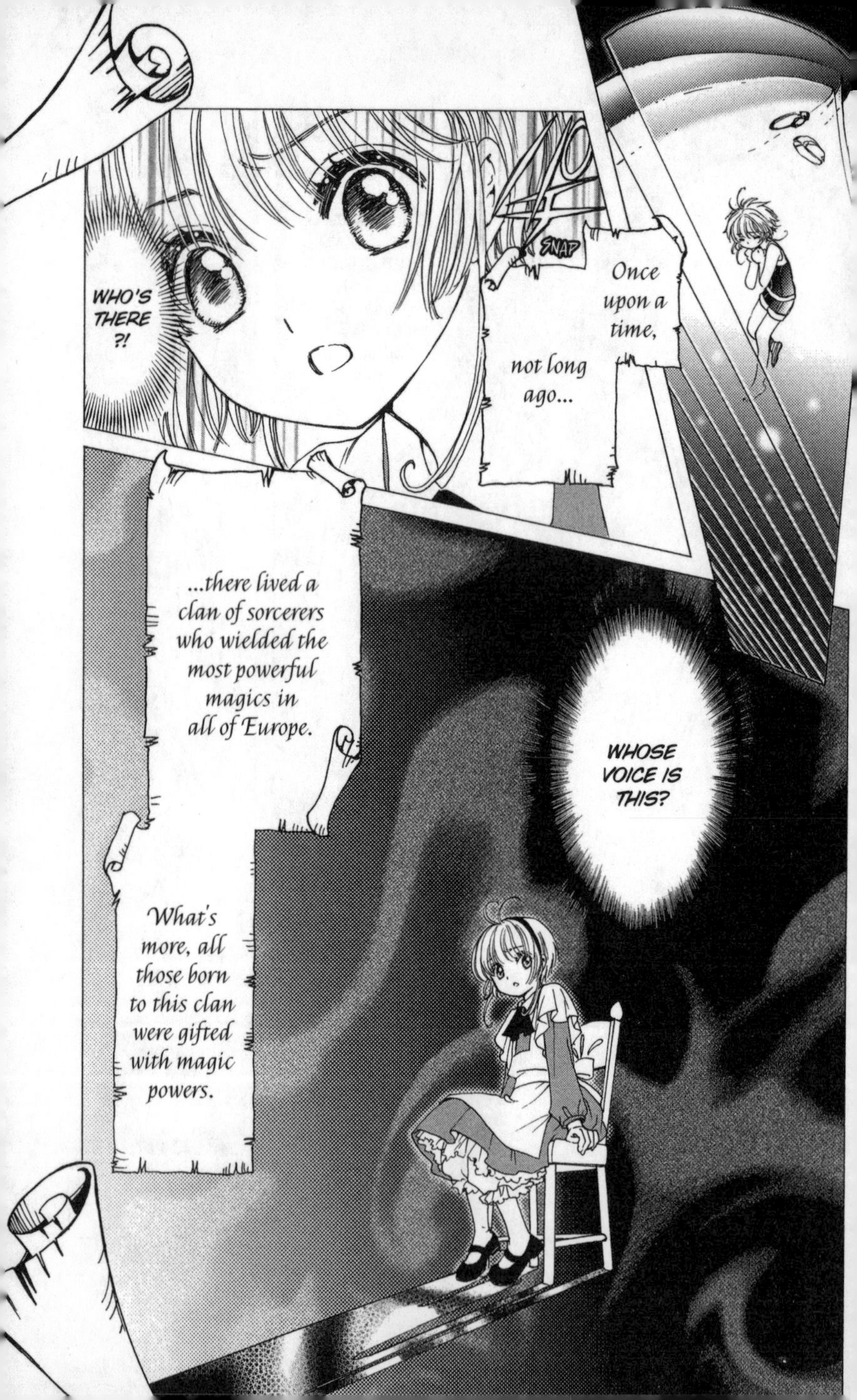
SNAP
Once upon a time,
not long ago...
WHO'S THERE ?!
...there lived a clan of sorcerers who wielded the most powerful magics in all of Europe.
WHOSE VOICE IS THIS?
What's more, all those born to this clan were gifted with magic powers.

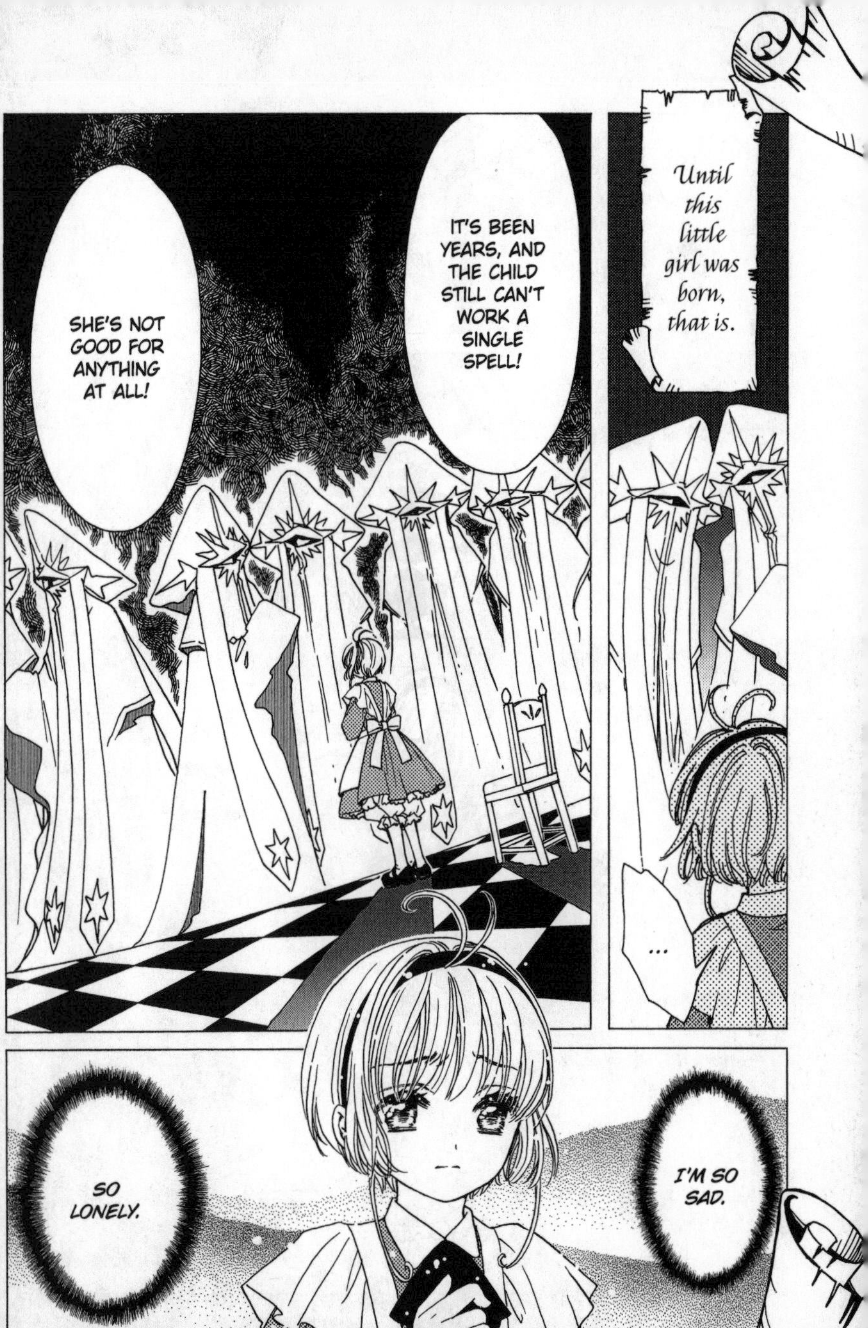
Until this little girl was born, that is.
...
IT'S BEEN YEARS, AND THE CHILD STILL CAN'T WORK A SINGLE SPELL!
SHE'S NOT GOOD FOR ANYTHING AT ALL!
I'M SO SAD.
SO LONELY.

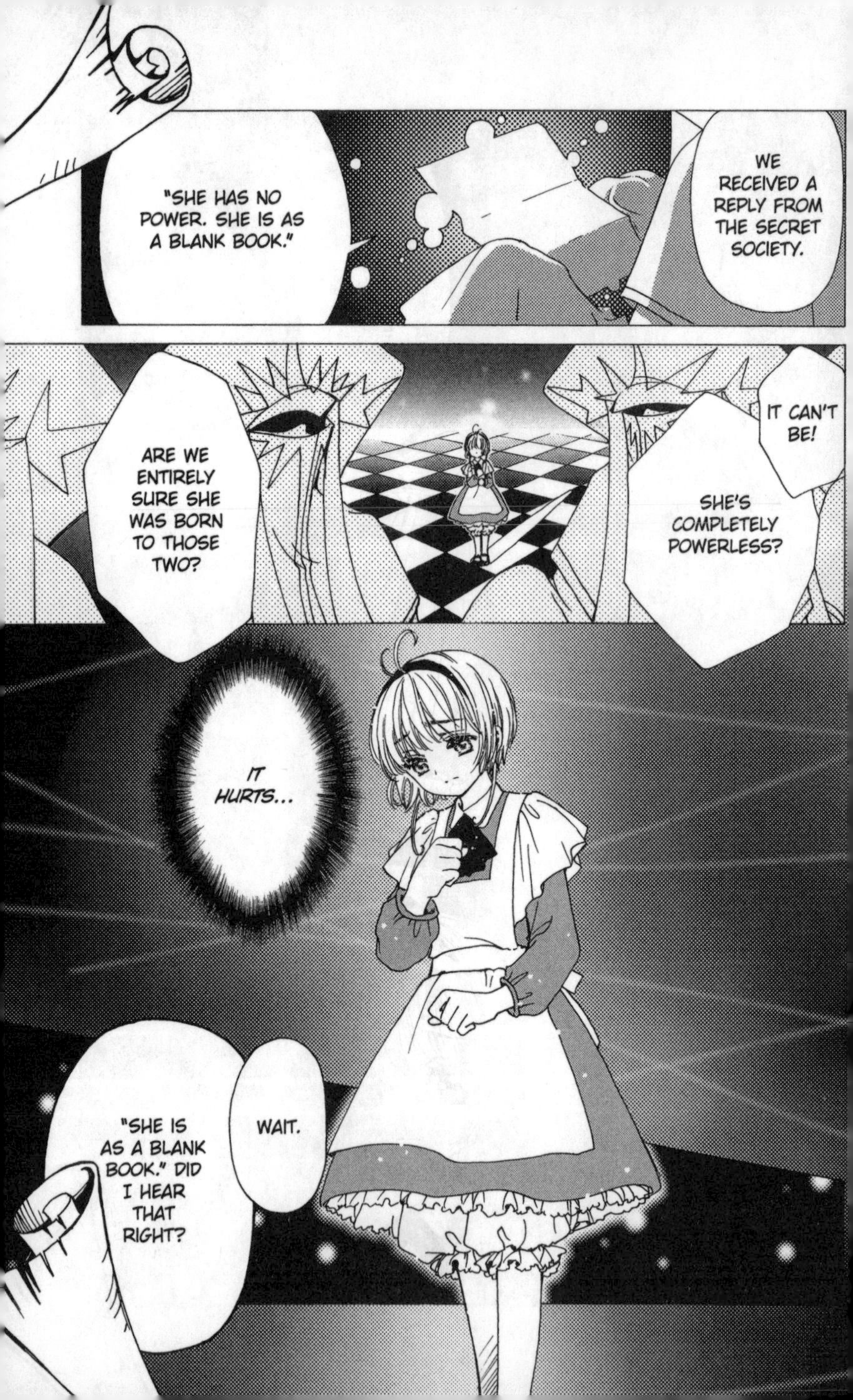
WE RECEIVED A REPLY FROM THE SECRET SOCIETY.
"SHE HAS NO POWER. SHE IS AS A BLANK BOOK."
IT CAN'T BE!
SHE'S COMPLETELY POWERLESS?
ARE WE ENTIRELY SURE SHE WAS BORN TO THOSE TWO?
IT HURTS...
WAIT.
"SHE IS AS A BLANK BOOK." DID I HEAR THAT RIGHT?

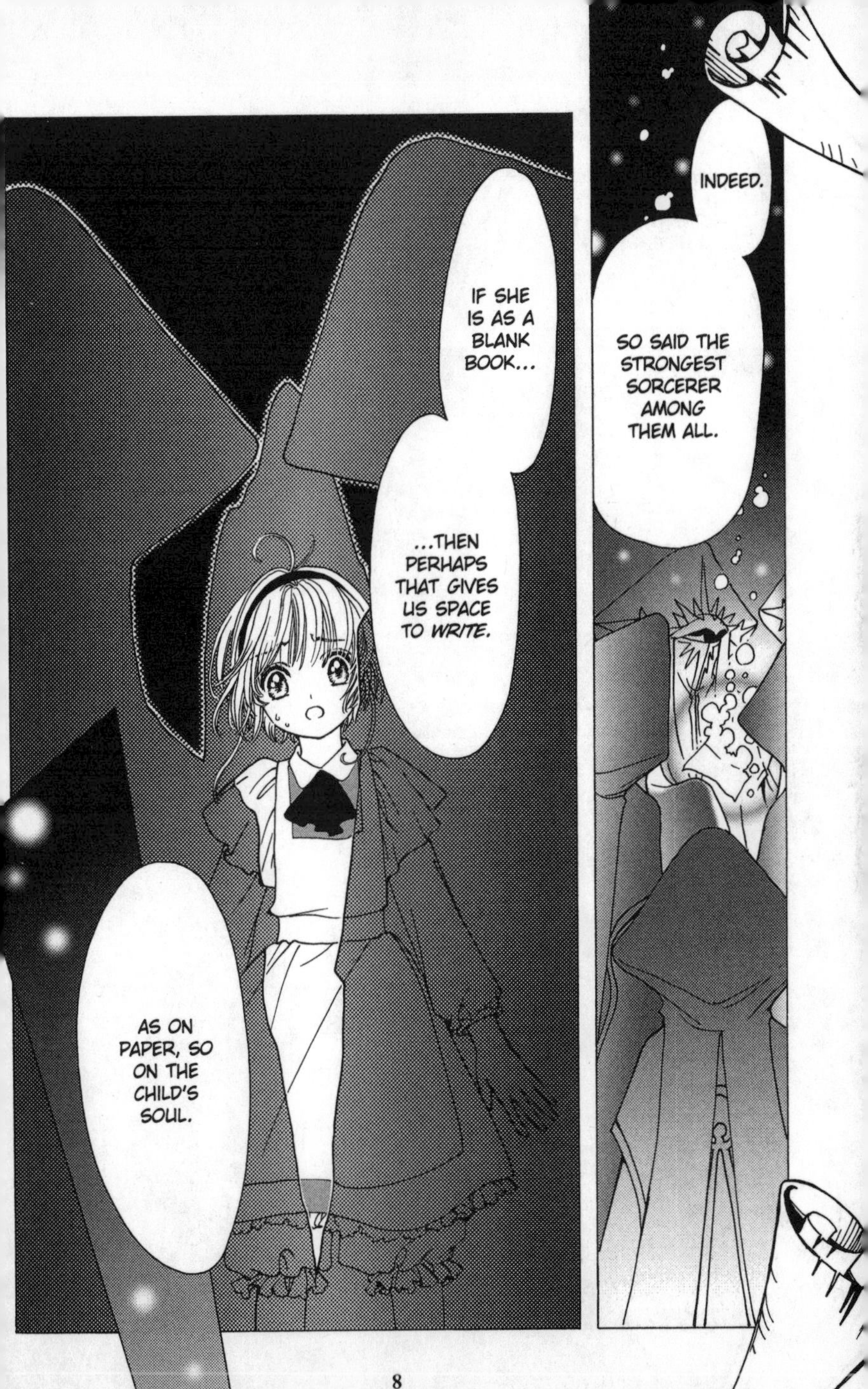
INDEED.
SO SAID THE STRONGEST SORCERER AMONG THEM ALL.
IF SHE IS AS A BLANK BOOK...
...THEN PERHAPS THAT GIVES US SPACE TO *WRITE*.
AS ON PAPER, SO ON THE CHILD'S SOUL.

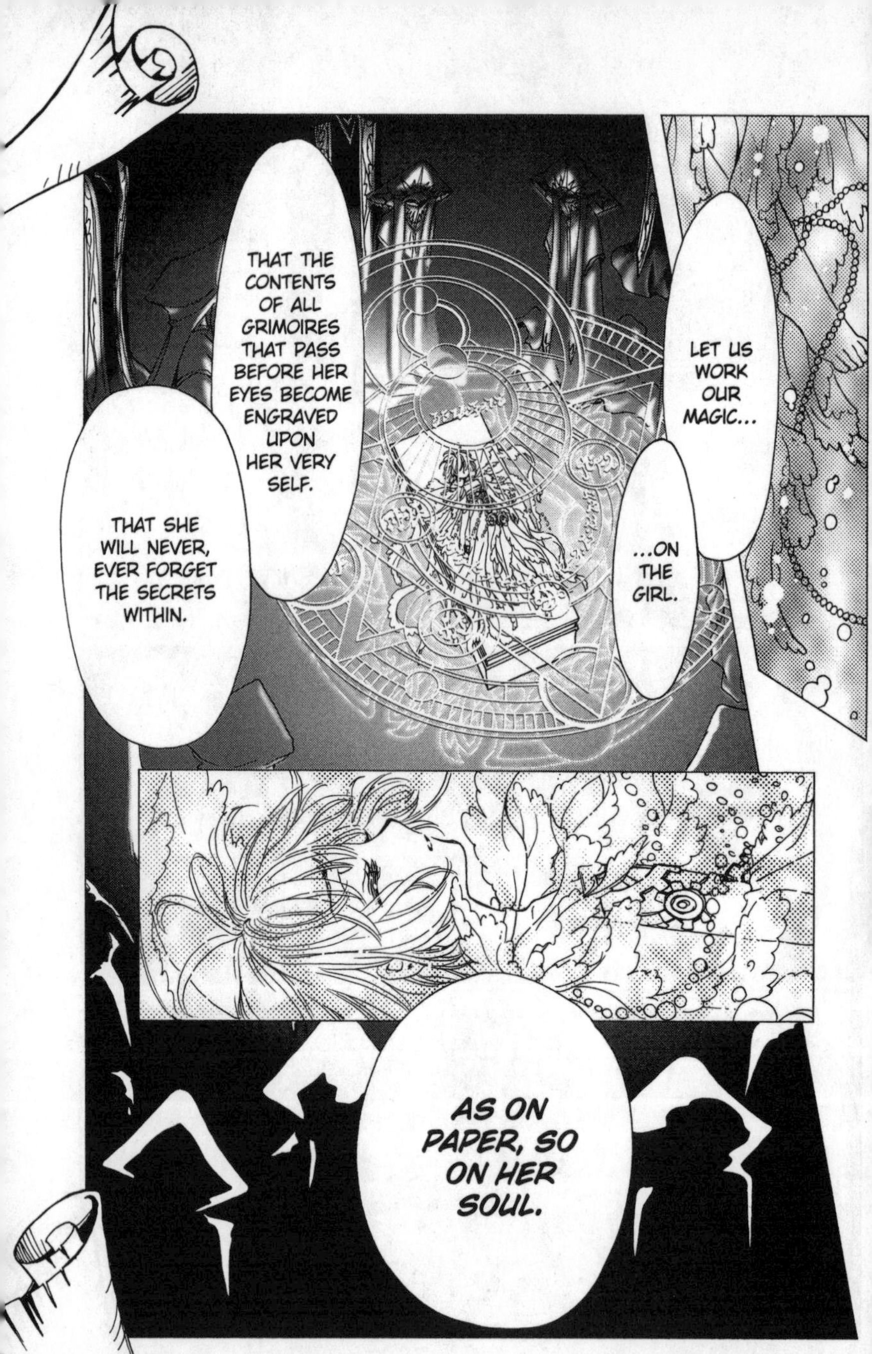
LET US WORK OUR MAGIC...
...ON THE GIRL.
THAT THE CONTENTS OF ALL GRIMOIRES THAT PASS BEFORE HER EYES BECOME ENGRAVED UPON HER VERY SELF.
THAT SHE WILL NEVER, EVER FORGET THE SECRETS WITHIN.
AS ON PAPER, SO ON HER SOUL.

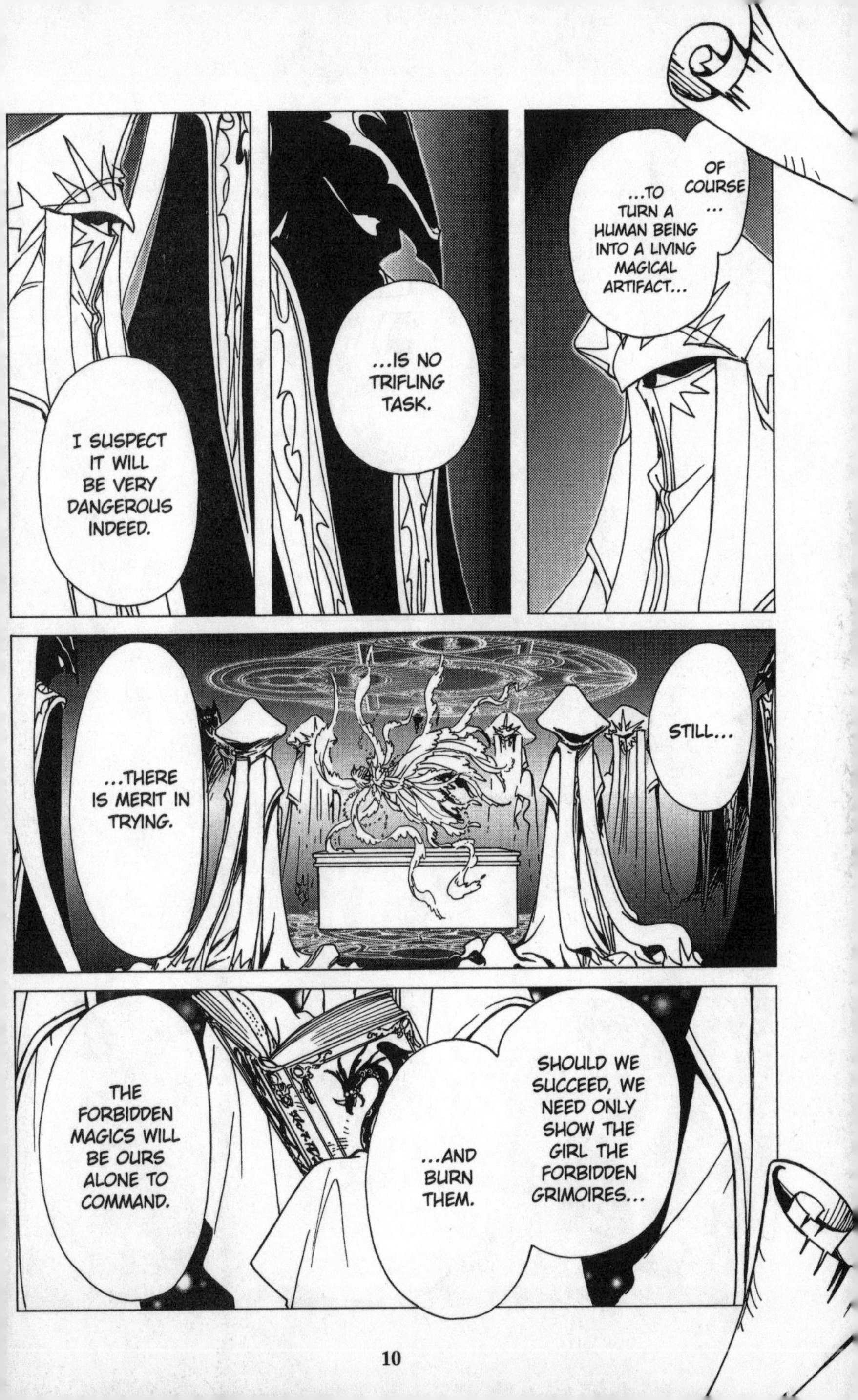
OF COURSE...
...TO TURN A HUMAN BEING INTO A LIVING MAGICAL ARTIFACT...
...IS NO TRIFLING TASK.
I SUSPECT IT WILL BE VERY DANGEROUS INDEED.
STILL...
...THERE IS MERIT IN TRYING.
SHOULD WE SUCCEED, WE NEED ONLY SHOW THE GIRL THE FORBIDDEN GRIMOIRES...
...AND BURN THEM.
THE FORBIDDEN MAGICS WILL BE OURS ALONE TO COMMAND.

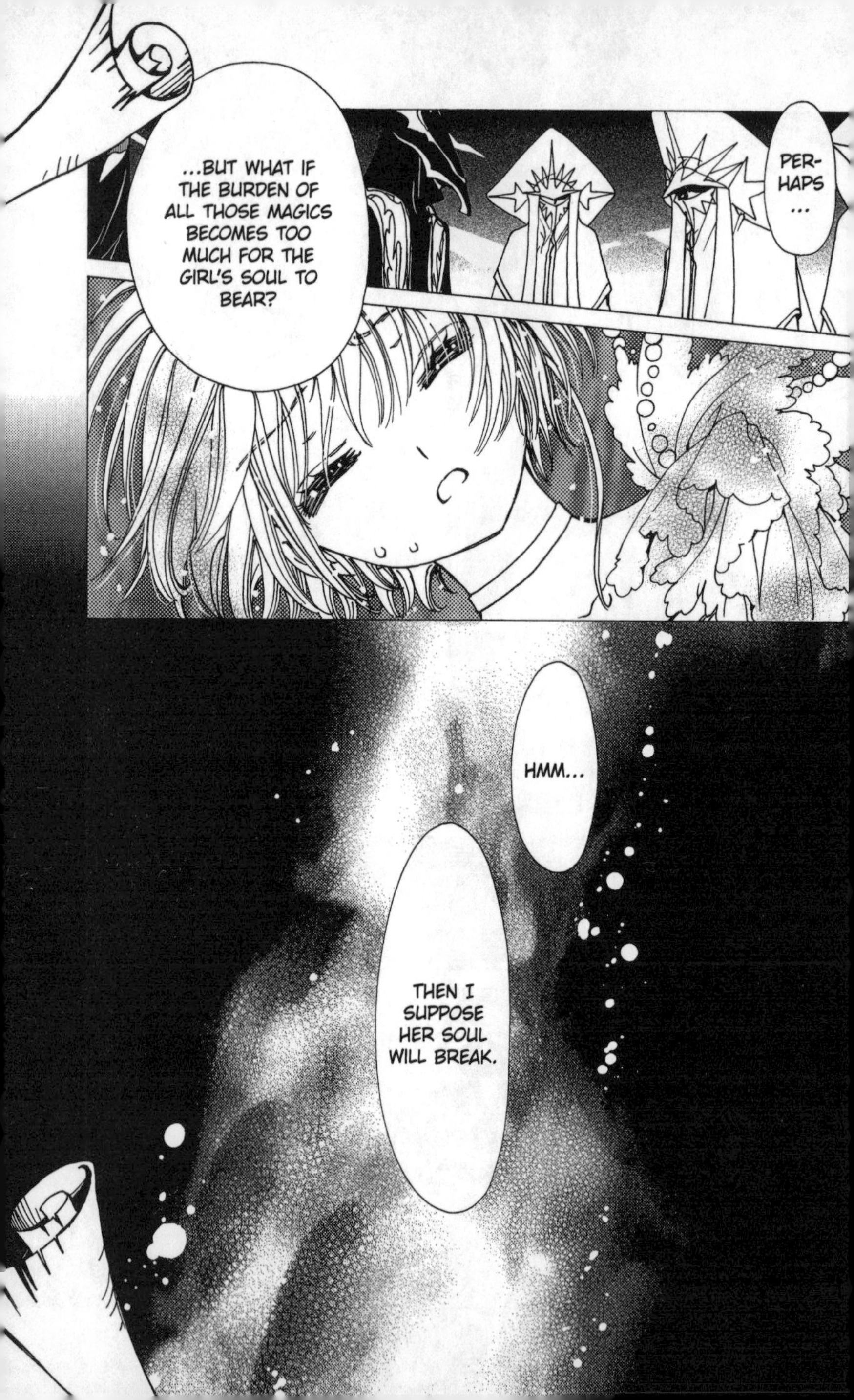
PER-HAPS...
...BUT WHAT IF THE BURDEN OF ALL THOSE MAGICS BECOMES TOO MUCH FOR THE GIRL'S SOUL TO BEAR?
HMM...
THEN I SUPPOSE HER SOUL WILL BREAK.

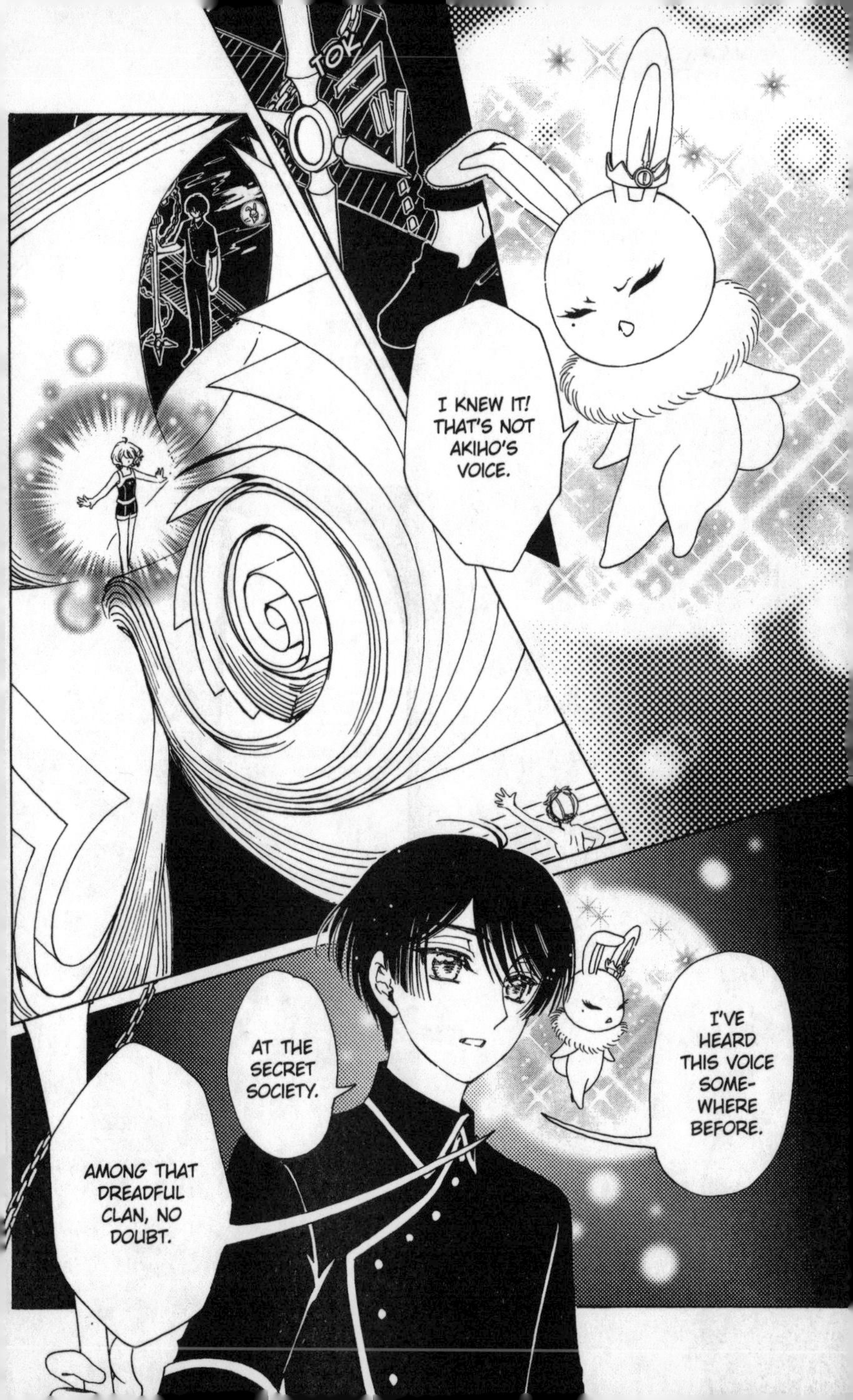
I KNEW IT! THAT'S NOT AKIHO'S VOICE.
TOK
I'VE HEARD THIS VOICE SOME-WHERE BEFORE.
AT THE SECRET SOCIETY.
AMONG THAT DREADFUL CLAN, NO DOUBT.

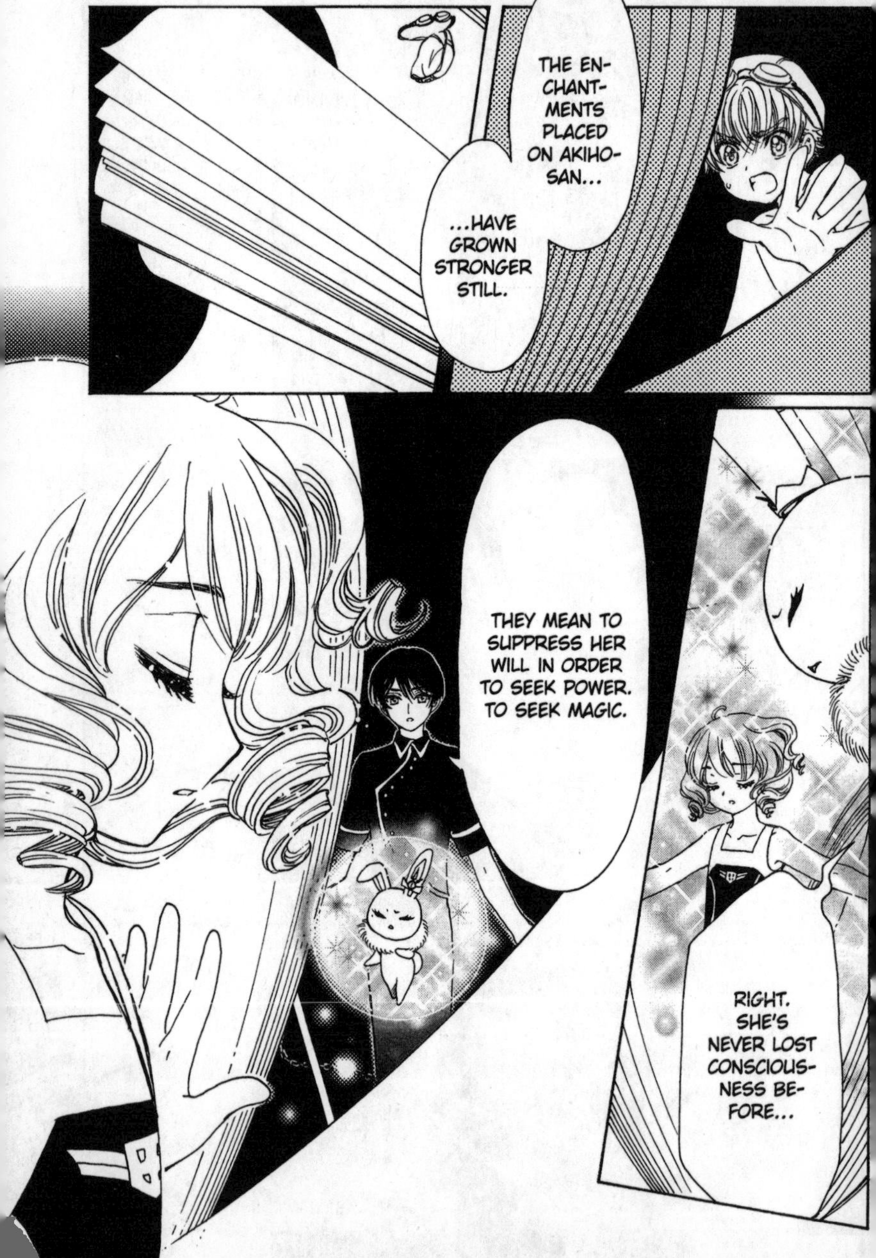
THE EN-CHANT-MENTS PLACED ON AKIHO-SAN...
...HAVE GROWN STRONGER STILL.
RIGHT. SHE'S NEVER LOST CONSCIOUS-NESS BE-FORE...
THEY MEAN TO SUPPRESS HER WILL IN ORDER TO SEEK POWER. TO SEEK MAGIC.

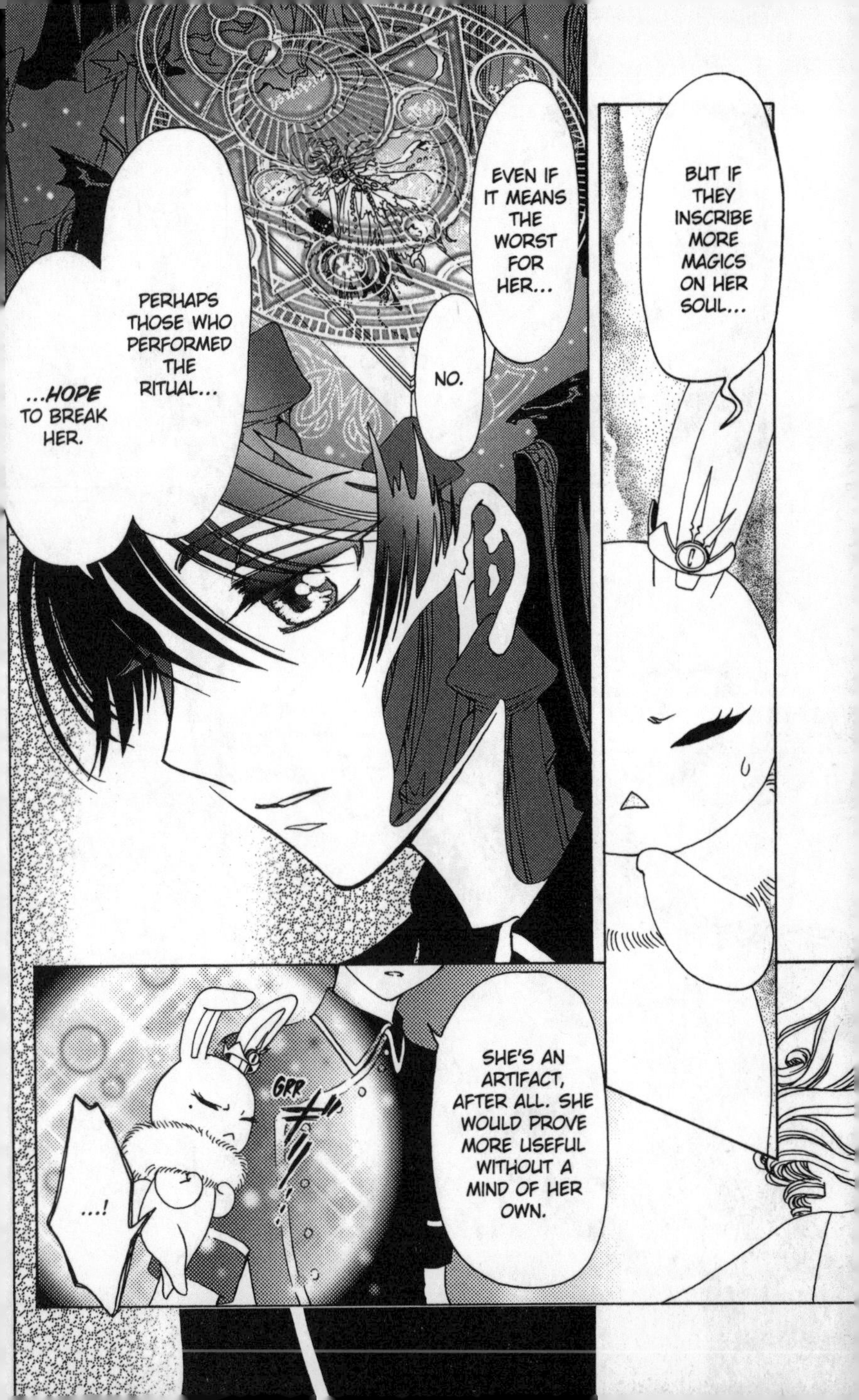
BUT IF THEY INSCRIBE MORE MAGICS ON HER SOUL...
EVEN IF IT MEANS THE WORST FOR HER...
NO.
PERHAPS THOSE WHO PERFORMED THE RITUAL...
...HOPE TO BREAK HER.
SHE'S AN ARTIFACT, AFTER ALL. SHE WOULD PROVE MORE USEFUL WITHOUT A MIND OF HER OWN.
GRR
...!

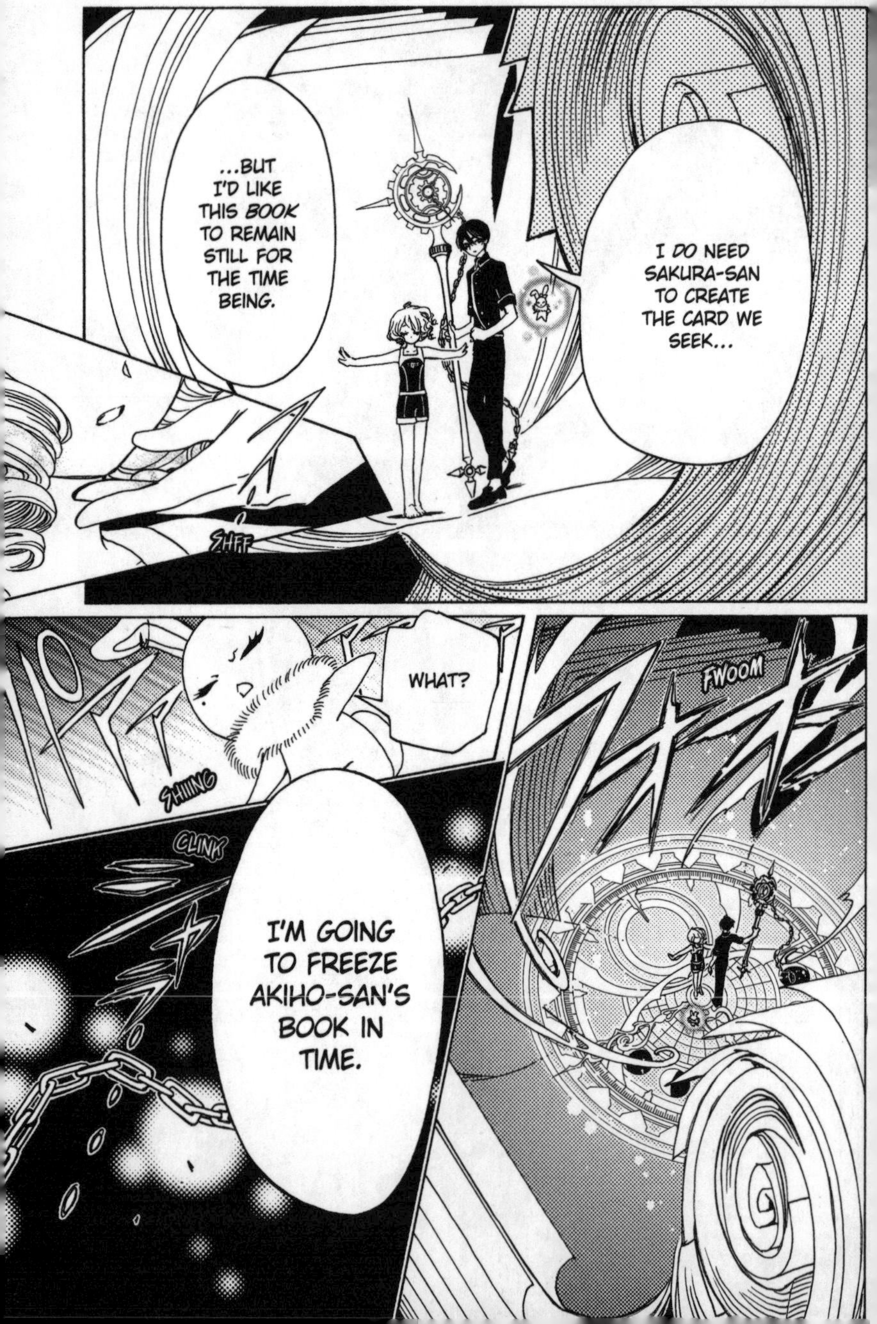
I DO NEED SAKURA-SAN TO CREATE THE CARD WE SEEK...
...BUT I'D LIKE THIS *BOOK* TO REMAIN STILL FOR THE TIME BEING.
SHFF
FWOOM
WHAT?
SHIIING
CLINK
I'M GOING TO FREEZE AKIHO-SAN'S BOOK IN TIME.

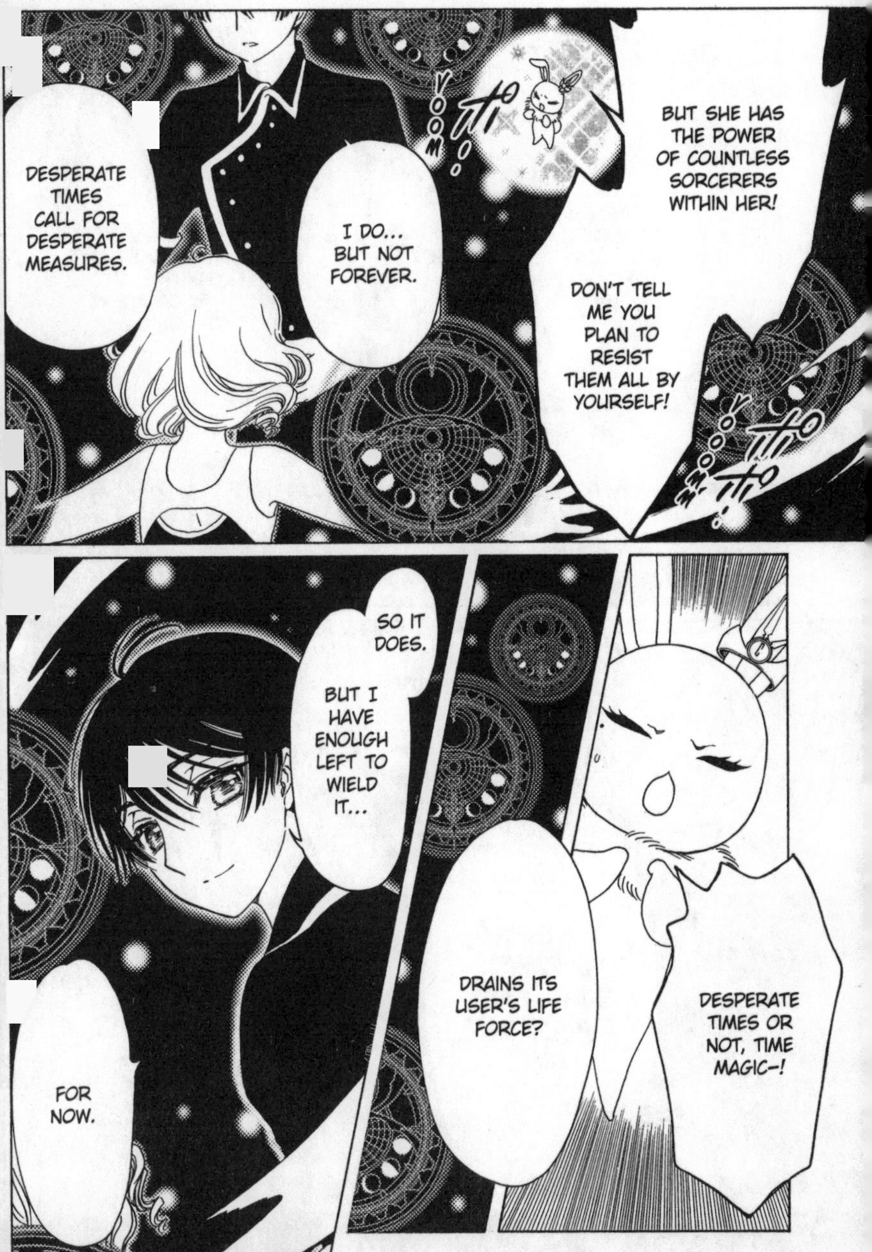
BUT SHE HAS THE POWER OF COUNTLESS SORCERERS WITHIN HER!
VOOOM
DON'T TELL ME YOU PLAN TO RESIST THEM ALL BY YOURSELF!
I DO... BUT NOT FOREVER.
DESPERATE TIMES CALL FOR DESPERATE MEASURES.
DESPERATE TIMES OR NOT, TIME MAGIC—!
DRAINS ITS USER'S LIFE FORCE?
SO IT DOES.
BUT I HAVE ENOUGH LEFT TO WIELD IT...
FOR NOW.

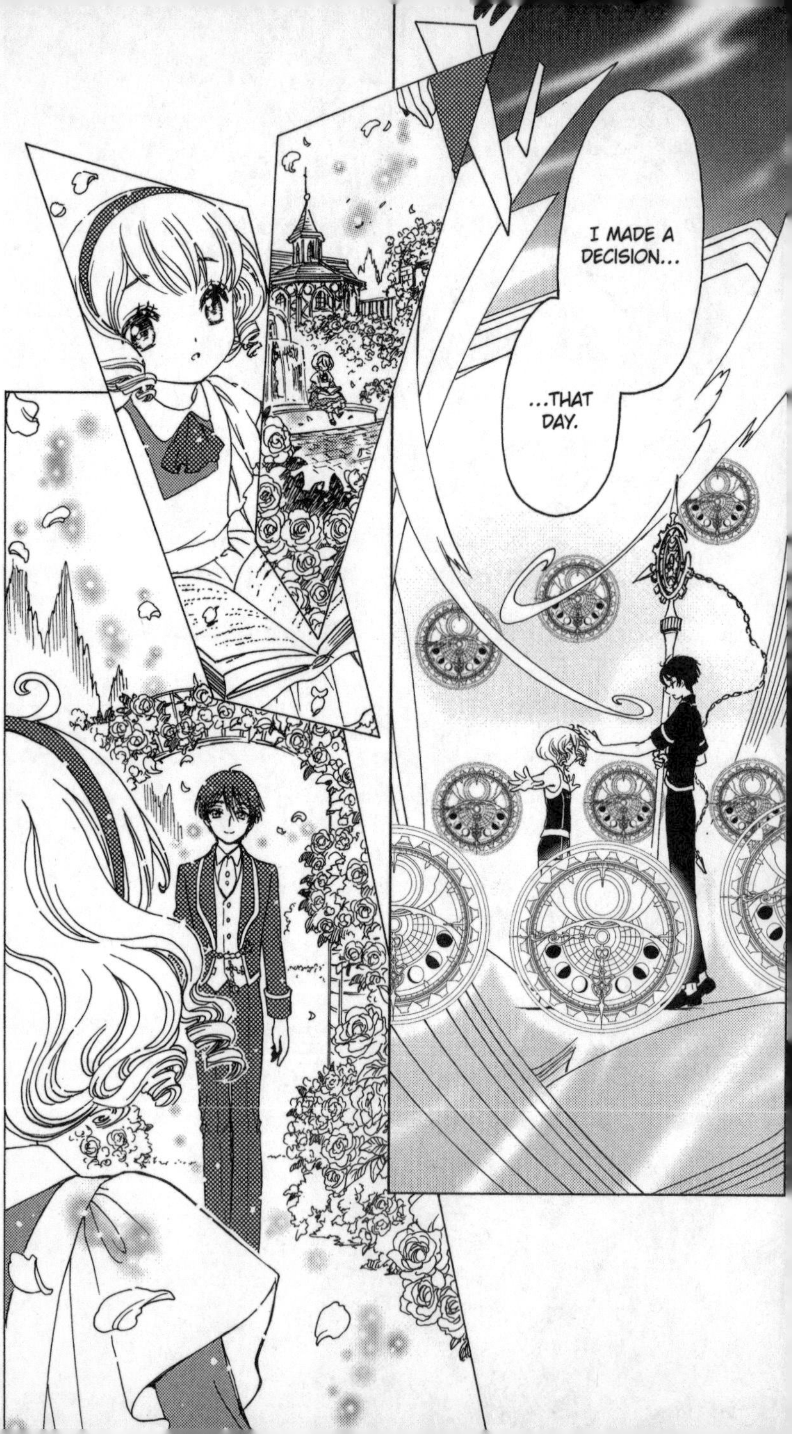
I MADE A DECISION...
...THAT DAY.

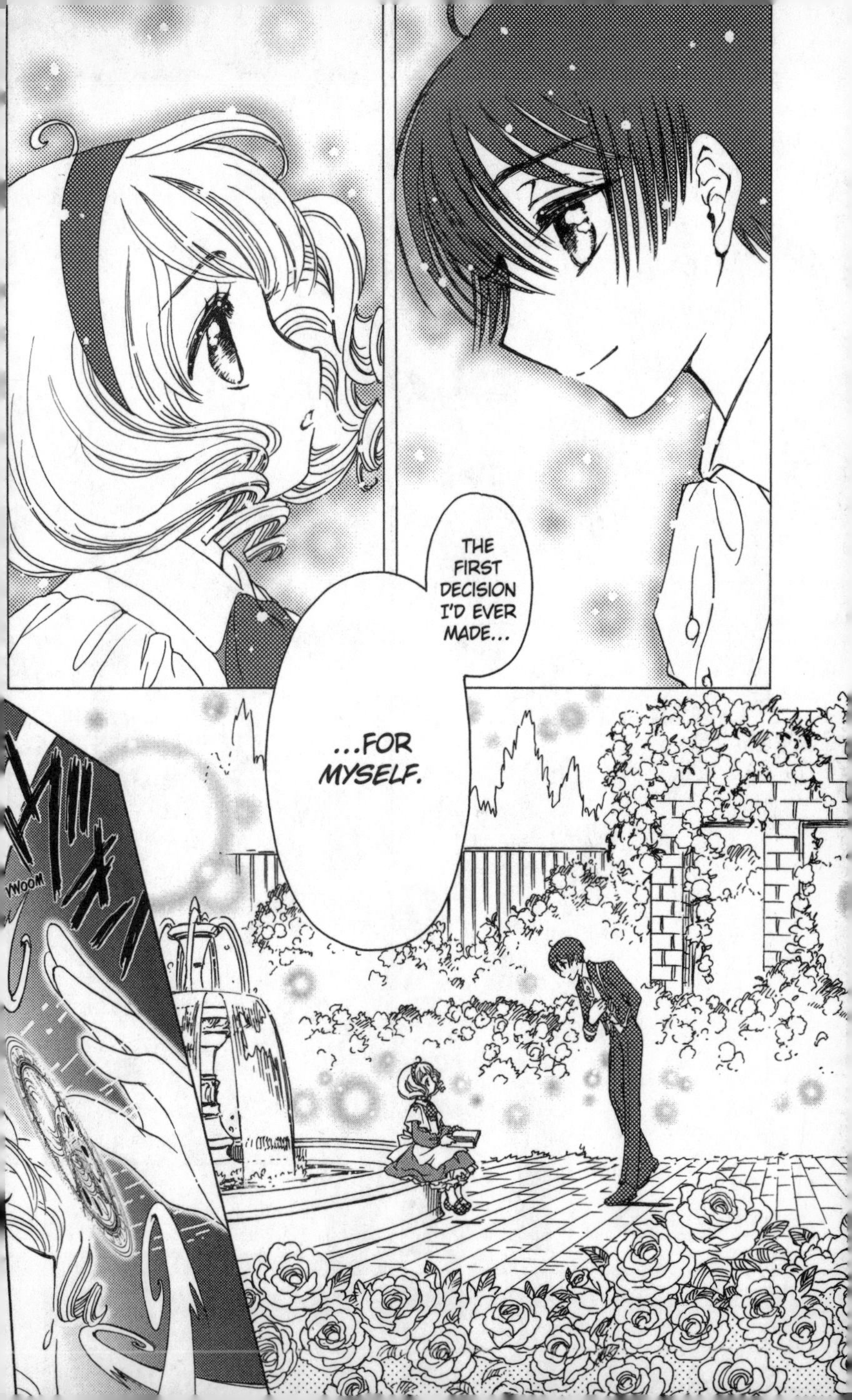
THE FIRST DECISION I'D EVER MADE...
...FOR MYSELF.

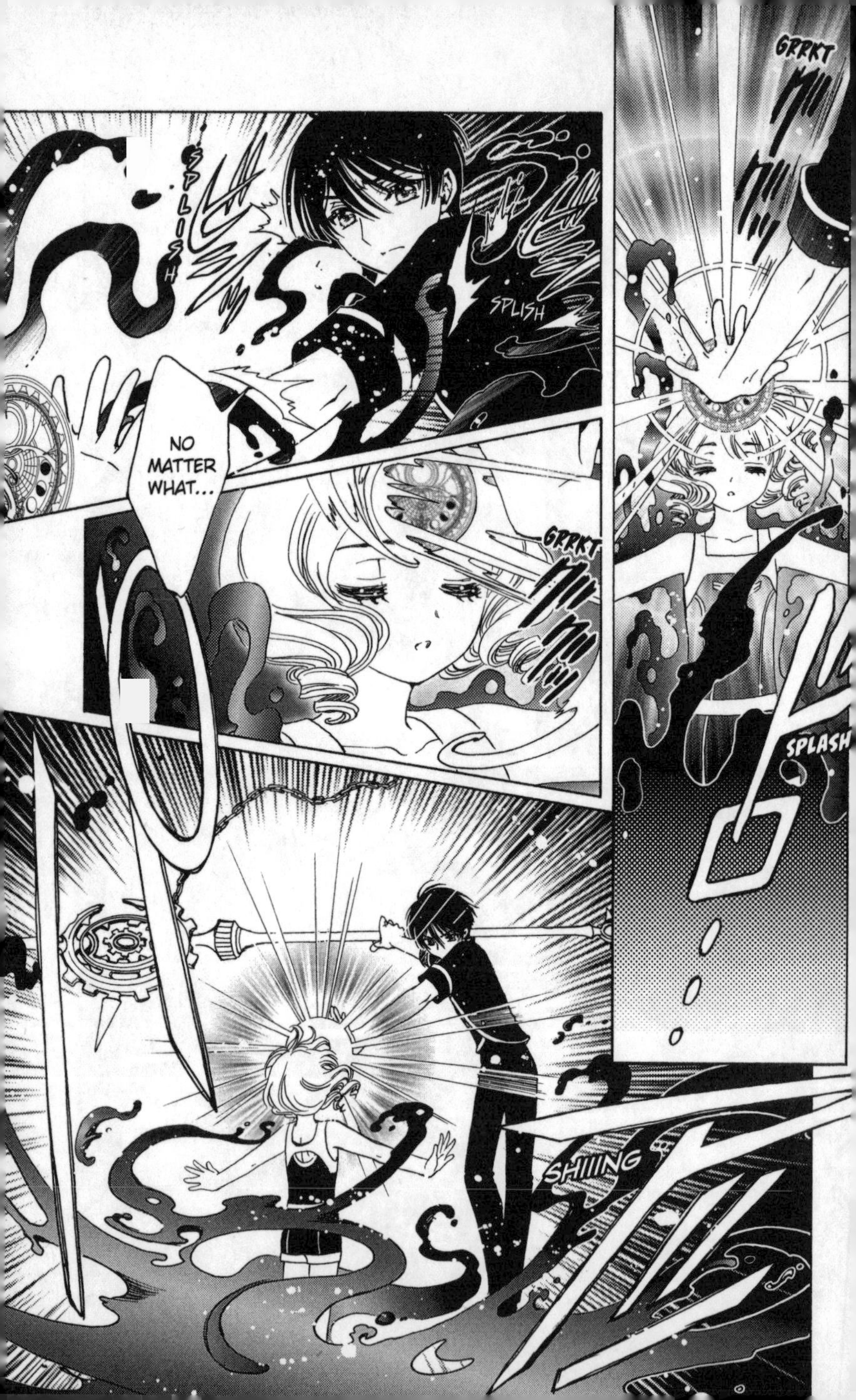
GRRKT
SPLASH
SPLISH
SPLISH
NO MATTER WHAT...
GRRKT
SHIIING

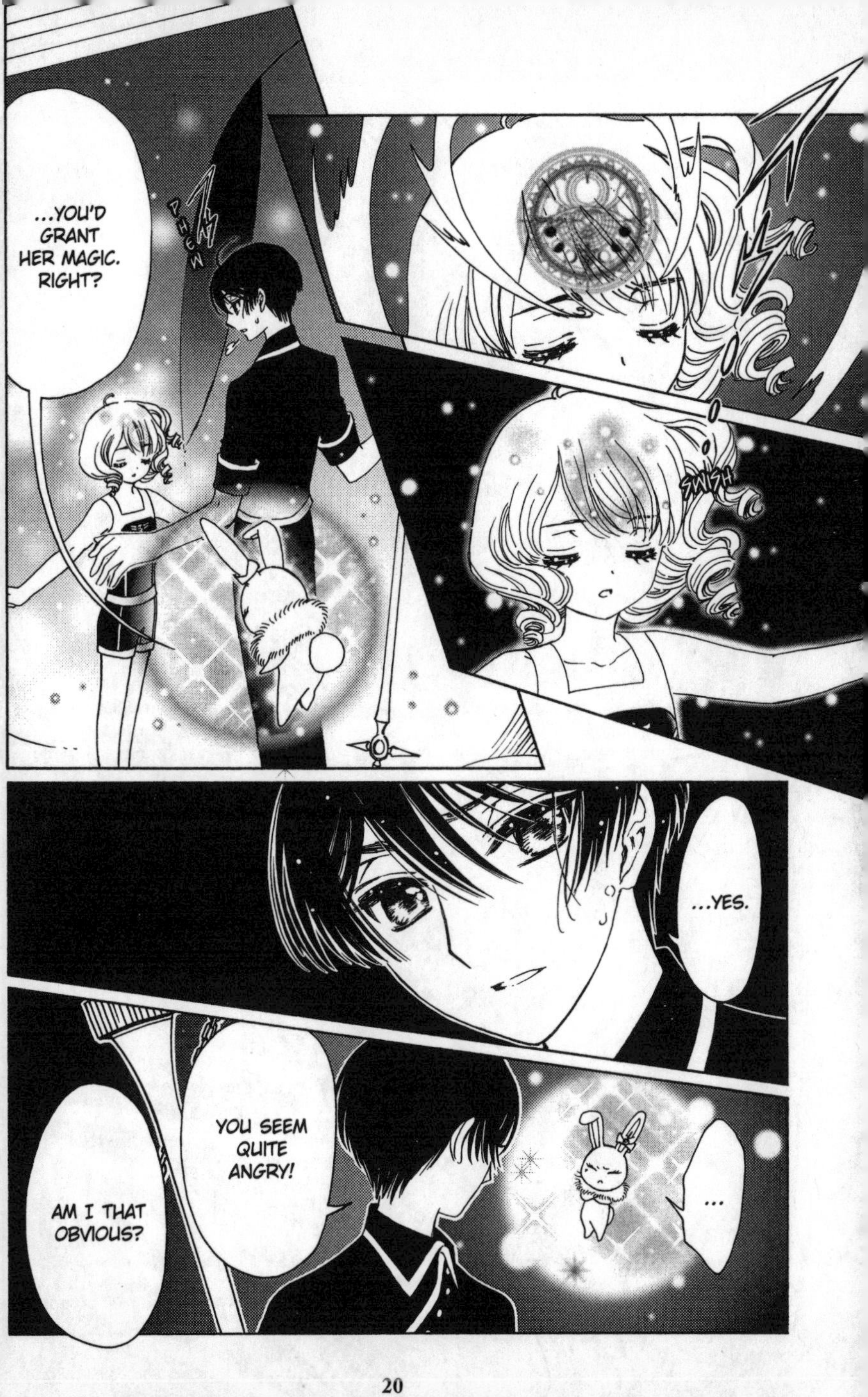
SWISH
...YOU'D GRANT HER MAGIC. RIGHT?
PHEW
...YES.
...
YOU SEEM QUITE ANGRY!
AM I THAT OBVIOUS?

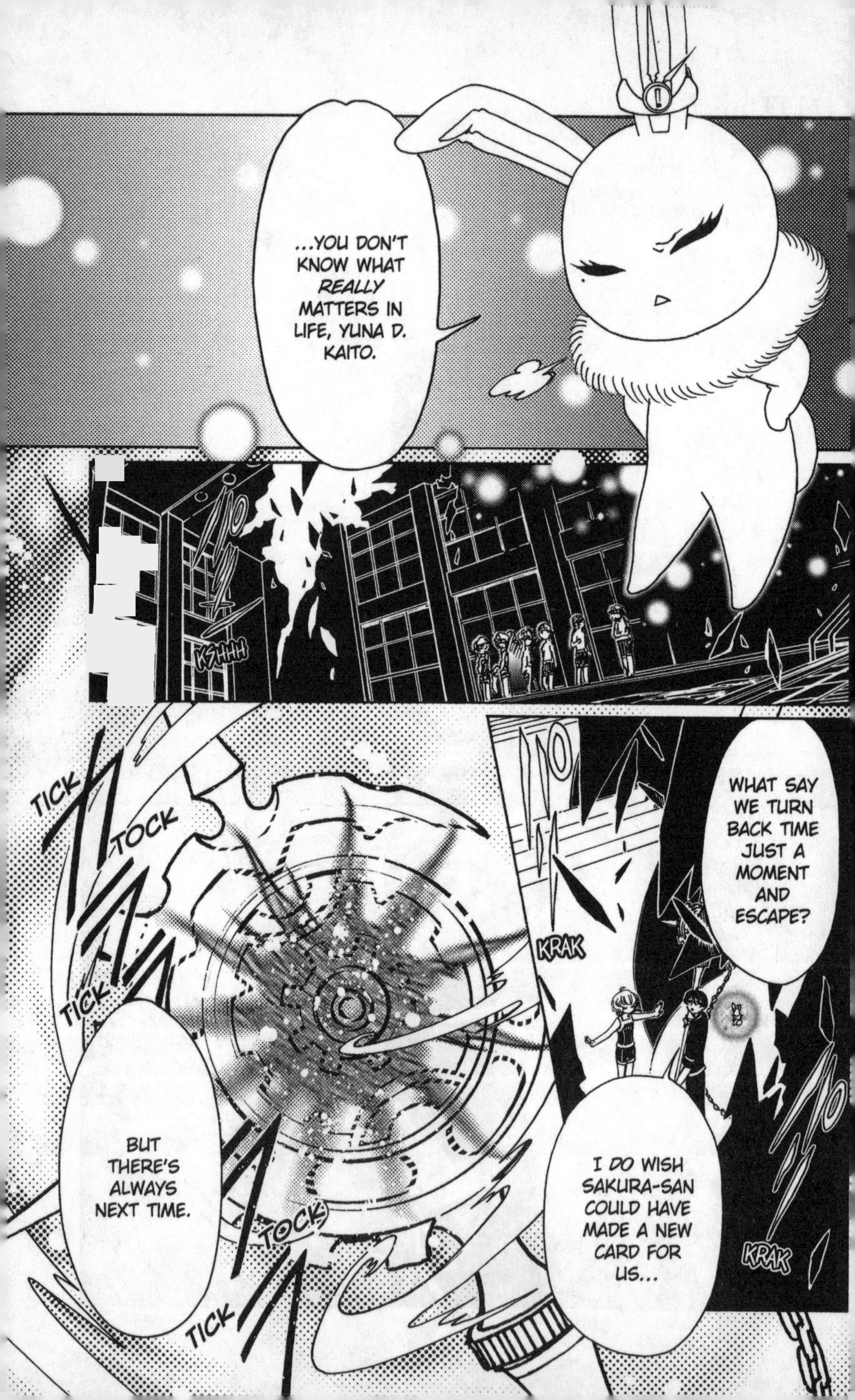
...YOU DON'T KNOW WHAT *REALLY* MATTERS IN LIFE, YUNA D. KAITO.
KSHHH
WHAT SAY WE TURN BACK TIME JUST A MOMENT AND ESCAPE?
KRAK
I *DO* WISH SAKURA-SAN COULD HAVE MADE A NEW CARD FOR US...
KRAK
TICK
TOCK
TICK
BUT THERE'S ALWAYS NEXT TIME.
TOCK
TICK

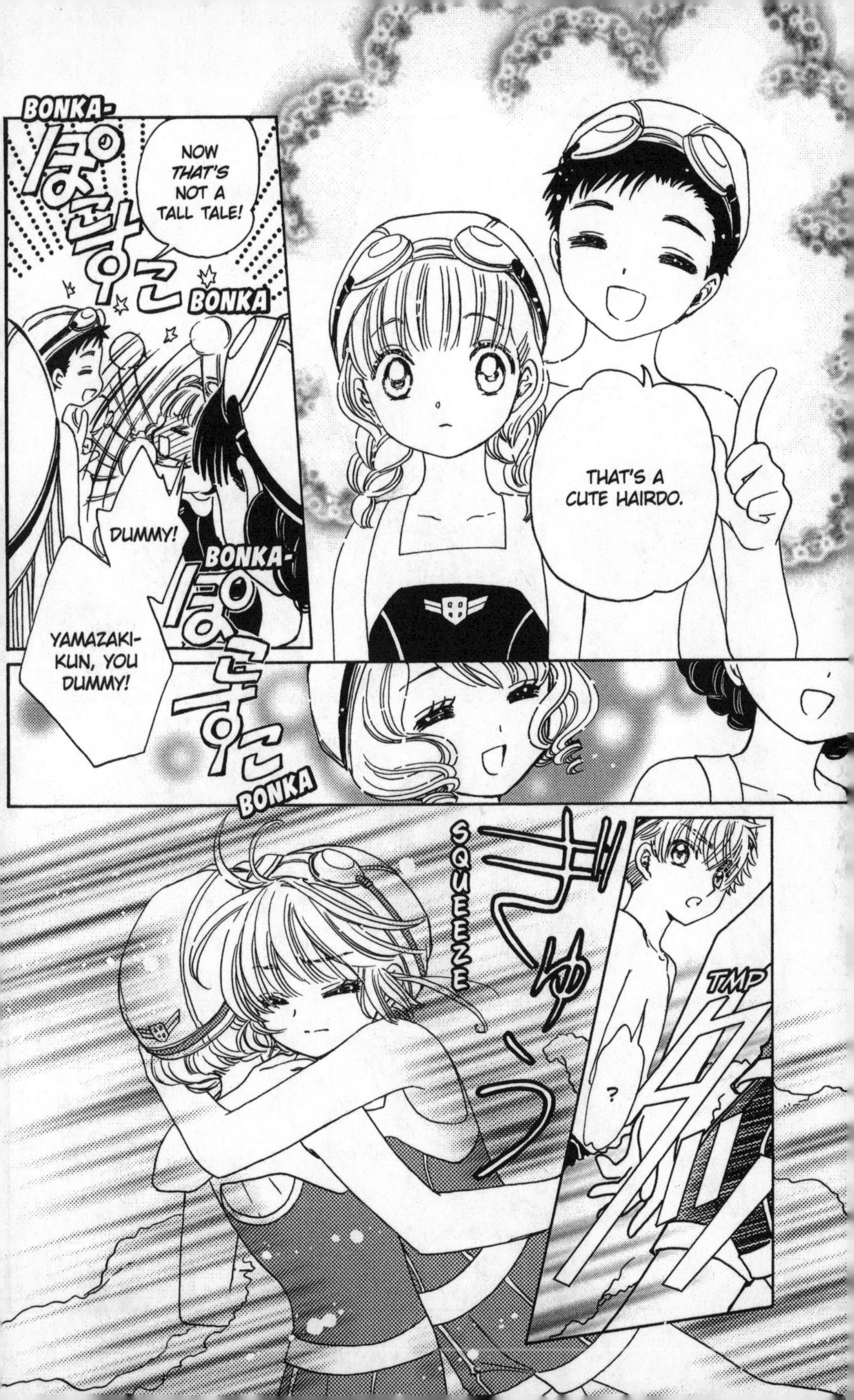
THAT'S A CUTE HAIRDO.
NOW THAT'S NOT A TALL TALE!
BONKA-
BONKA
DUMMY!
BONKA-
YAMAZAKI-KUN, YOU DUMMY!
BONKA
SQUEEZE
TMP
?

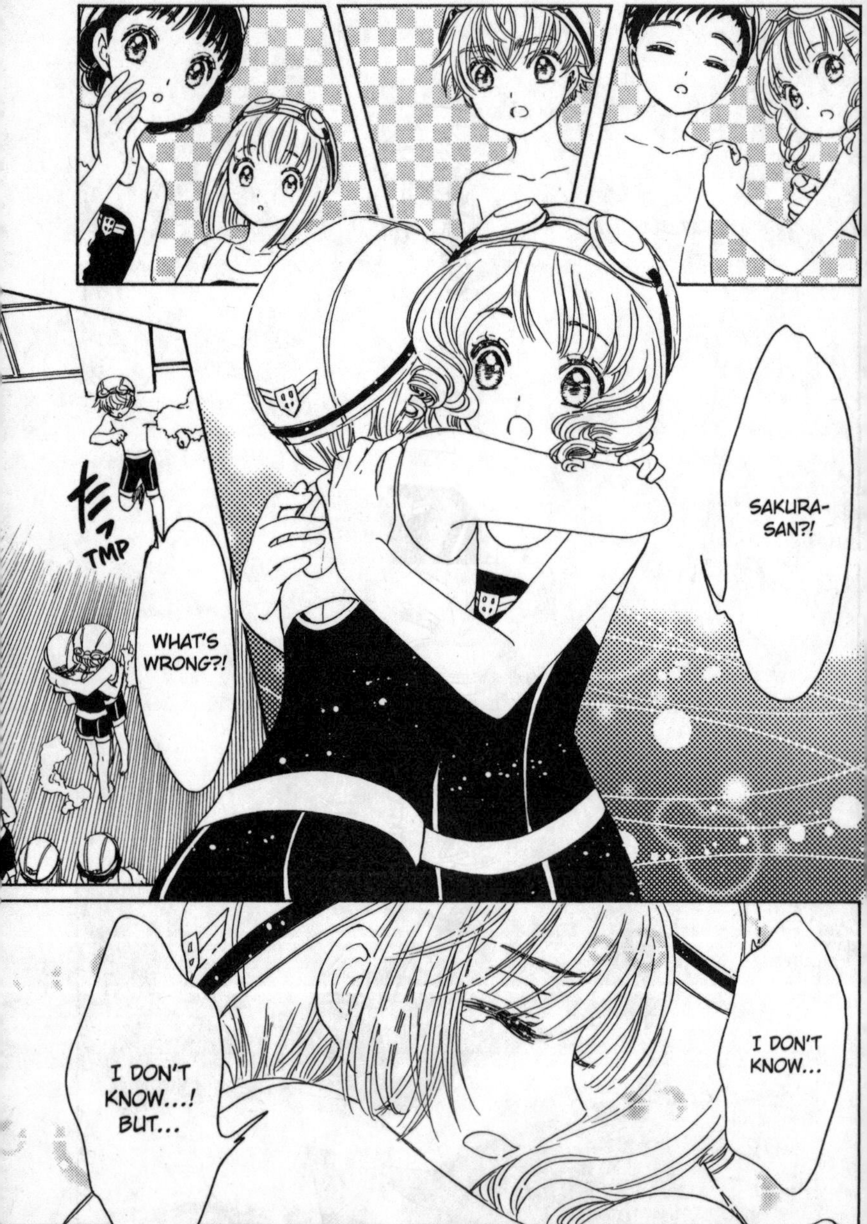
SAKURA-SAN?!
たっ
TMP
WHAT'S WRONG?!
I DON'T KNOW...
I DON'T KNOW...! BUT...

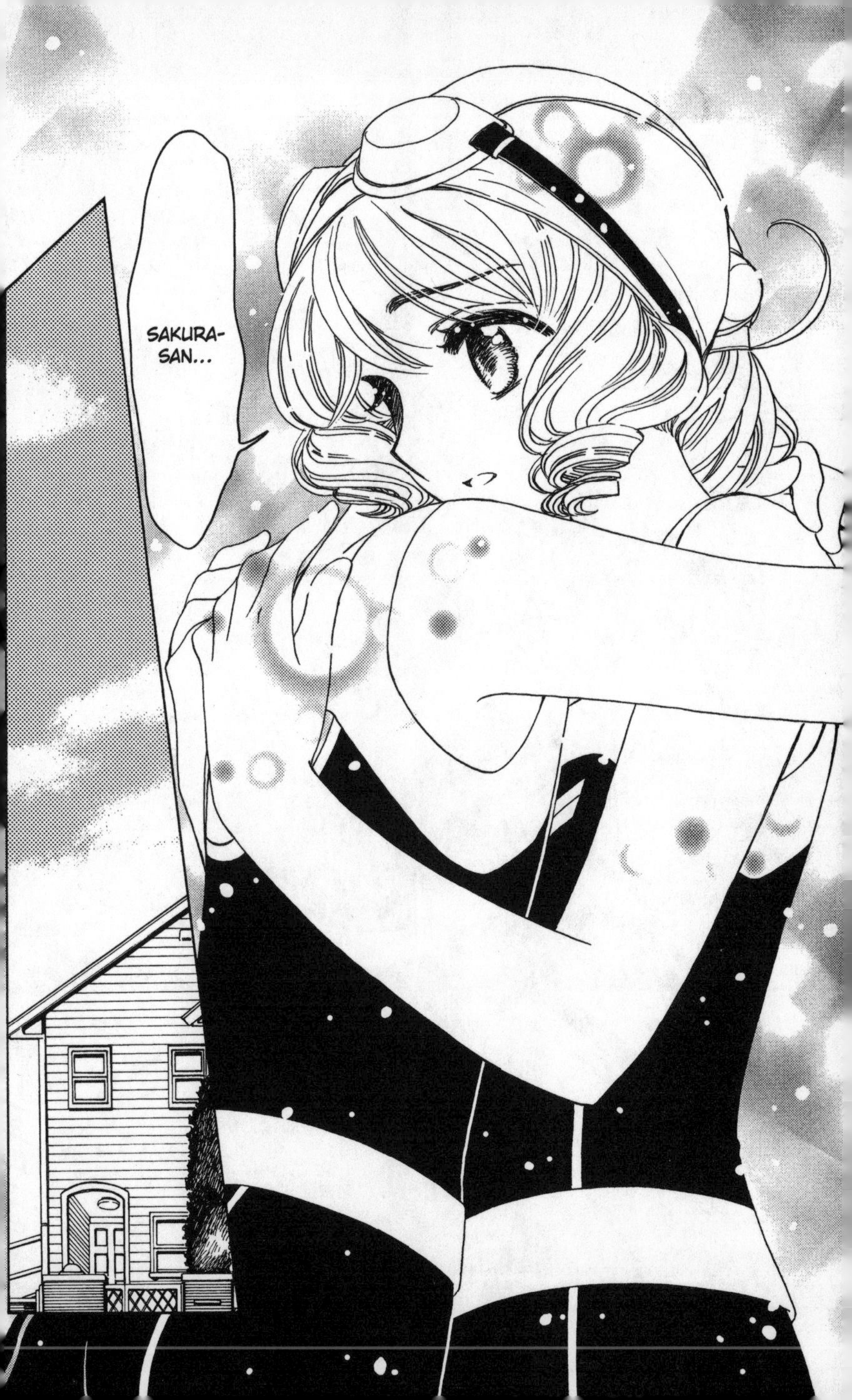
SAKURA-SAN...

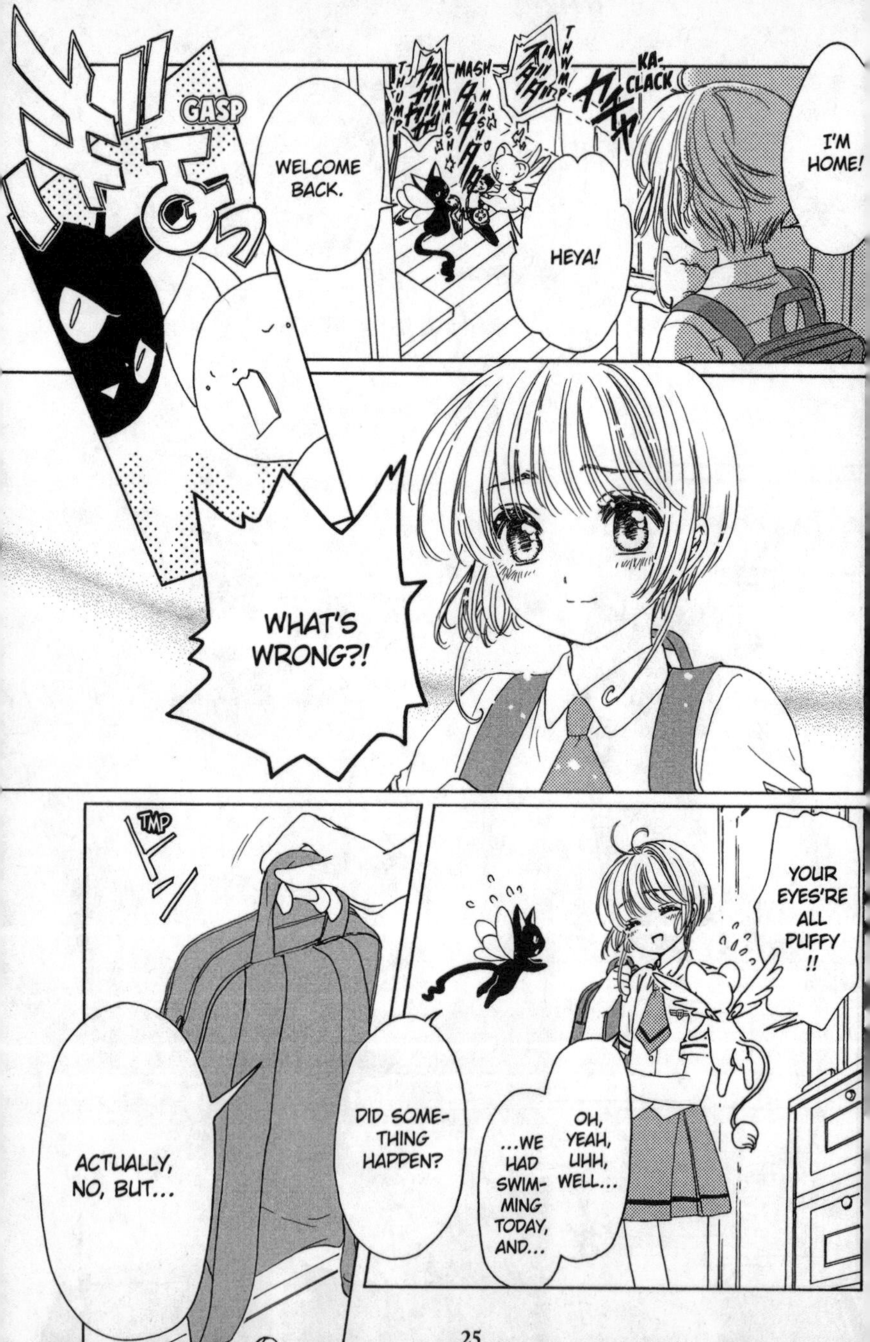
I'M HOME!
KA-CLACK
THWMP
MASH MASH
THUMP
HEYA!
WELCOME BACK.
GASP
WHAT'S WRONG?!
YOUR EYES'RE ALL PUFFY !!
OH, YEAH, UHH, WELL...
...WE HAD SWIMMING TODAY, AND...
DID SOMETHING HAPPEN?
TMP
ACTUALLY, NO, BUT...

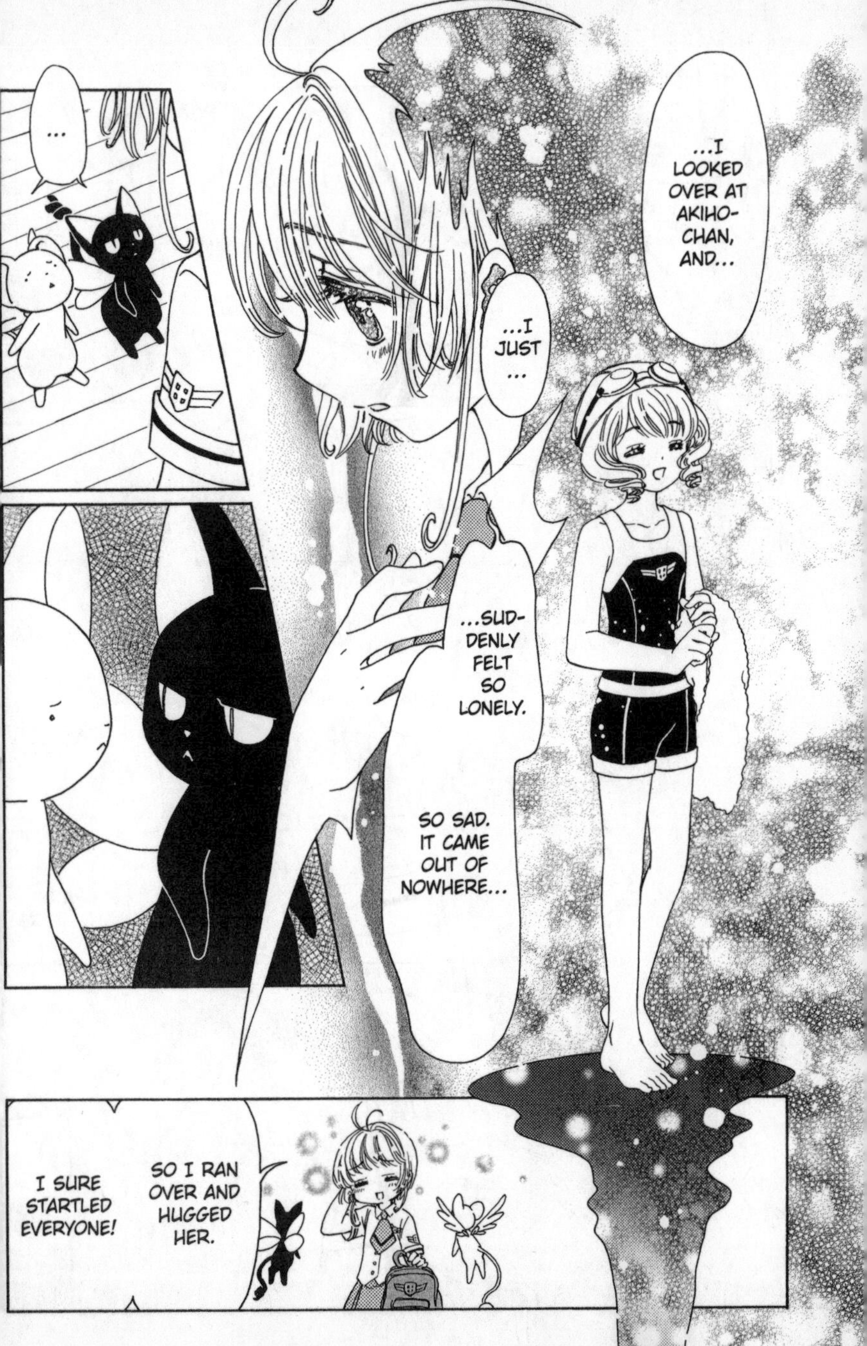
...I LOOKED OVER AT AKIHO-CHAN, AND...
...I JUST...
...SUDDENLY FELT SO LONELY.
SO SAD. IT CAME OUT OF NOWHERE...
...
SO I RAN OVER AND HUGGED HER.
I SURE STARTLED EVERYONE!

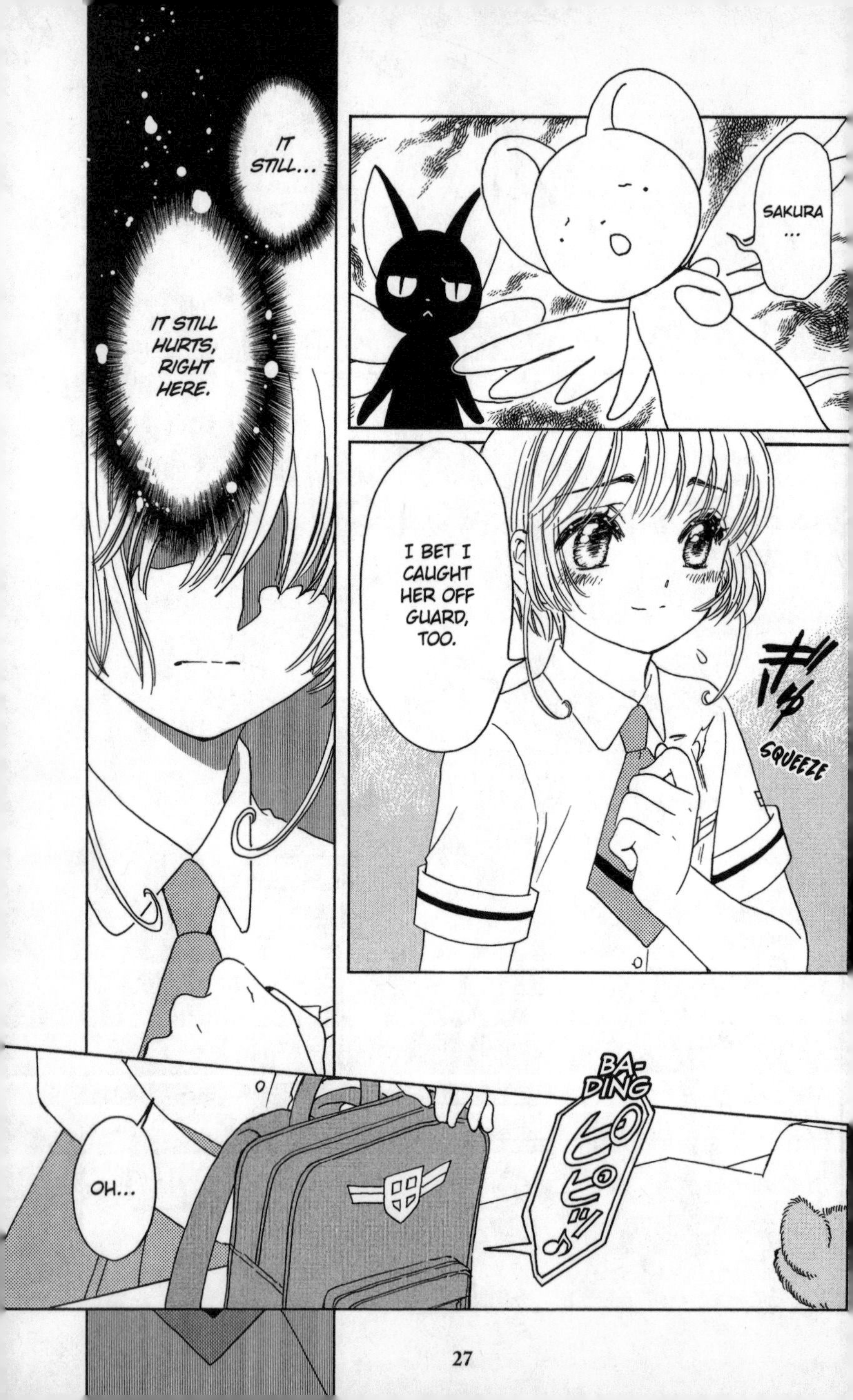
SAKURA …
I BET I CAUGHT HER OFF GUARD, TOO.
SQUEEZE
IT STILL…
IT STILL HURTS, RIGHT HERE.
BA-DING
OH…

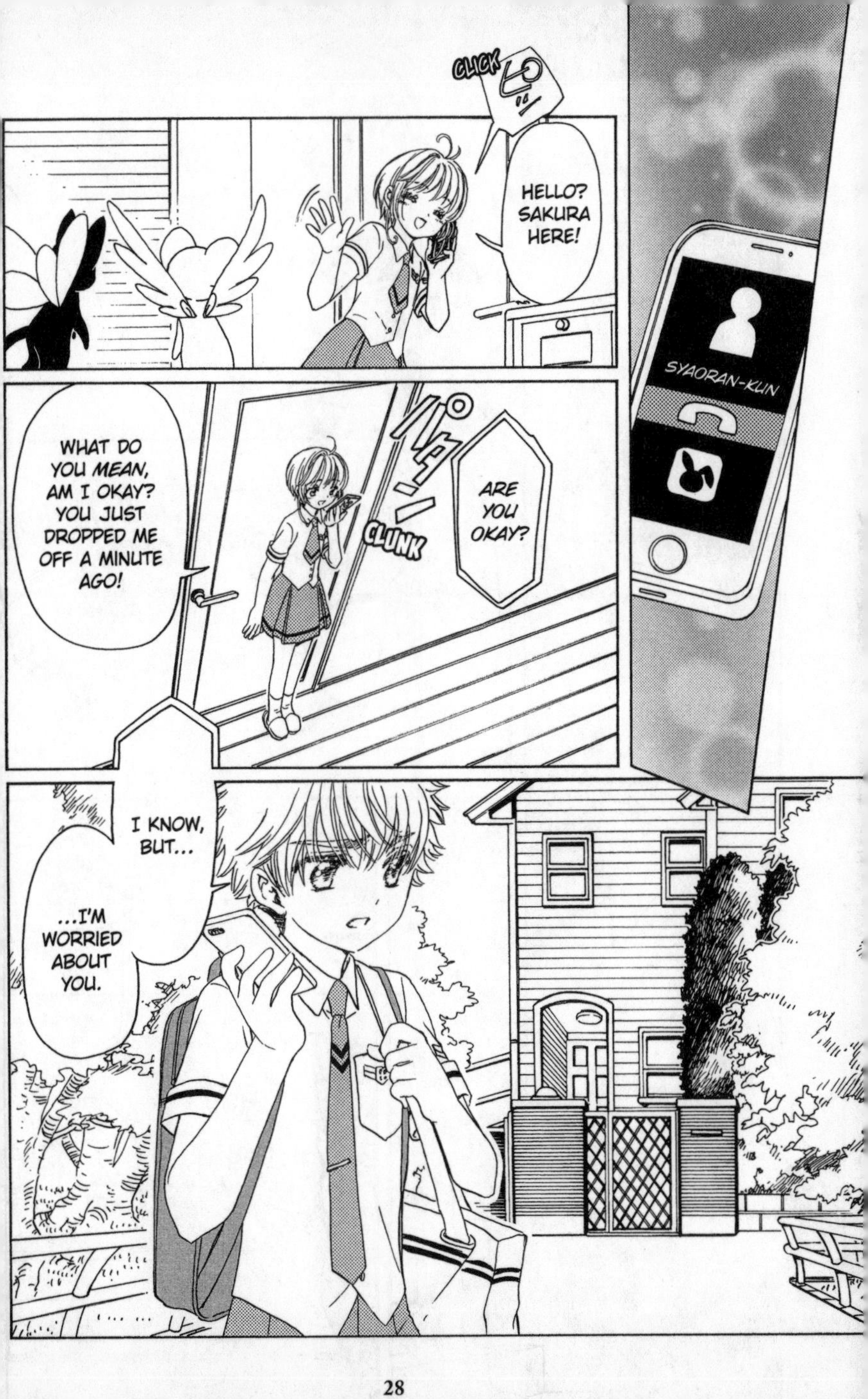
SYAORAN-KUN
CLICK
HELLO? SAKURA HERE!
CLUNK
ARE YOU OKAY?
WHAT DO YOU MEAN, AM I OKAY? YOU JUST DROPPED ME OFF A MINUTE AGO!
I KNOW, BUT...
...I'M WORRIED ABOUT YOU.

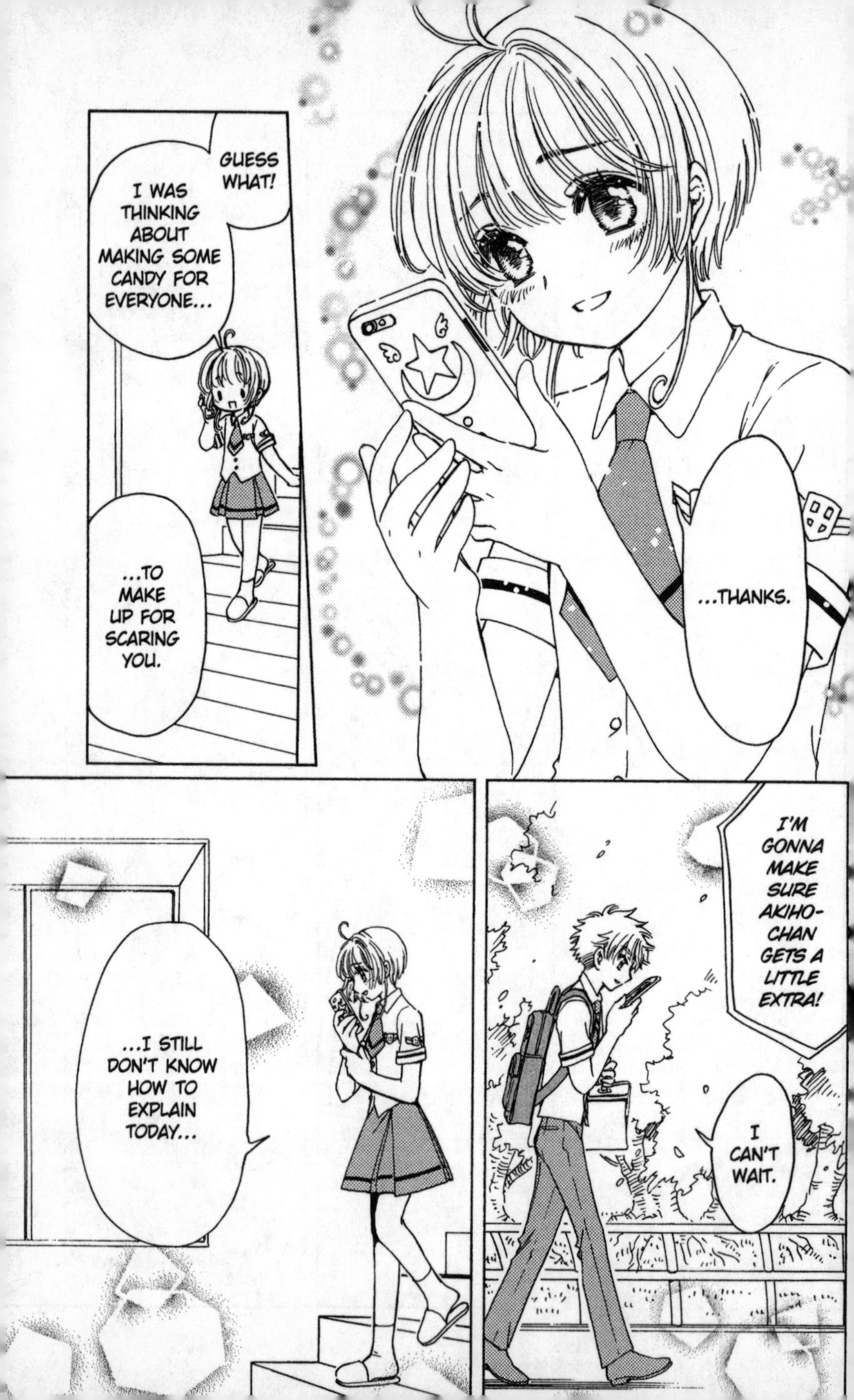
...THANKS.
GUESS WHAT!
I WAS THINKING ABOUT MAKING SOME CANDY FOR EVERYONE...
...TO MAKE UP FOR SCARING YOU.
I'M GONNA MAKE SURE AKIHO-CHAN GETS A LITTLE EXTRA!
I CAN'T WAIT.
...I STILL DON'T KNOW HOW TO EXPLAIN TODAY...

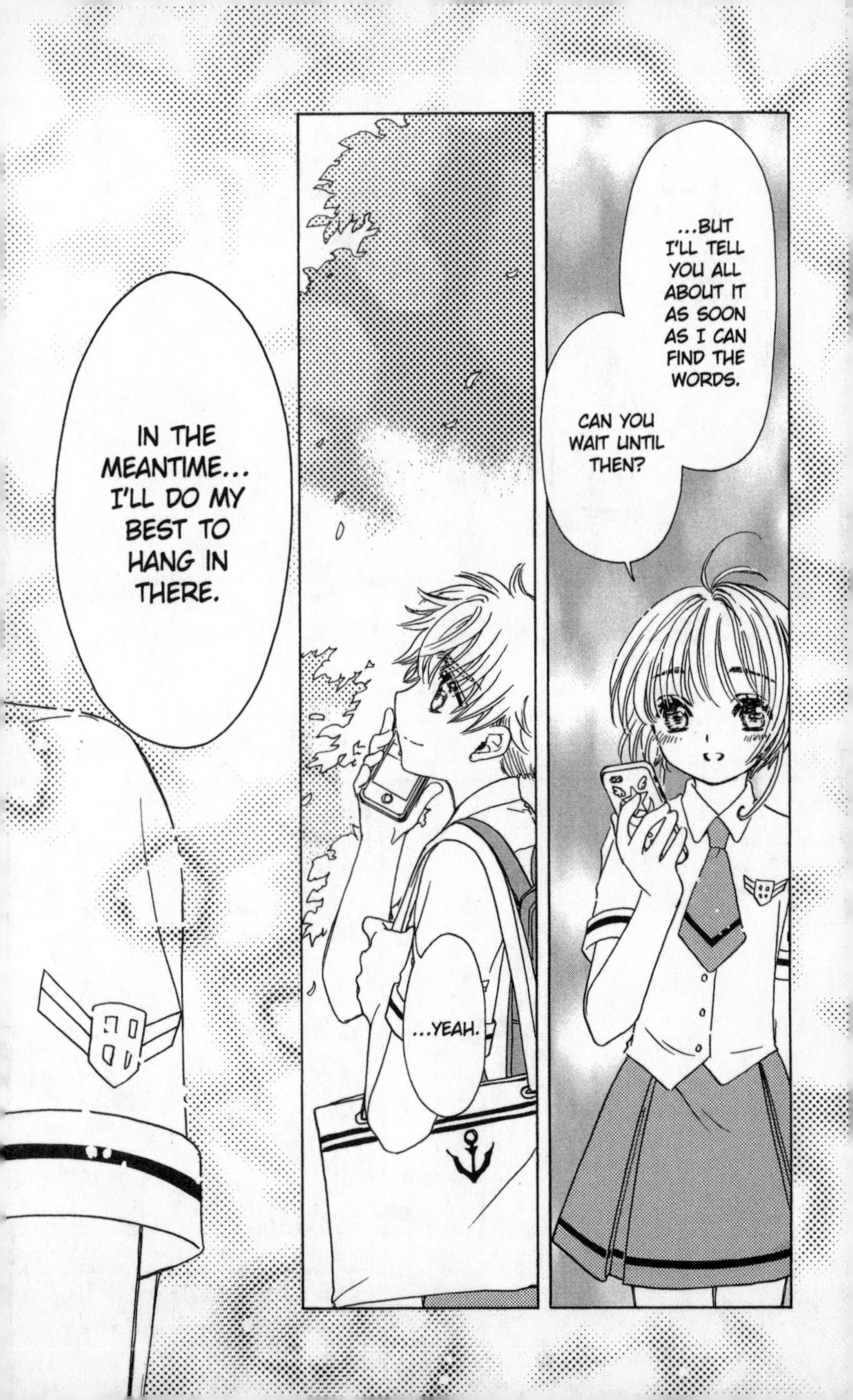
...BUT I'LL TELL YOU ALL ABOUT IT AS SOON AS I CAN FIND THE WORDS.
CAN YOU WAIT UNTIL THEN?
...YEAH.
IN THE MEANTIME... I'LL DO MY BEST TO HANG IN THERE.

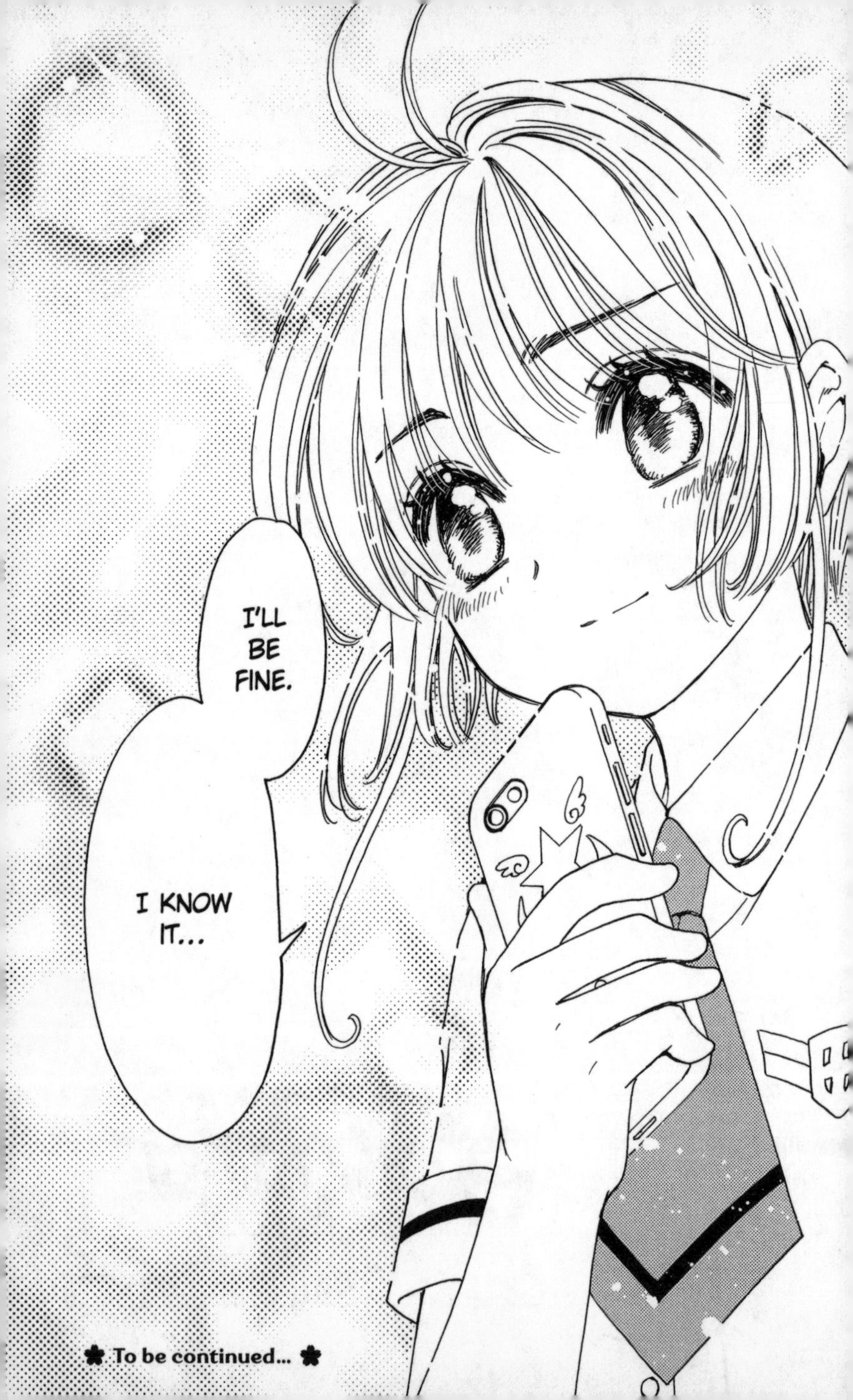
I'LL BE FINE.
I KNOW IT...
To be continued...

Cardcaptor
Sakura
CLEAR CARD

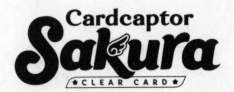

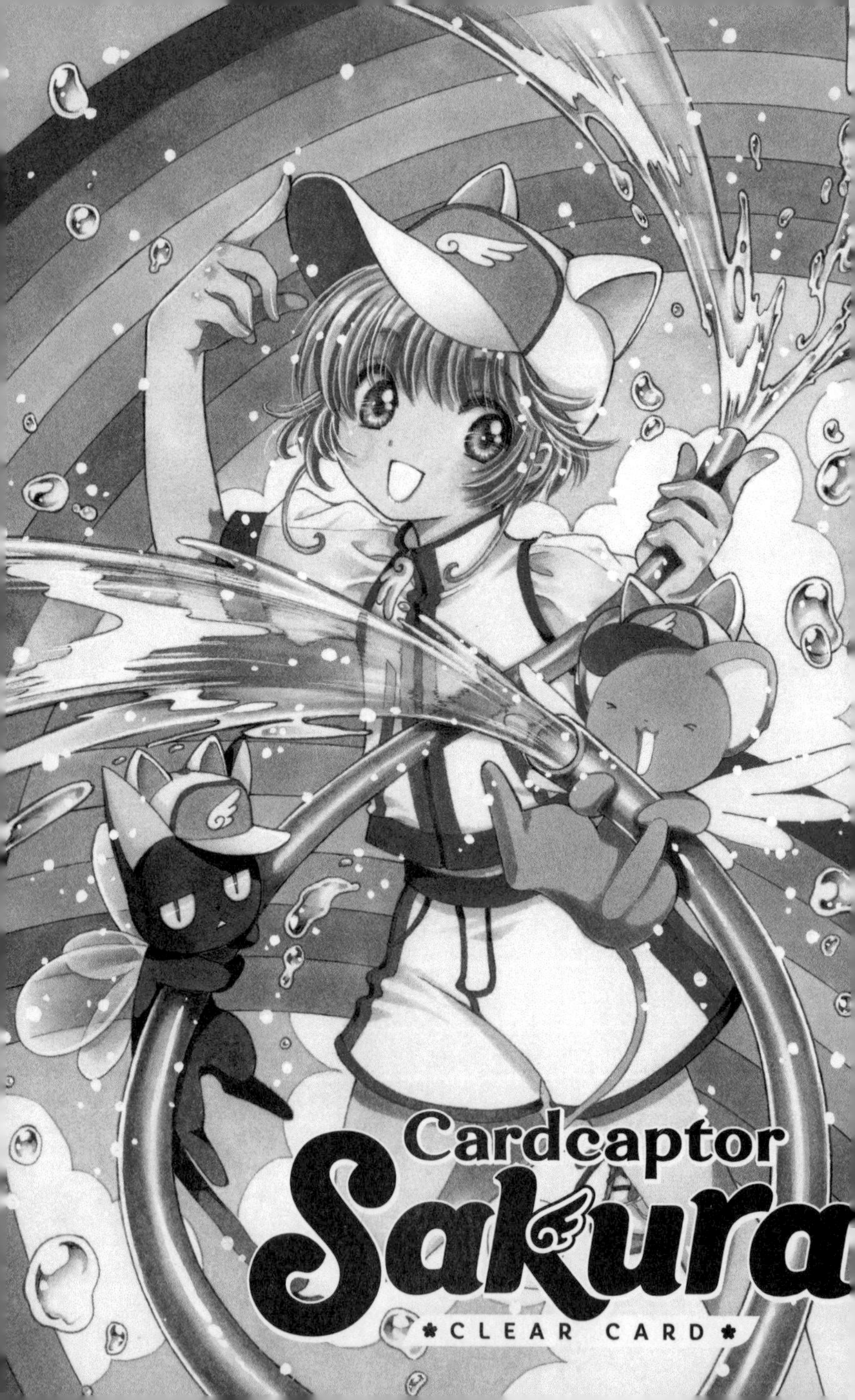
Cardcaptor
Sakura
CLEAR CARD

Cardcaptor Sakura

CLEAR CARD

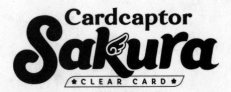

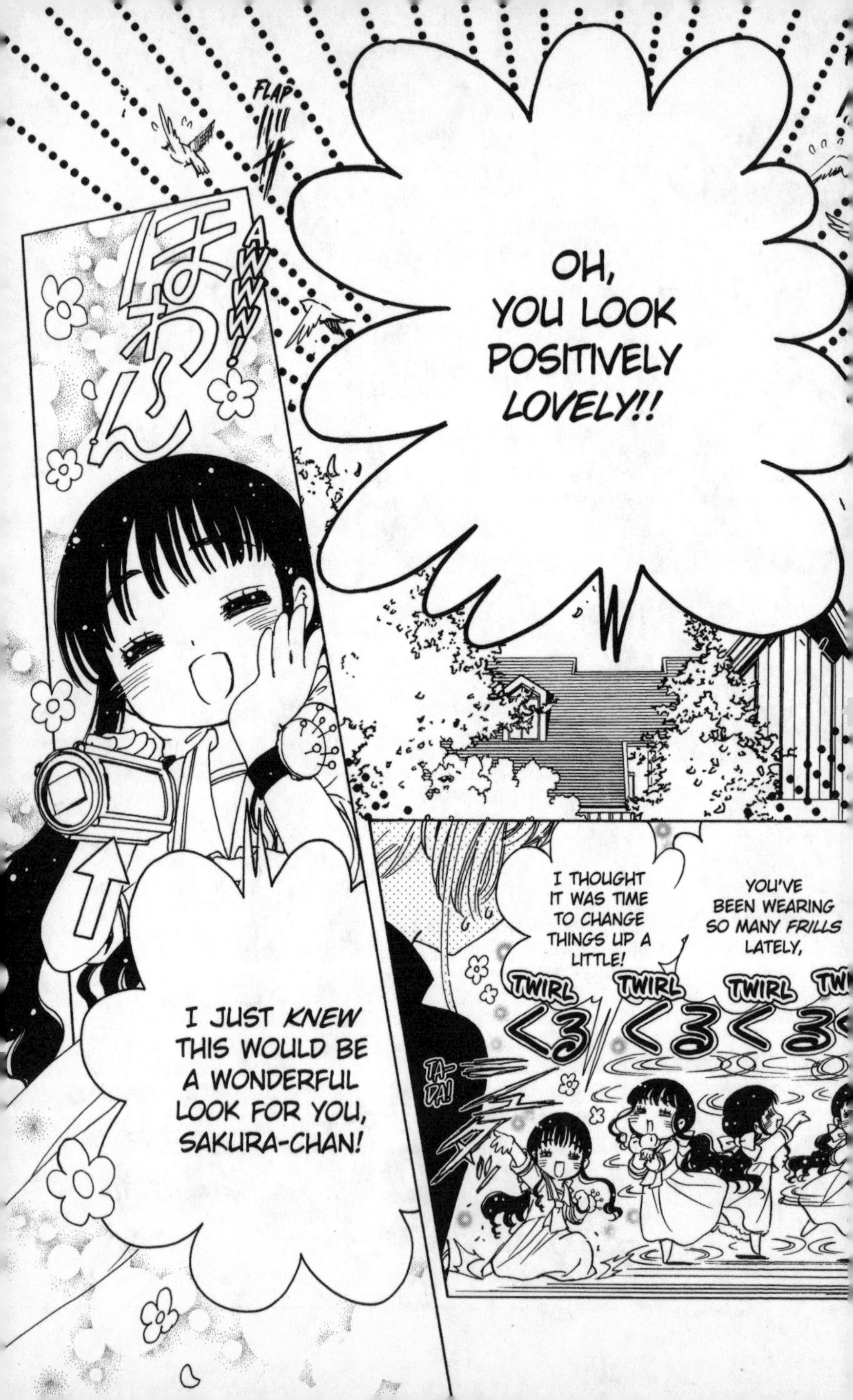
FLAP
OH, YOU LOOK POSITIVELY LOVELY!!
YOU'VE BEEN WEARING SO MANY FRILLS LATELY,
I THOUGHT IT WAS TIME TO CHANGE THINGS UP A LITTLE!
TWIRL TWIRL TWIRL TW
くるくるくる
TA-DA!
ほわ〜ん
AWWW!
I JUST KNEW THIS WOULD BE A WONDERFUL LOOK FOR YOU, SAKURA-CHAN!

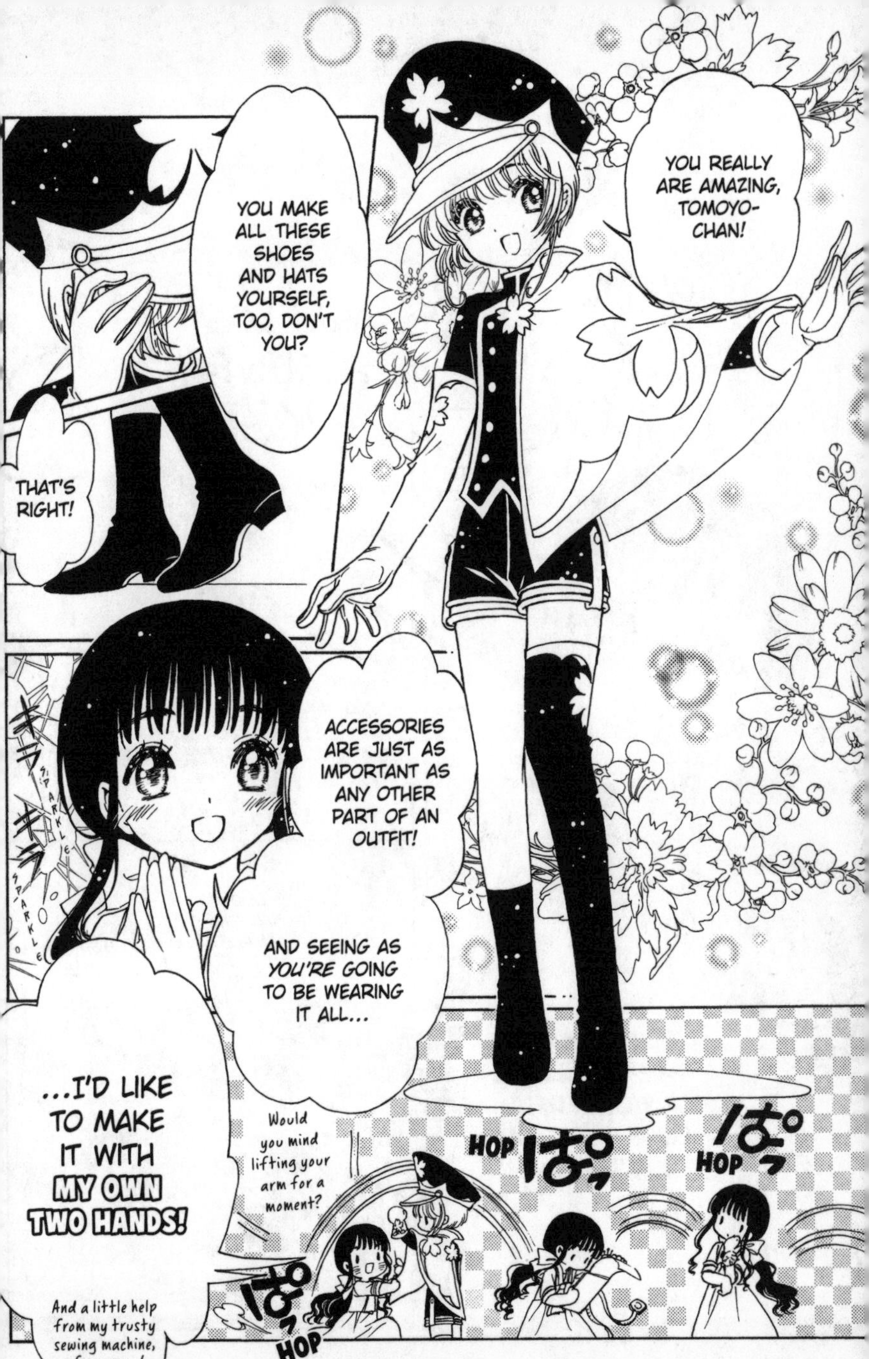
YOU REALLY ARE AMAZING, TOMOYO-CHAN!
YOU MAKE ALL THESE SHOES AND HATS YOURSELF, TOO, DON'T YOU?
THAT'S RIGHT!
キラ キラ
SPARKLE SPARKLE
ACCESSORIES ARE JUST AS IMPORTANT AS ANY OTHER PART OF AN OUTFIT!
AND SEEING AS *YOU'RE* GOING TO BE WEARING IT ALL...
...I'D LIKE TO MAKE IT WITH **MY OWN TWO HANDS!**
And a little help from my trusty sewing machine, of course...!
ぱっ HOP
HOP ぱっ
Would you mind lifting your arm for a moment?
ぱっ HOP

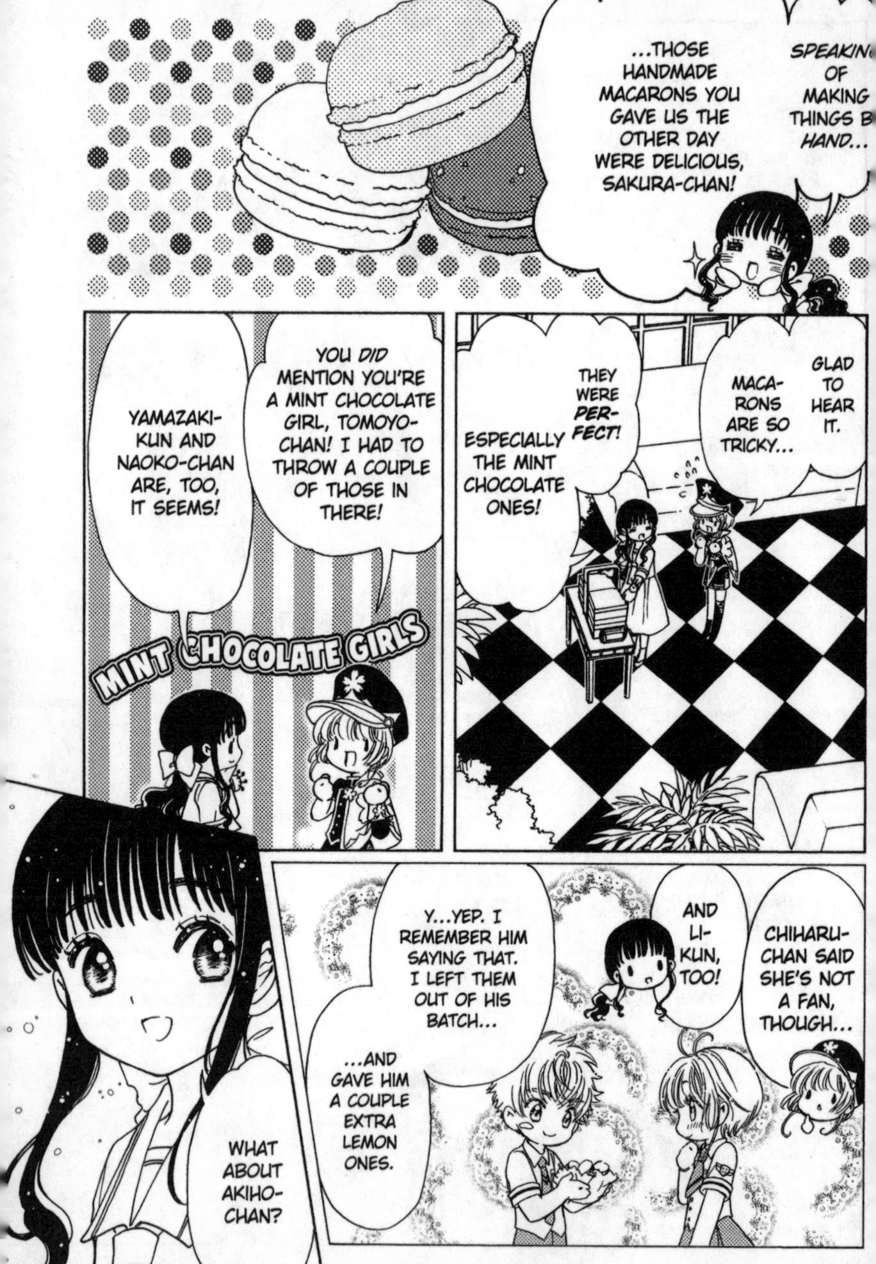
SPEAKIN OF MAKING THINGS B HAND...
...THOSE HANDMADE MACARONS YOU GAVE US THE OTHER DAY WERE DELICIOUS, SAKURA-CHAN!
GLAD TO HEAR IT.
MACARONS ARE SO TRICKY...
THEY WERE PERFECT!
ESPECIALLY THE MINT CHOCOLATE ONES!
YOU DID MENTION YOU'RE A MINT CHOCOLATE GIRL, TOMOYO-CHAN! I HAD TO THROW A COUPLE OF THOSE IN THERE!
YAMAZAKI-KUN AND NAOKO-CHAN ARE, TOO, IT SEEMS!
MINT CHOCOLATE GIRLS
CHIHARU-CHAN SAID SHE'S NOT A FAN, THOUGH...
AND LI-KUN, TOO!
Y...YEP. I REMEMBER HIM SAYING THAT. I LEFT THEM OUT OF HIS BATCH...
...AND GAVE HIM A COUPLE EXTRA LEMON ONES.
WHAT ABOUT AKIHO-CHAN?

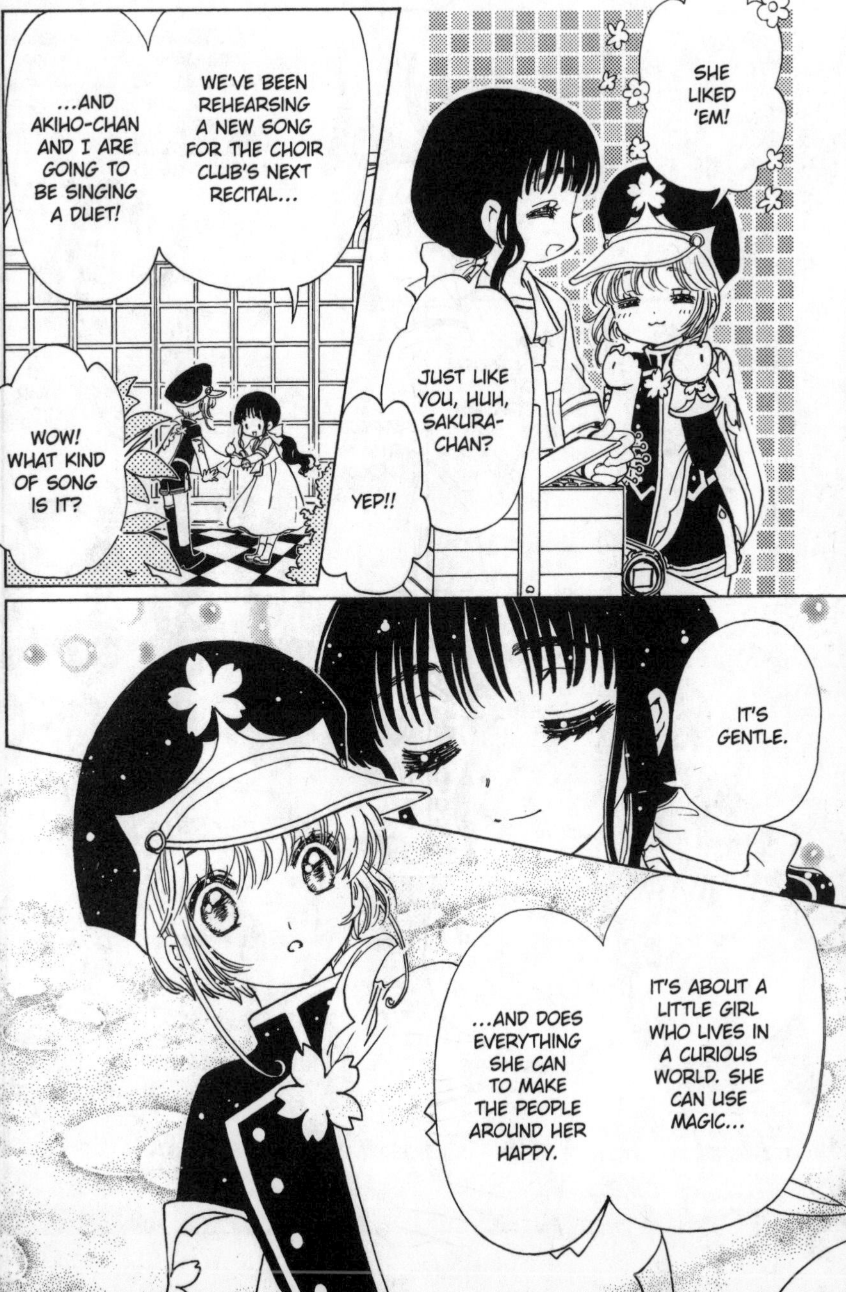
SHE LIKED 'EM!
JUST LIKE YOU, HUH, SAKURA-CHAN?
YEP!!
WE'VE BEEN REHEARSING A NEW SONG FOR THE CHOIR CLUB'S NEXT RECITAL...
...AND AKIHO-CHAN AND I ARE GOING TO BE SINGING A DUET!
WOW! WHAT KIND OF SONG IS IT?
IT'S GENTLE.
IT'S ABOUT A LITTLE GIRL WHO LIVES IN A CURIOUS WORLD. SHE CAN USE MAGIC...
...AND DOES EVERYTHING SHE CAN TO MAKE THE PEOPLE AROUND HER HAPPY.

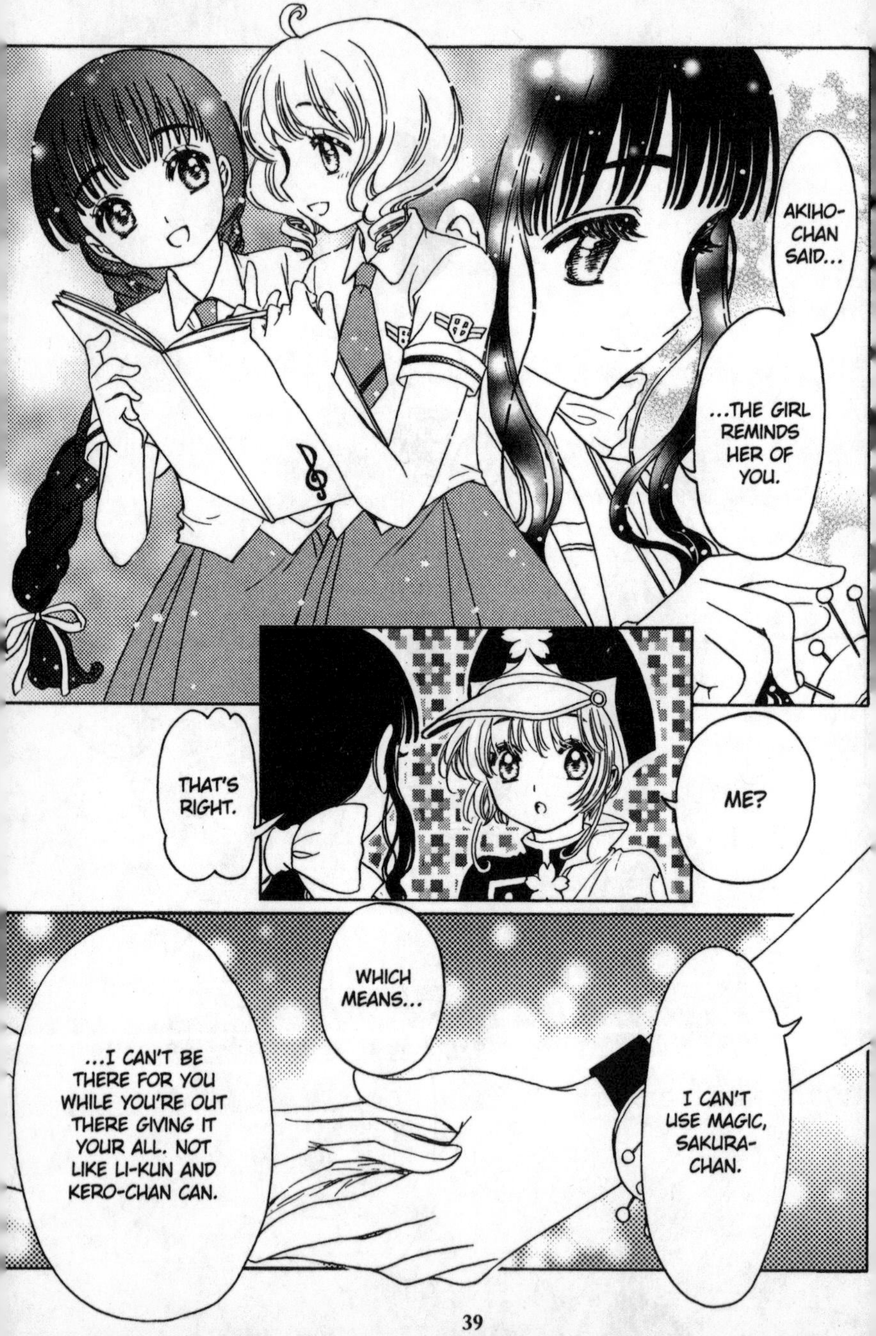
AKIHO-CHAN SAID...
...THE GIRL REMINDS HER OF YOU.
ME?
THAT'S RIGHT.
I CAN'T USE MAGIC, SAKURA-CHAN.
WHICH MEANS...
...I CAN'T BE THERE FOR YOU WHILE YOU'RE OUT THERE GIVING IT YOUR ALL. NOT LIKE LI-KUN AND KERO-CHAN CAN.

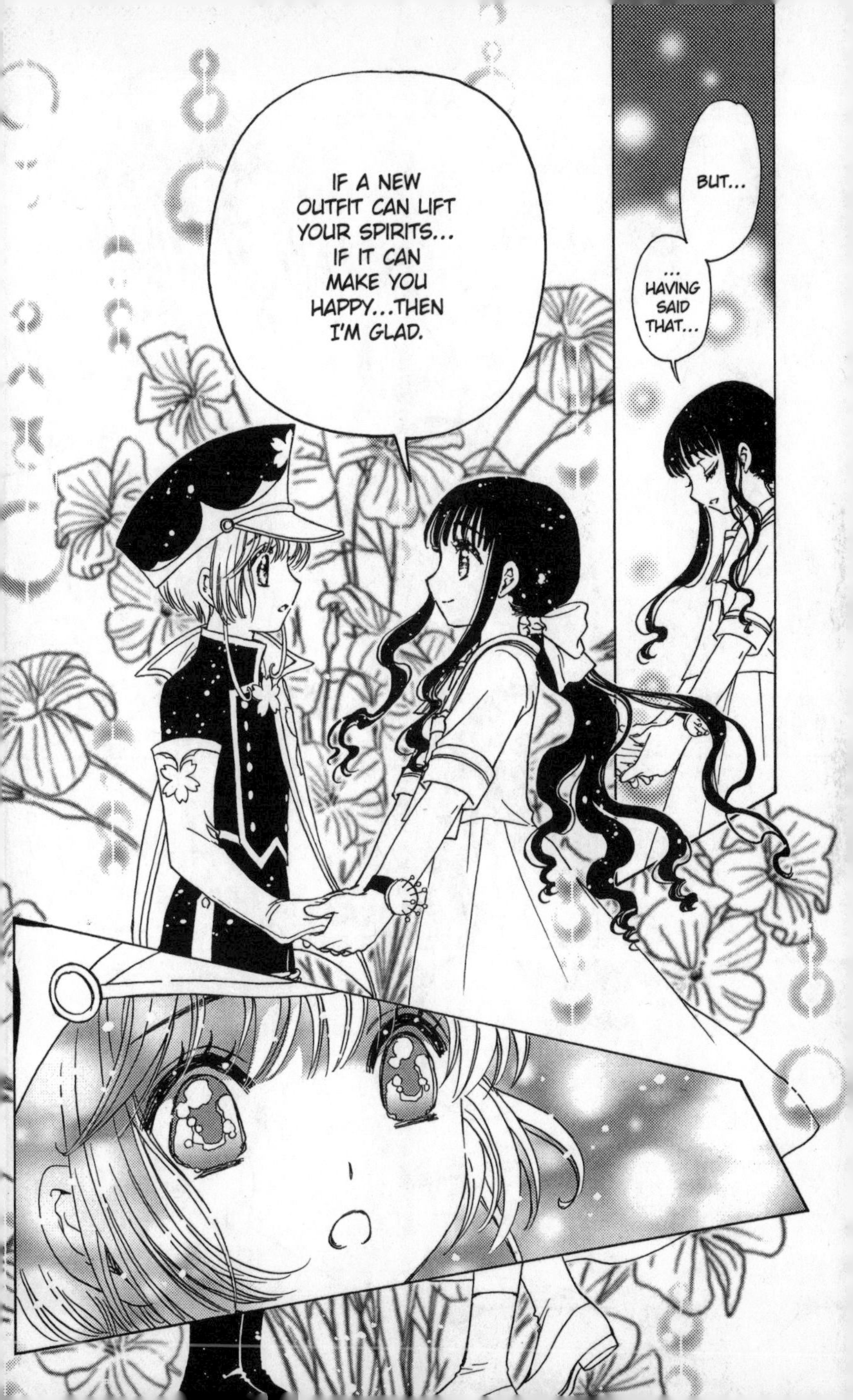
BUT...
...HAVING SAID THAT...
IF A NEW OUTFIT CAN LIFT YOUR SPIRITS... IF IT CAN MAKE YOU HAPPY...THEN I'M GLAD.

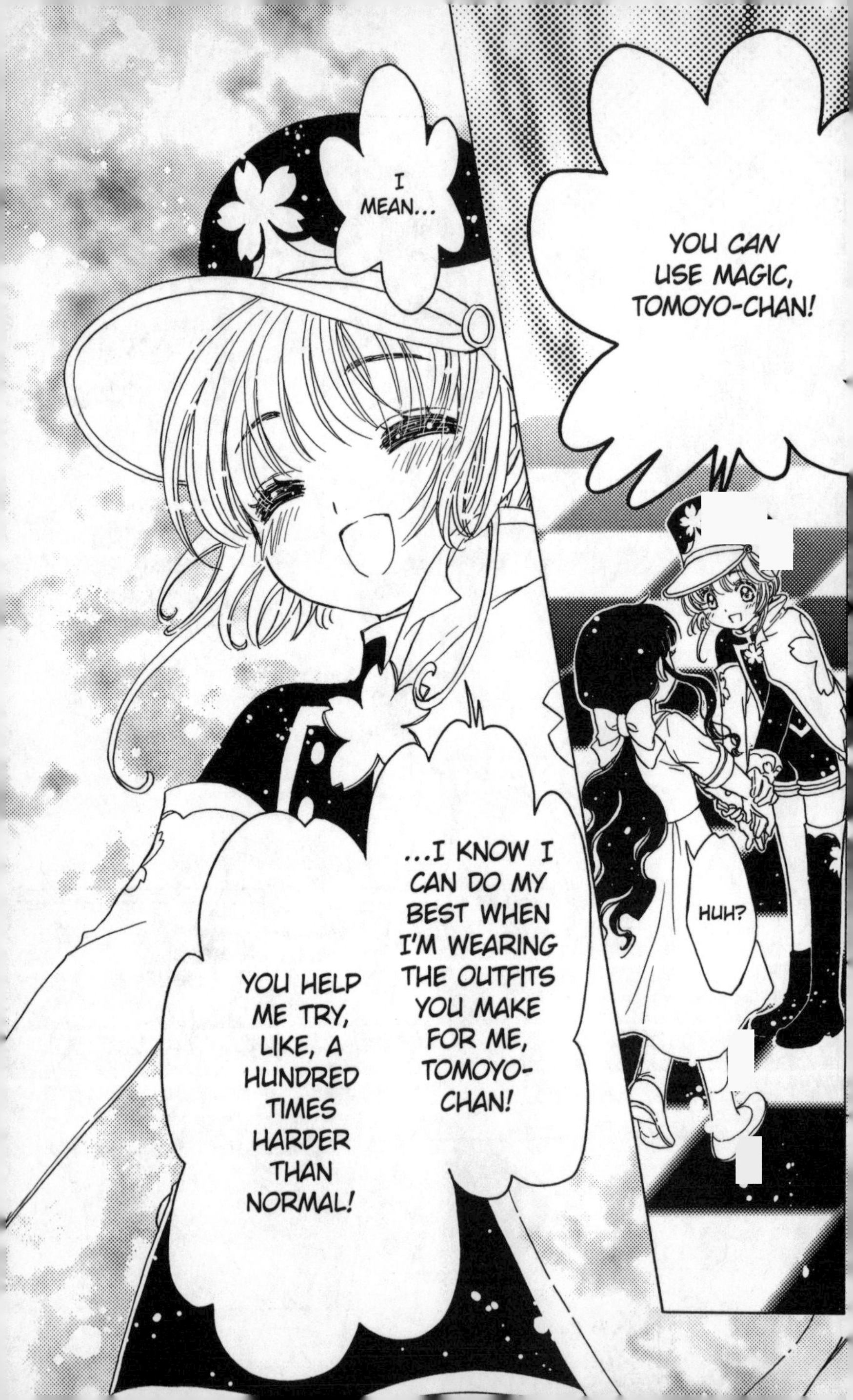
YOU CAN USE MAGIC, TOMOYO-CHAN!
HUH?
I MEAN...
...I KNOW I CAN DO MY BEST WHEN I'M WEARING THE OUTFITS YOU MAKE FOR ME, TOMOYO-CHAN!
YOU HELP ME TRY, LIKE, A HUNDRED TIMES HARDER THAN NORMAL!

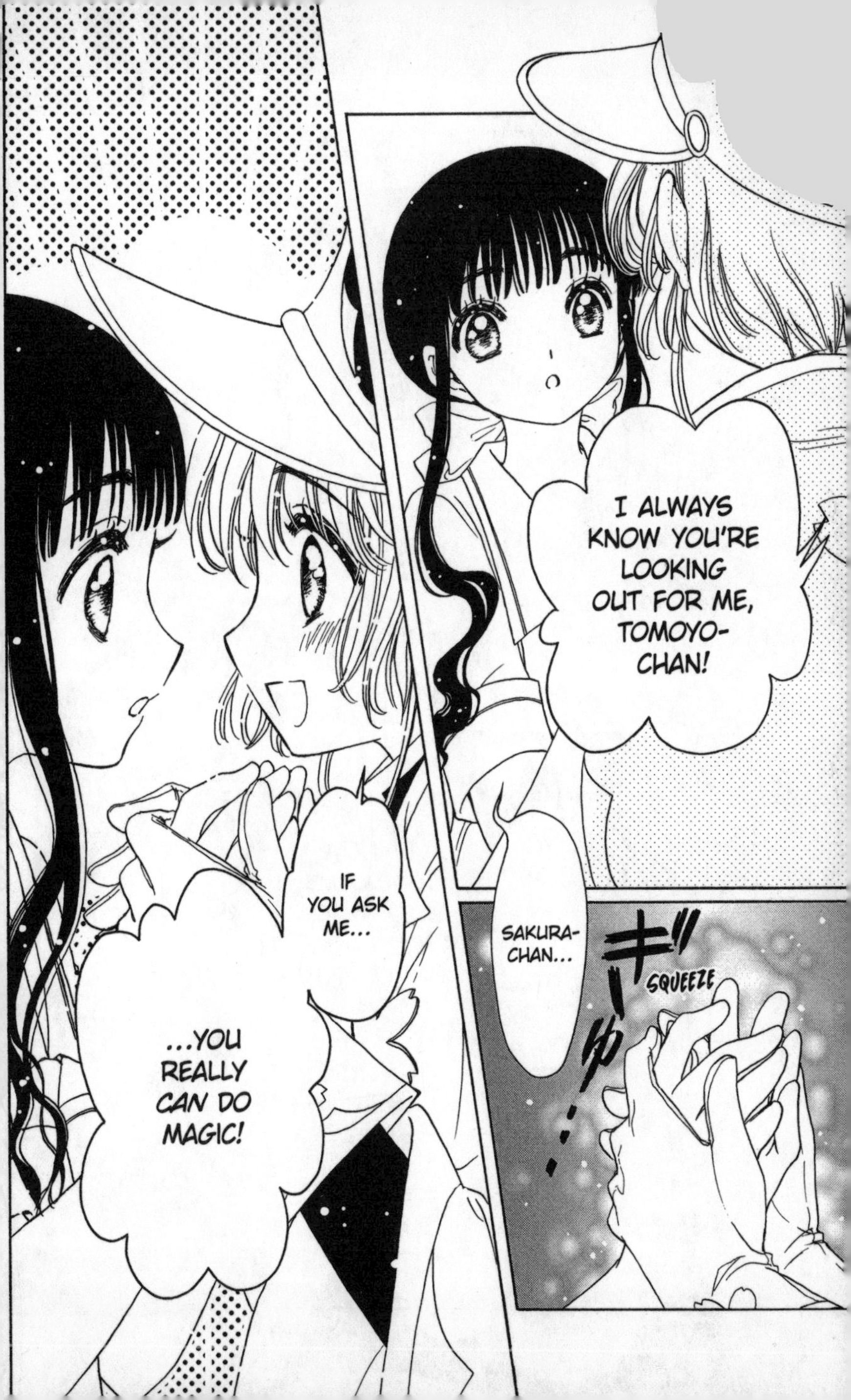
I ALWAYS KNOW YOU'RE LOOKING OUT FOR ME, TOMOYO-CHAN!
SAKURA-CHAN...
SQUEEZE
IF YOU ASK ME...
...YOU REALLY CAN DO MAGIC!

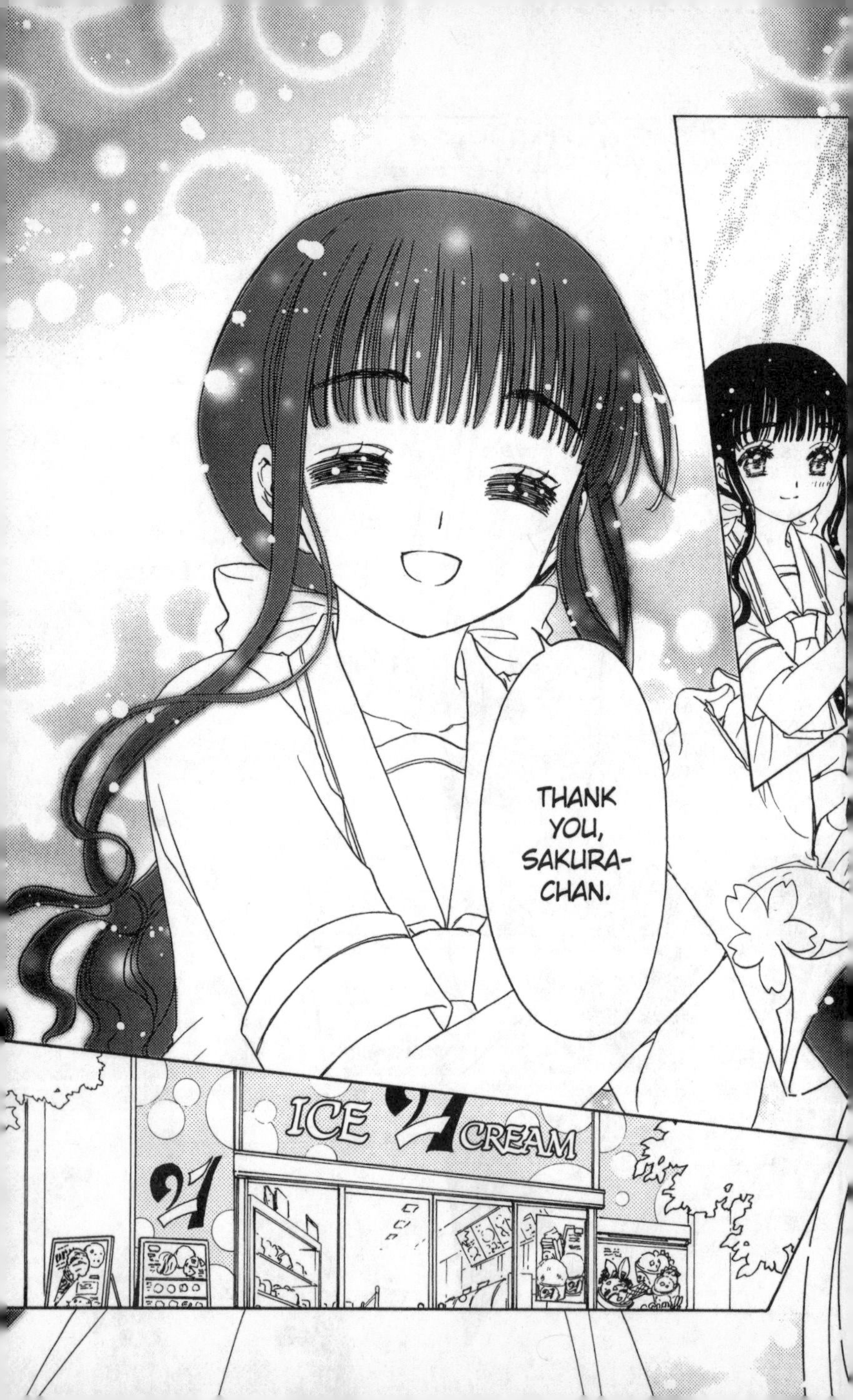
THANK YOU, SAKURA-CHAN.
ICE 21 CREAM
21

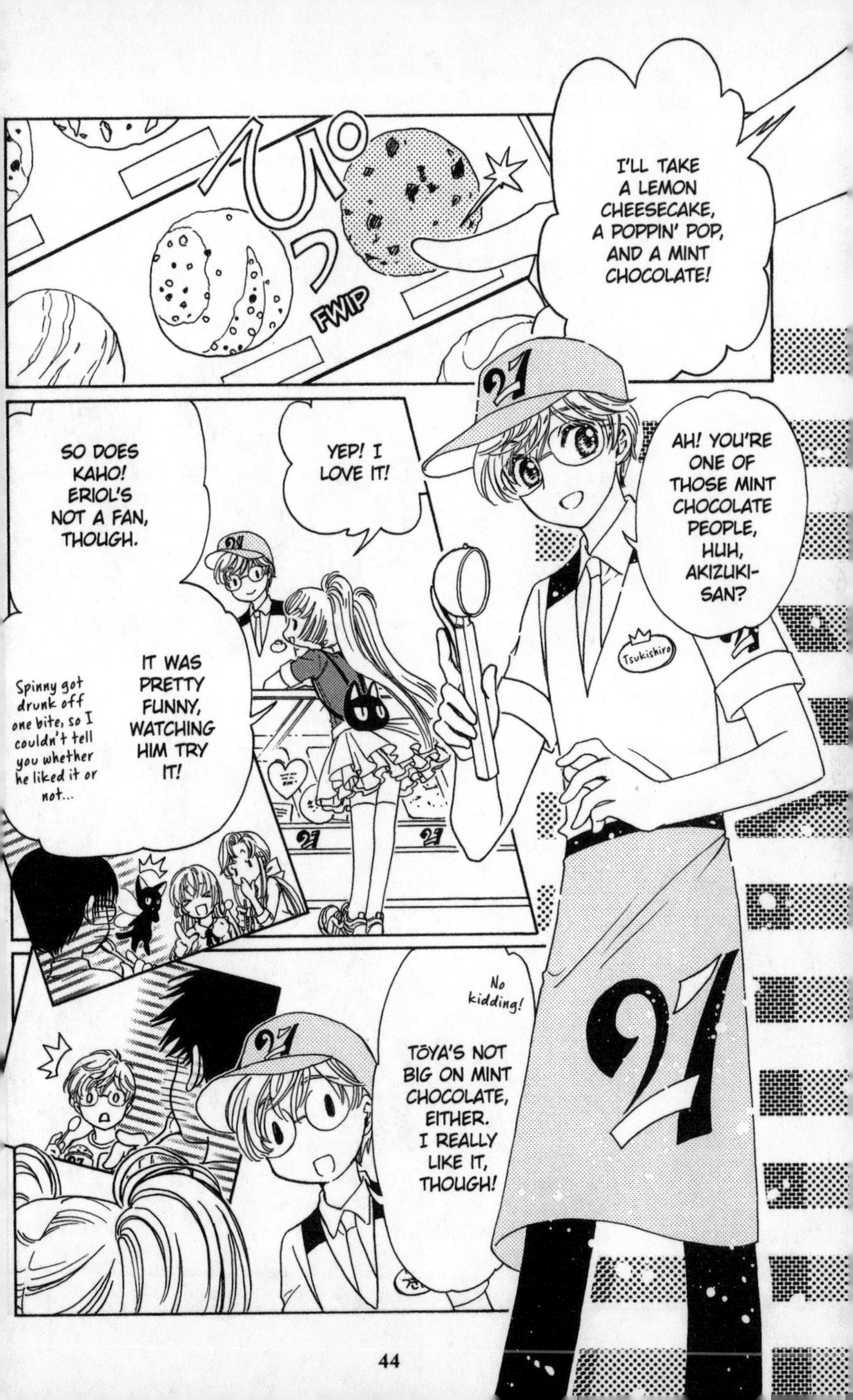
I'LL TAKE A LEMON CHEESECAKE, A POPPIN' POP, AND A MINT CHOCOLATE!
FWIP
AH! YOU'RE ONE OF THOSE MINT CHOCOLATE PEOPLE, HUH, AKIZUKI-SAN?
Tsukishiro
YEP! I LOVE IT!
SO DOES KAHO! ERIOL'S NOT A FAN, THOUGH.
IT WAS PRETTY FUNNY, WATCHING HIM TRY IT!
Spinny got drunk off one bite, so I couldn't tell you whether he liked it or not...
No kidding!
TŌYA'S NOT BIG ON MINT CHOCOLATE, EITHER. I REALLY LIKE IT, THOUGH!

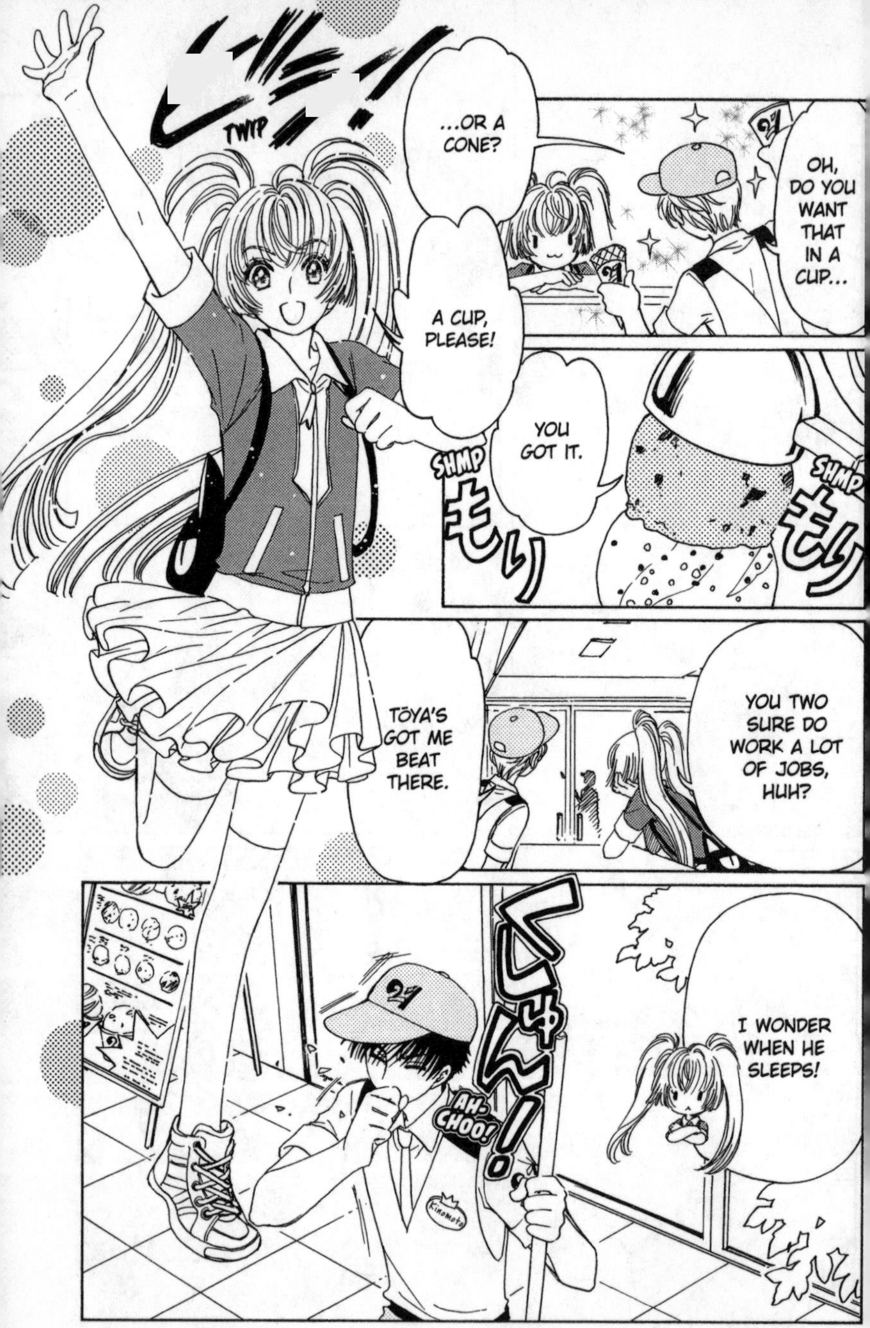
OH, DO YOU WANT THAT IN A CUP...
...OR A CONE?
A CUP, PLEASE!
TWIP
SHMP
もり
YOU GOT IT.
SHMP
もり
YOU TWO SURE DO WORK A LOT OF JOBS, HUH?
TŌYA'S GOT ME BEAT THERE.
I WONDER WHEN HE SLEEPS!
しゅん！
AH-CHOO!

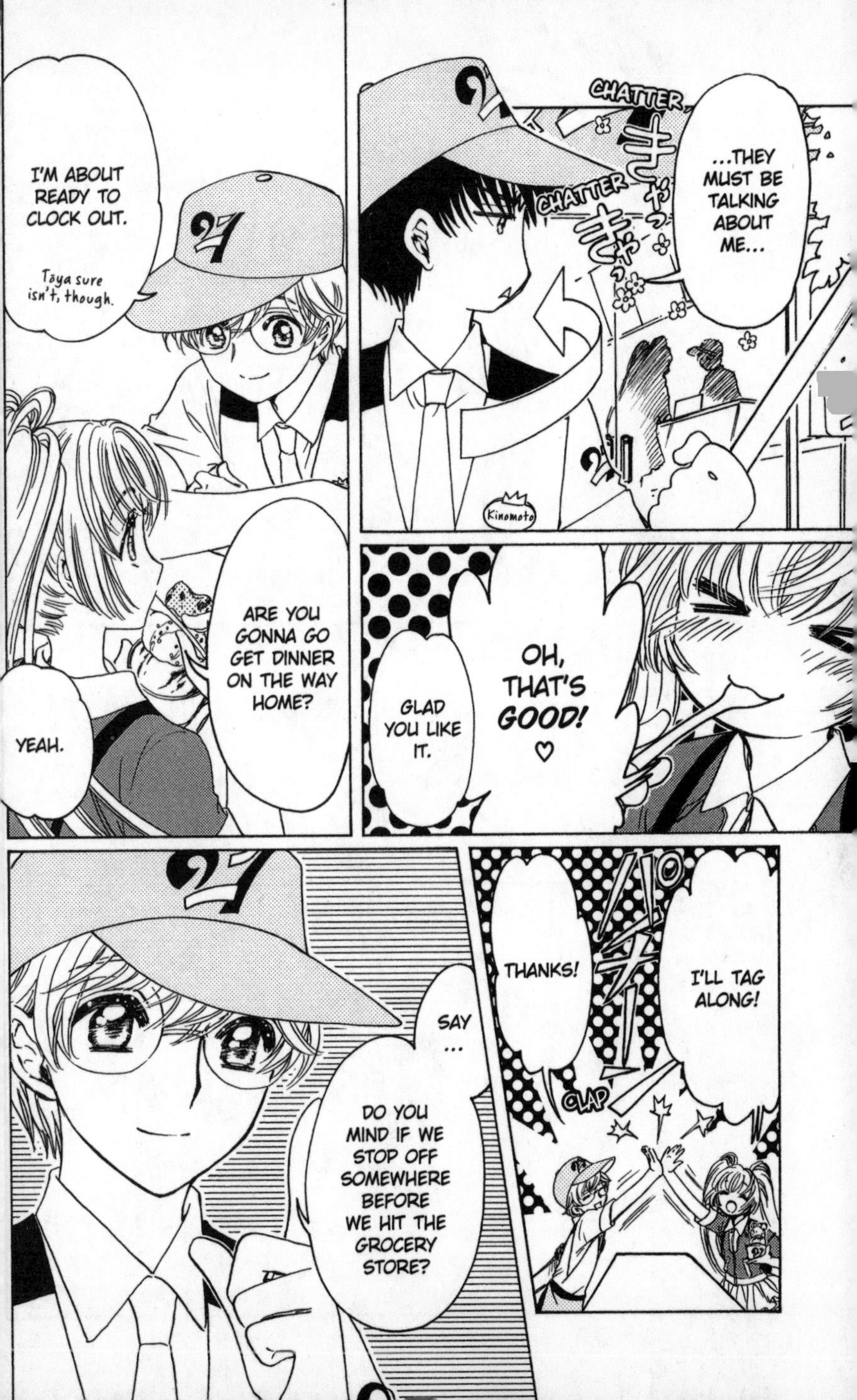
CHATTER
CHATTER
...THEY MUST BE TALKING ABOUT ME...
Kinomoto
OH, THAT'S GOOD! ♡
GLAD YOU LIKE IT.
I'M ABOUT READY TO CLOCK OUT.
Tōya sure isn't, though.
ARE YOU GONNA GO GET DINNER ON THE WAY HOME?
YEAH.
I'LL TAG ALONG!
THANKS!
CLAP
SAY...
DO YOU MIND IF WE STOP OFF SOMEWHERE BEFORE WE HIT THE GROCERY STORE?

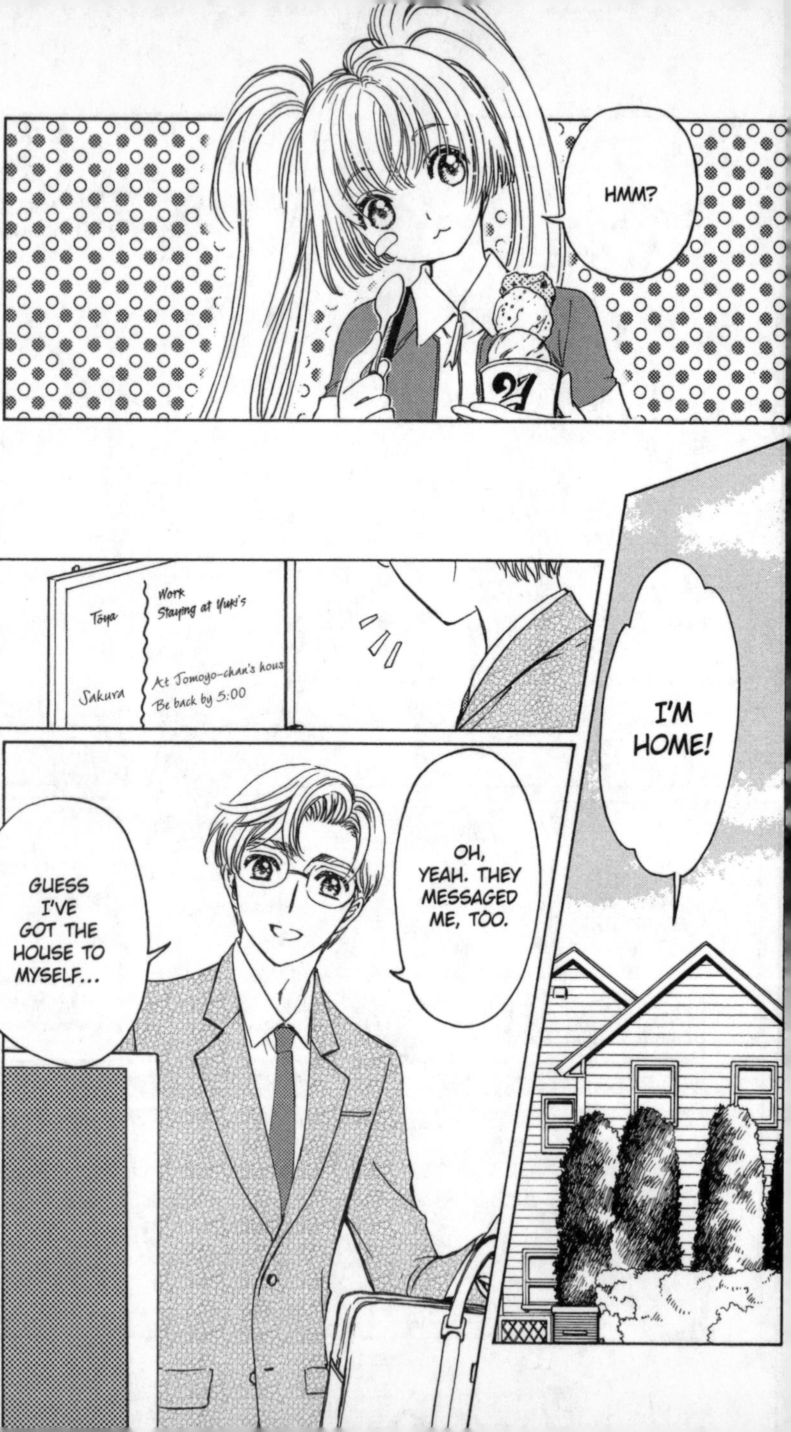
HMM?
I'M HOME!
Tōya
Work
Staying at Yuki's
Sakura
At Tomoyo-chan's hous
Be back by 5:00
OH, YEAH. THEY MESSAGED ME, TOO.
GUESS I'VE GOT THE HOUSE TO MYSELF...

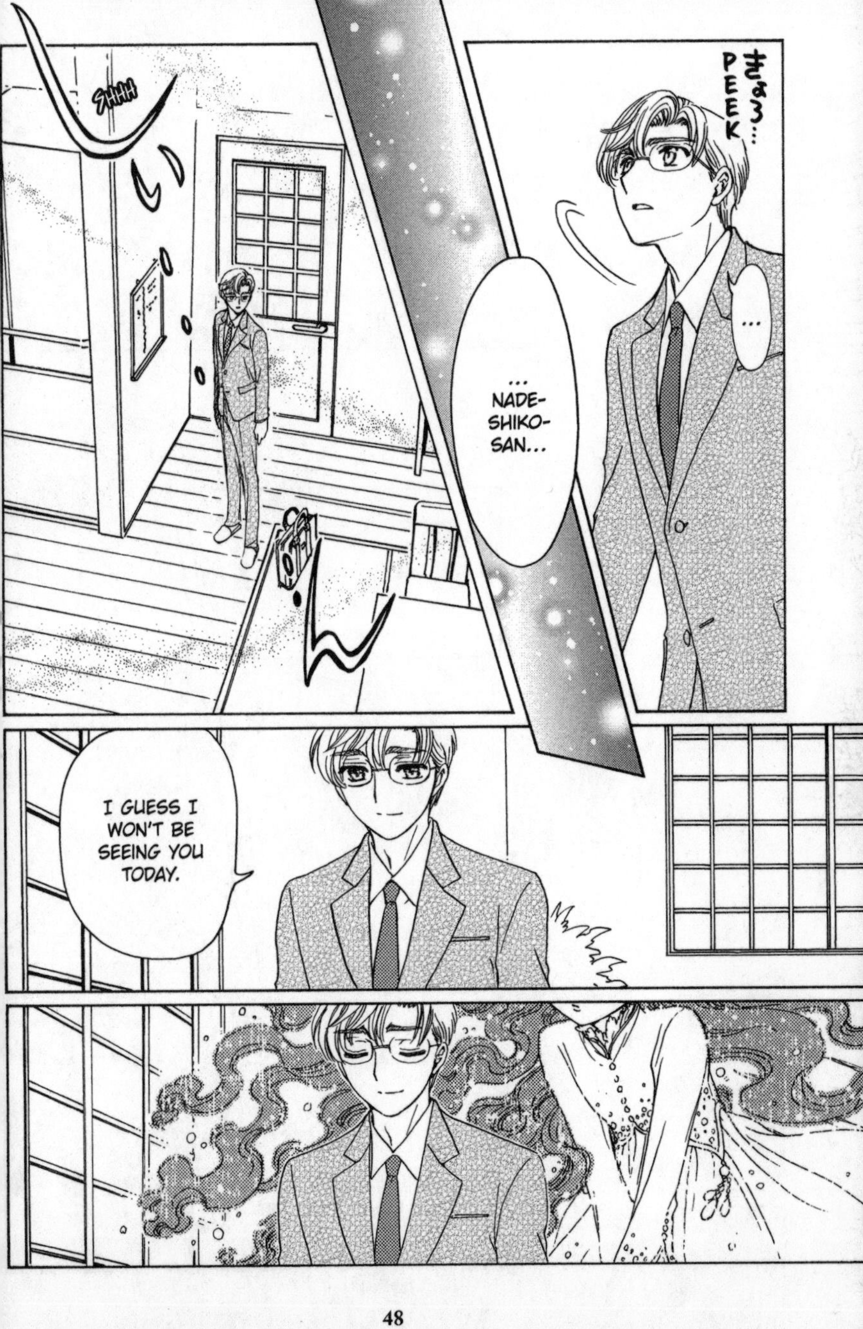
きょろ…
PEEK
...
... NADE-SHIKO-SAN...
SHHH
I GUESS I WON'T BE SEEING YOU TODAY.

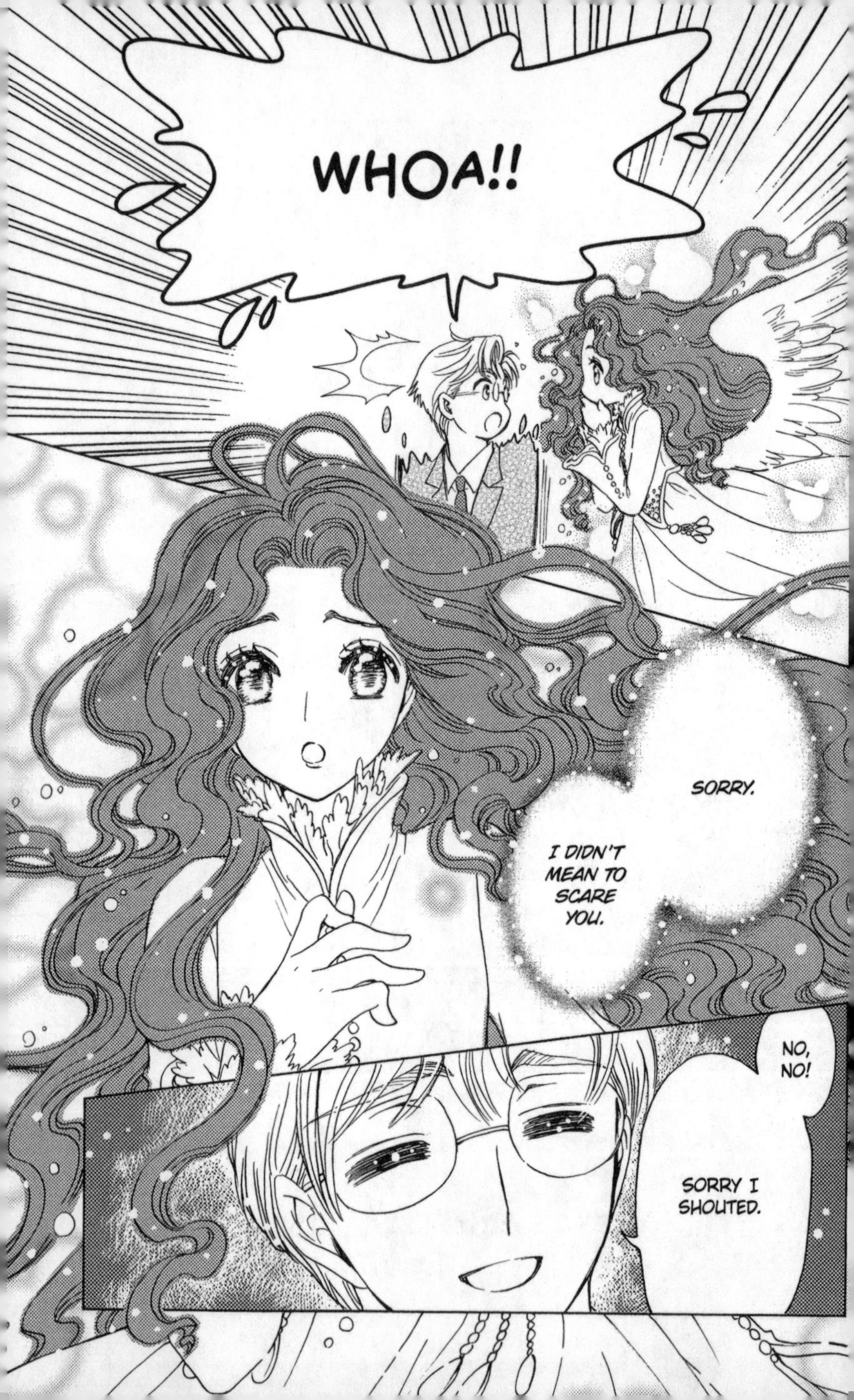
WHOA!!
SORRY.
I DIDN'T MEAN TO SCARE YOU.
NO, NO!
SORRY I SHOUTED.

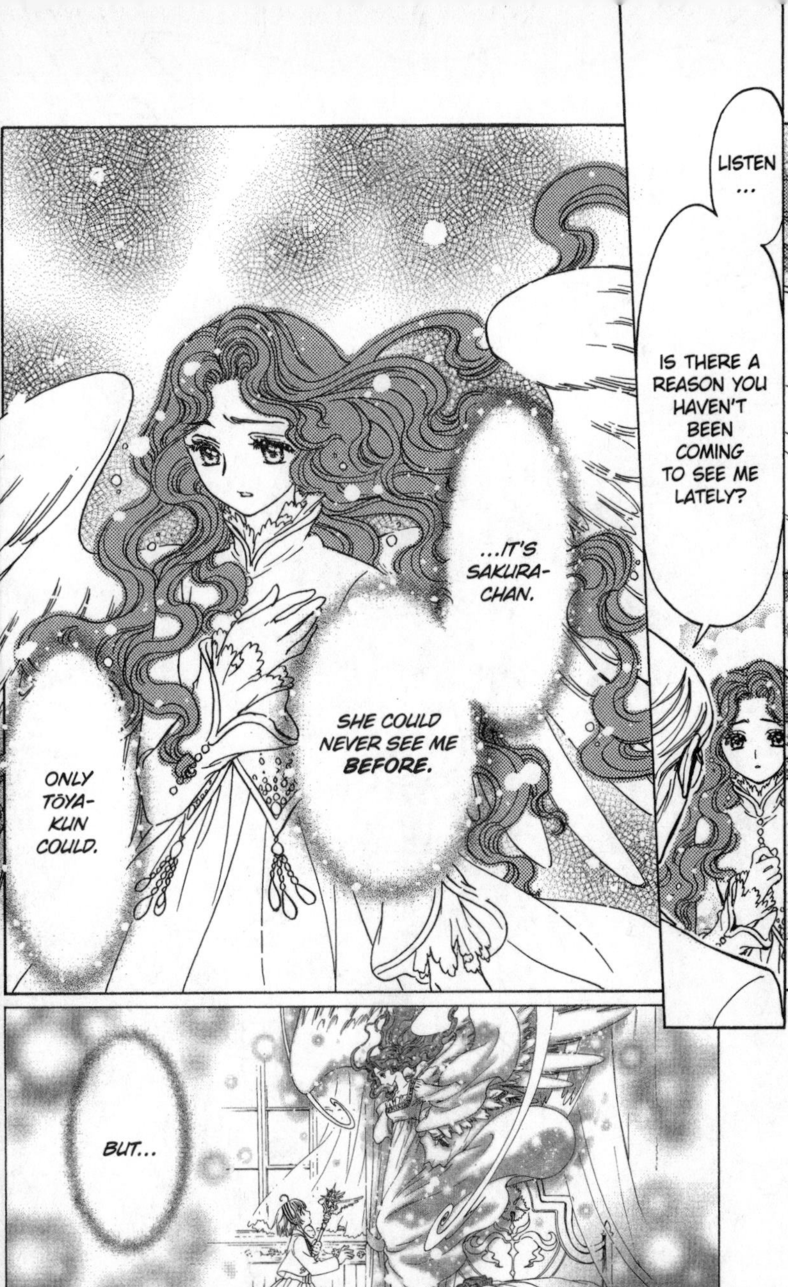
LISTEN...
IS THERE A REASON YOU HAVEN'T BEEN COMING TO SEE ME LATELY?
...IT'S SAKURA-CHAN.
SHE COULD NEVER SEE ME **BEFORE.**
ONLY TŌYA-KUN COULD.
BUT...

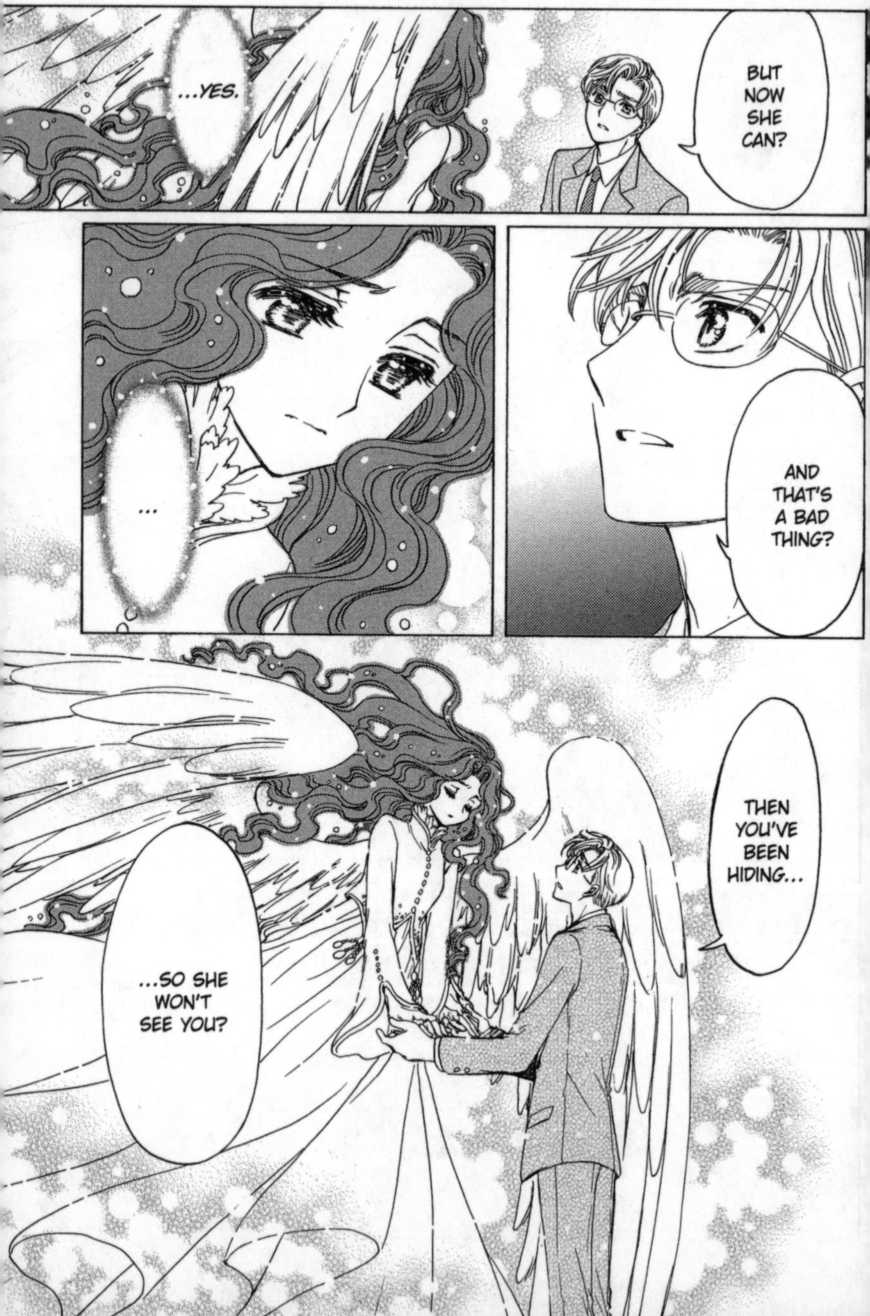
BUT NOW SHE CAN?
...YES.
AND THAT'S A BAD THING?
...
THEN YOU'VE BEEN HIDING...
...SO SHE WON'T SEE YOU?

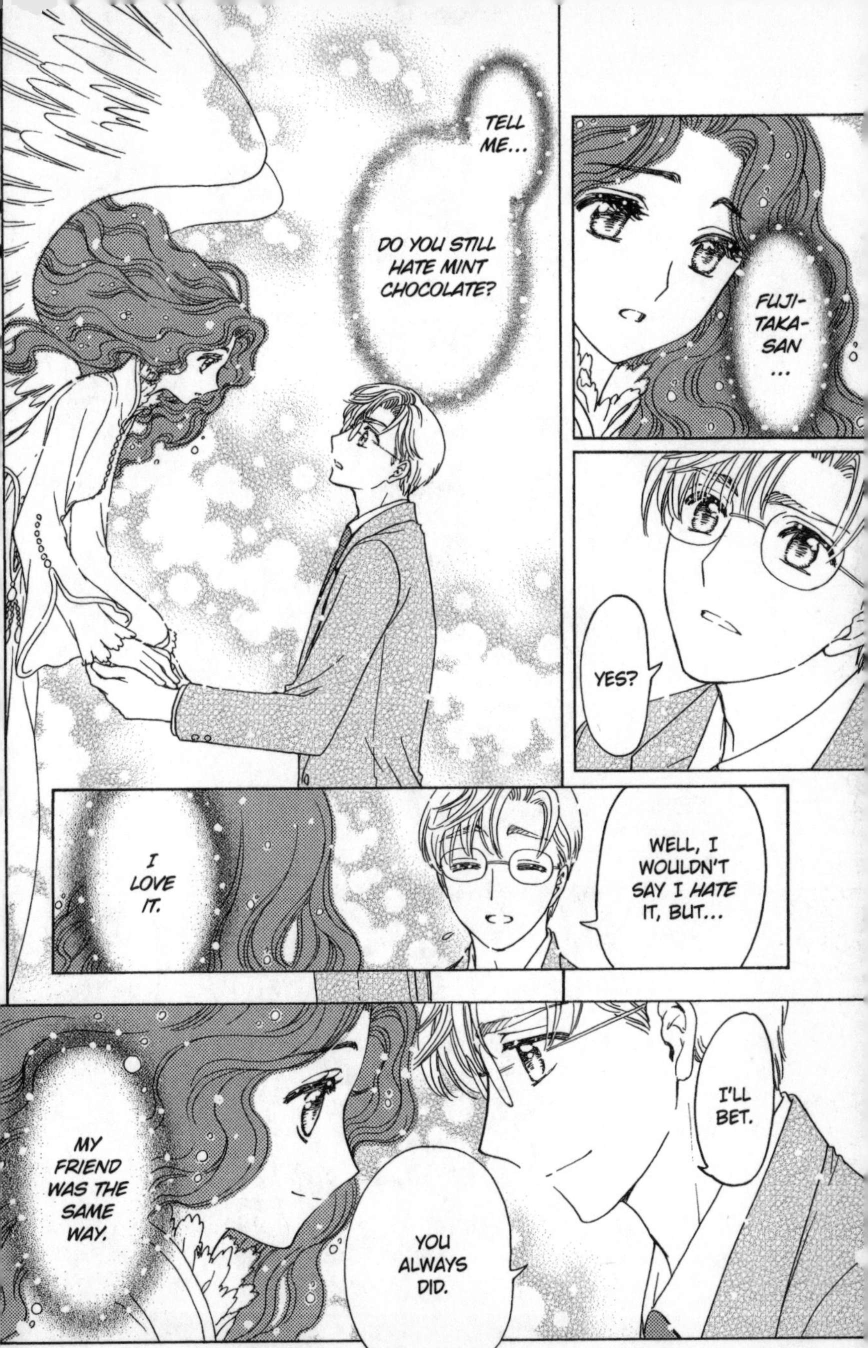
FUJI-TAKA-SAN...
YES?
TELL ME...
DO YOU STILL HATE MINT CHOCOLATE?
WELL, I WOULDN'T SAY I *HATE* IT, BUT...
I LOVE IT.
I'LL BET.
YOU ALWAYS DID.
MY FRIEND WAS THE SAME WAY.

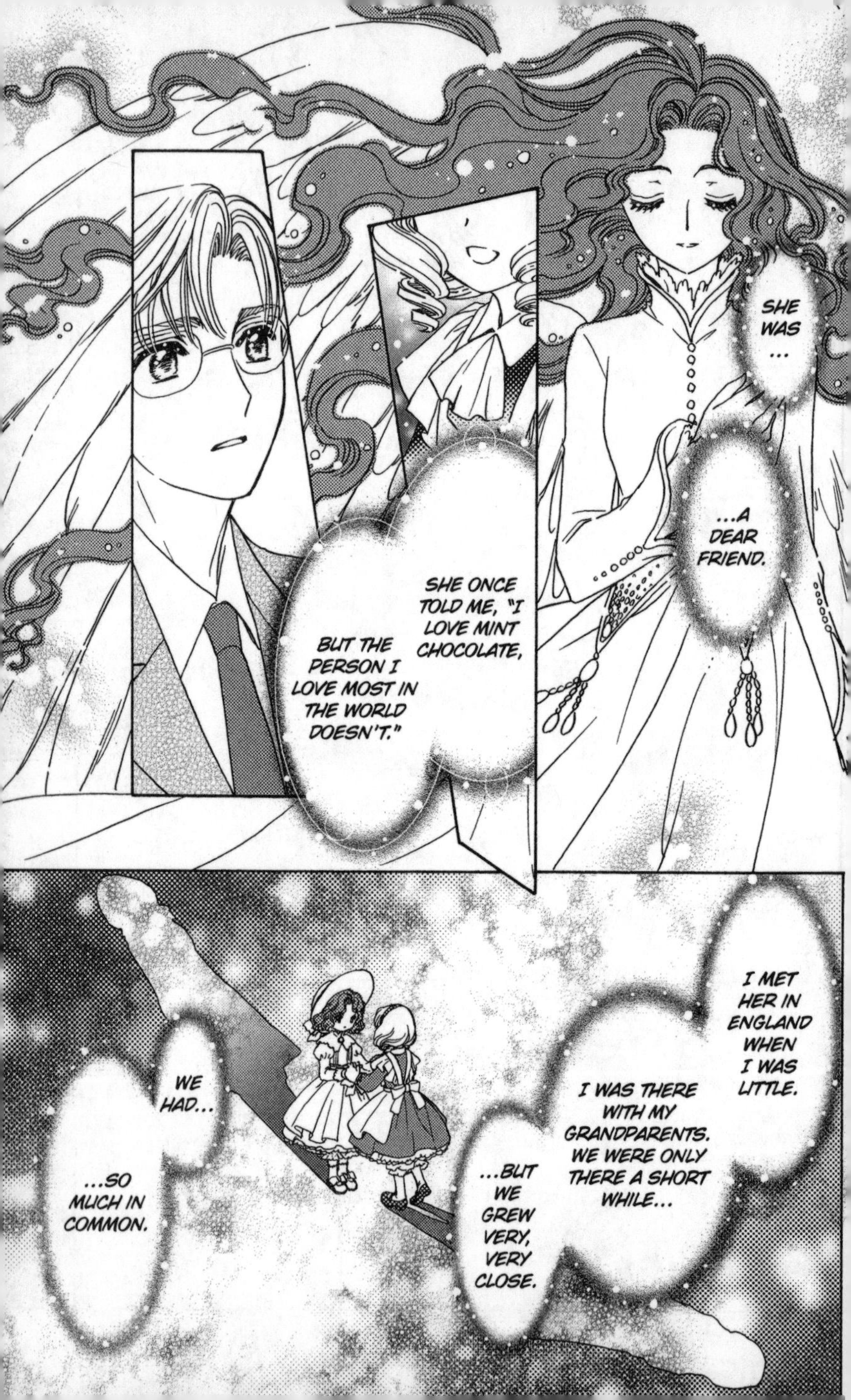
SHE WAS...
...A DEAR FRIEND.
SHE ONCE TOLD ME, "I LOVE MINT CHOCOLATE,
BUT THE PERSON I LOVE MOST IN THE WORLD DOESN'T."
I MET HER IN ENGLAND WHEN I WAS LITTLE.
I WAS THERE WITH MY GRANDPARENTS. WE WERE ONLY THERE A SHORT WHILE...
...BUT WE GREW VERY, VERY CLOSE.
WE HAD...
...SO MUCH IN COMMON.

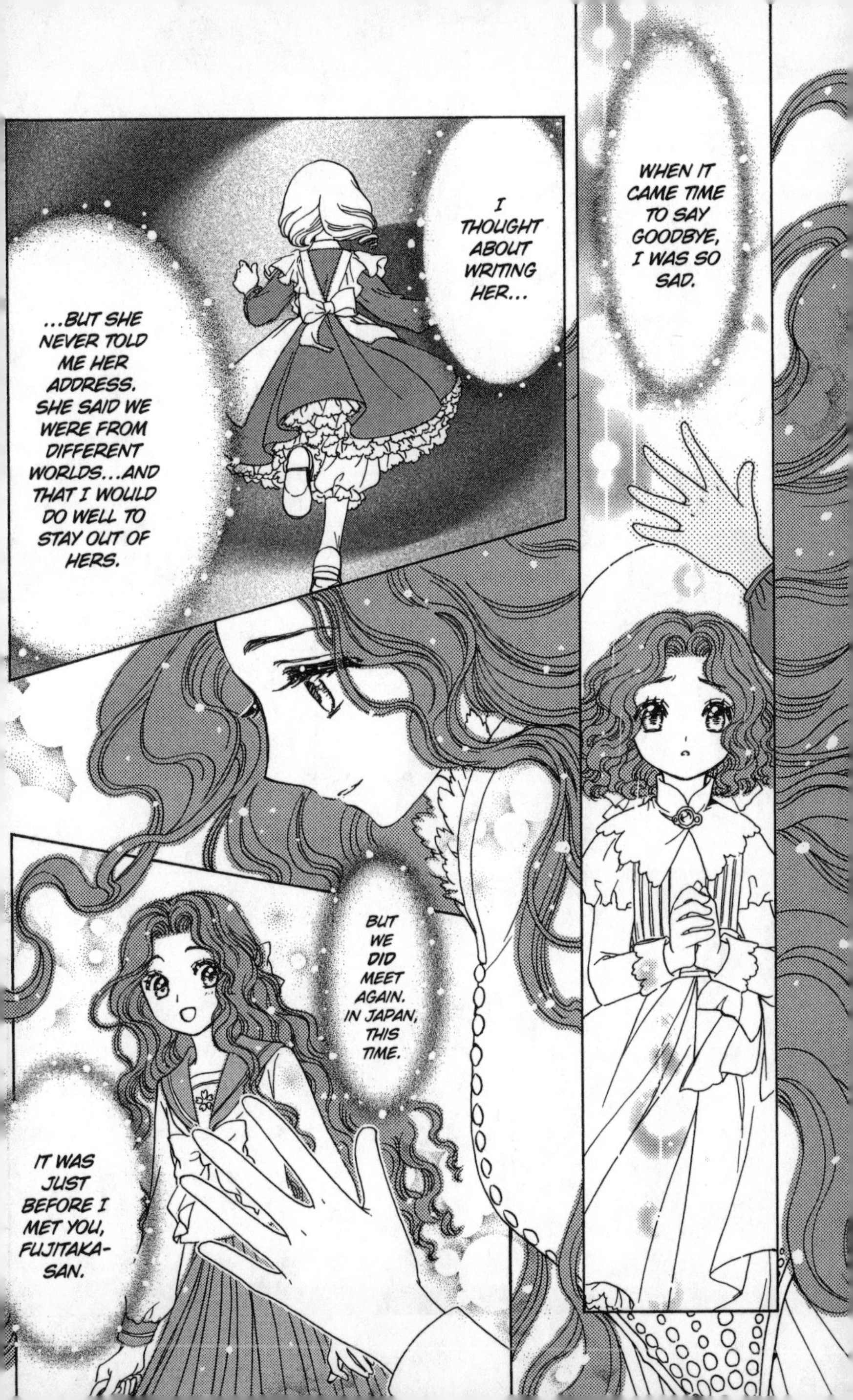
WHEN IT CAME TIME TO SAY GOODBYE, I WAS SO SAD.
I THOUGHT ABOUT WRITING HER...
...BUT SHE NEVER TOLD ME HER ADDRESS. SHE SAID WE WERE FROM DIFFERENT WORLDS...AND THAT I WOULD DO WELL TO STAY OUT OF HERS.
BUT WE DID MEET AGAIN. IN JAPAN, THIS TIME.
IT WAS JUST BEFORE I MET YOU, FUJITAKA-SAN.

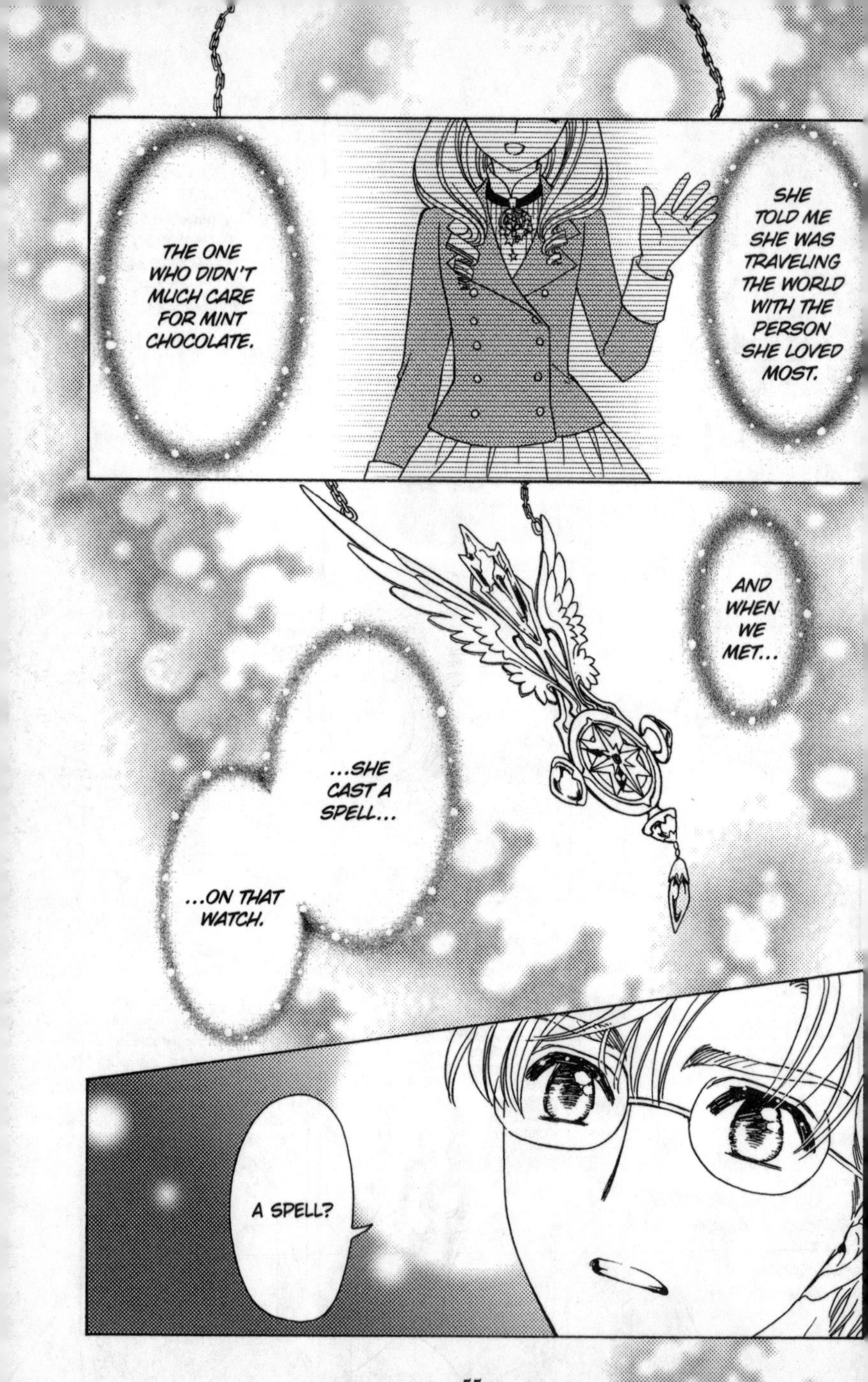
SHE TOLD ME SHE WAS TRAVELING THE WORLD WITH THE PERSON SHE LOVED MOST.
THE ONE WHO DIDN'T MUCH CARE FOR MINT CHOCOLATE.
AND WHEN WE MET...
...SHE CAST A SPELL...
...ON THAT WATCH.
A SPELL?

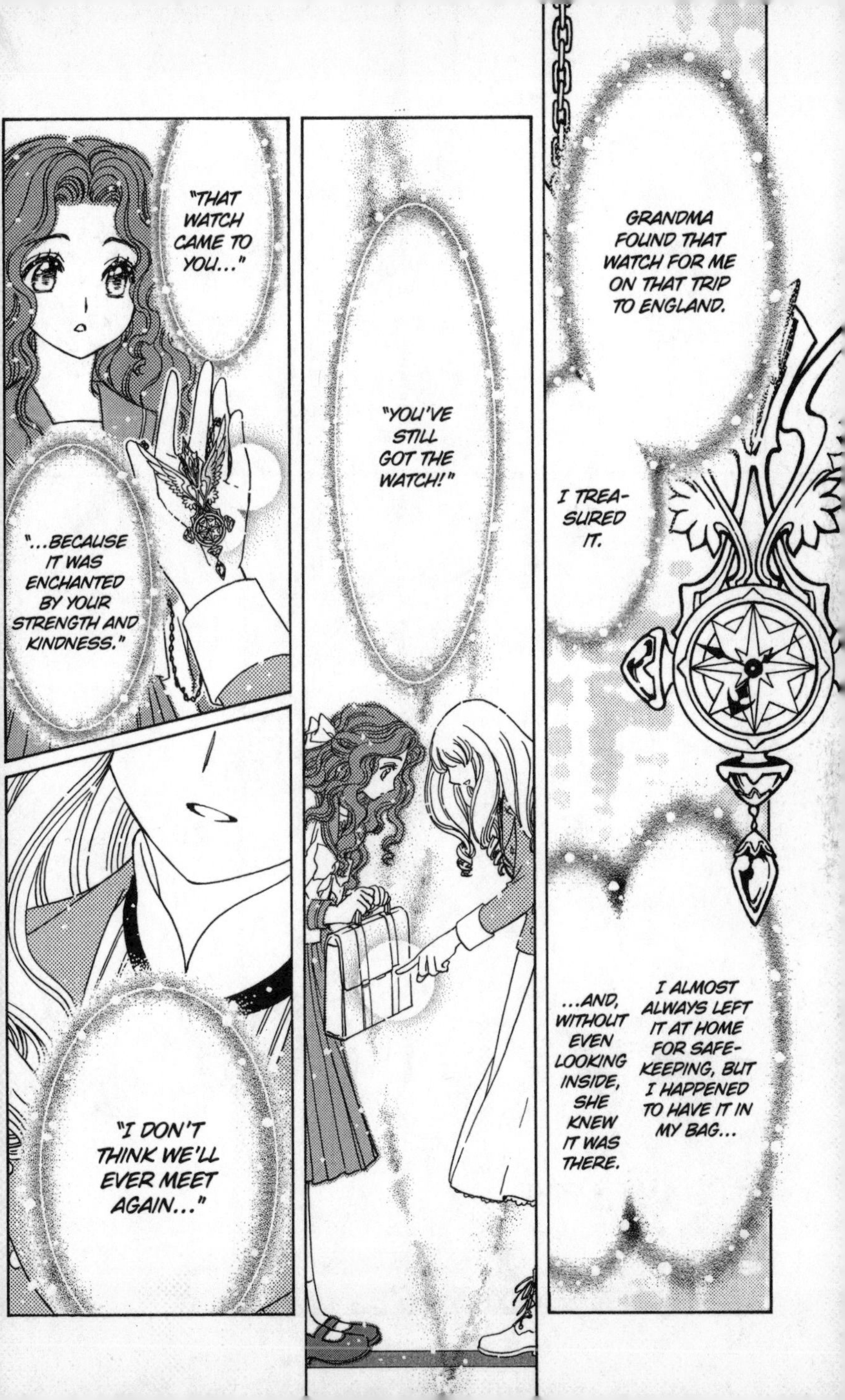
GRANDMA FOUND THAT WATCH FOR ME ON THAT TRIP TO ENGLAND.
I TREA-SURED IT.
I ALMOST ALWAYS LEFT IT AT HOME FOR SAFE-KEEPING, BUT I HAPPENED TO HAVE IT IN MY BAG...
...AND, WITHOUT EVEN LOOKING INSIDE, SHE KNEW IT WAS THERE.
"YOU'VE STILL GOT THE WATCH!"
"THAT WATCH CAME TO YOU..."
"...BECAUSE IT WAS ENCHANTED BY YOUR STRENGTH AND KINDNESS."
"I DON'T THINK WE'LL EVER MEET AGAIN..."

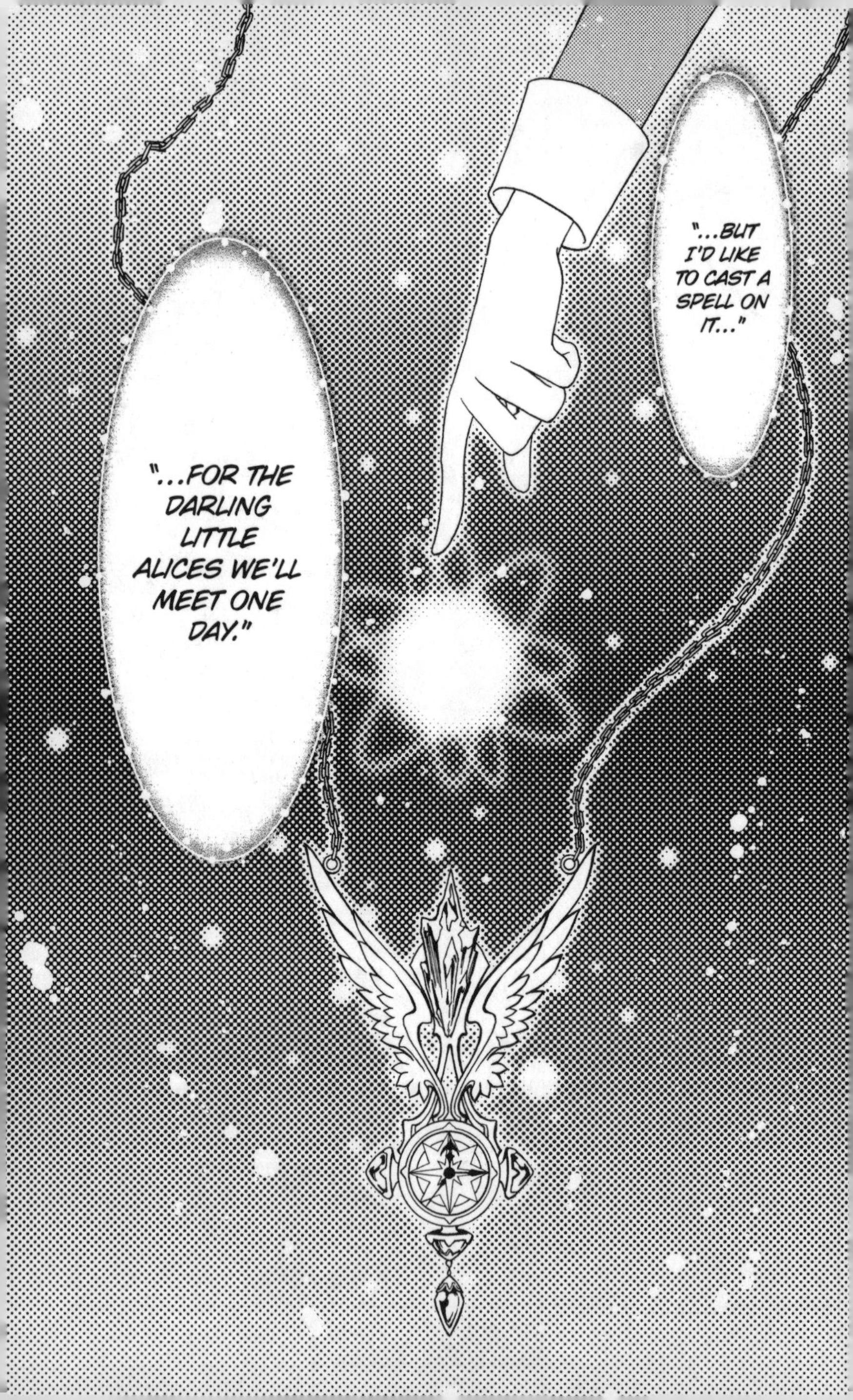
"...BUT I'D LIKE TO CAST A SPELL ON IT..."
"...FOR THE DARLING LITTLE ALICES WE'LL MEET ONE DAY."

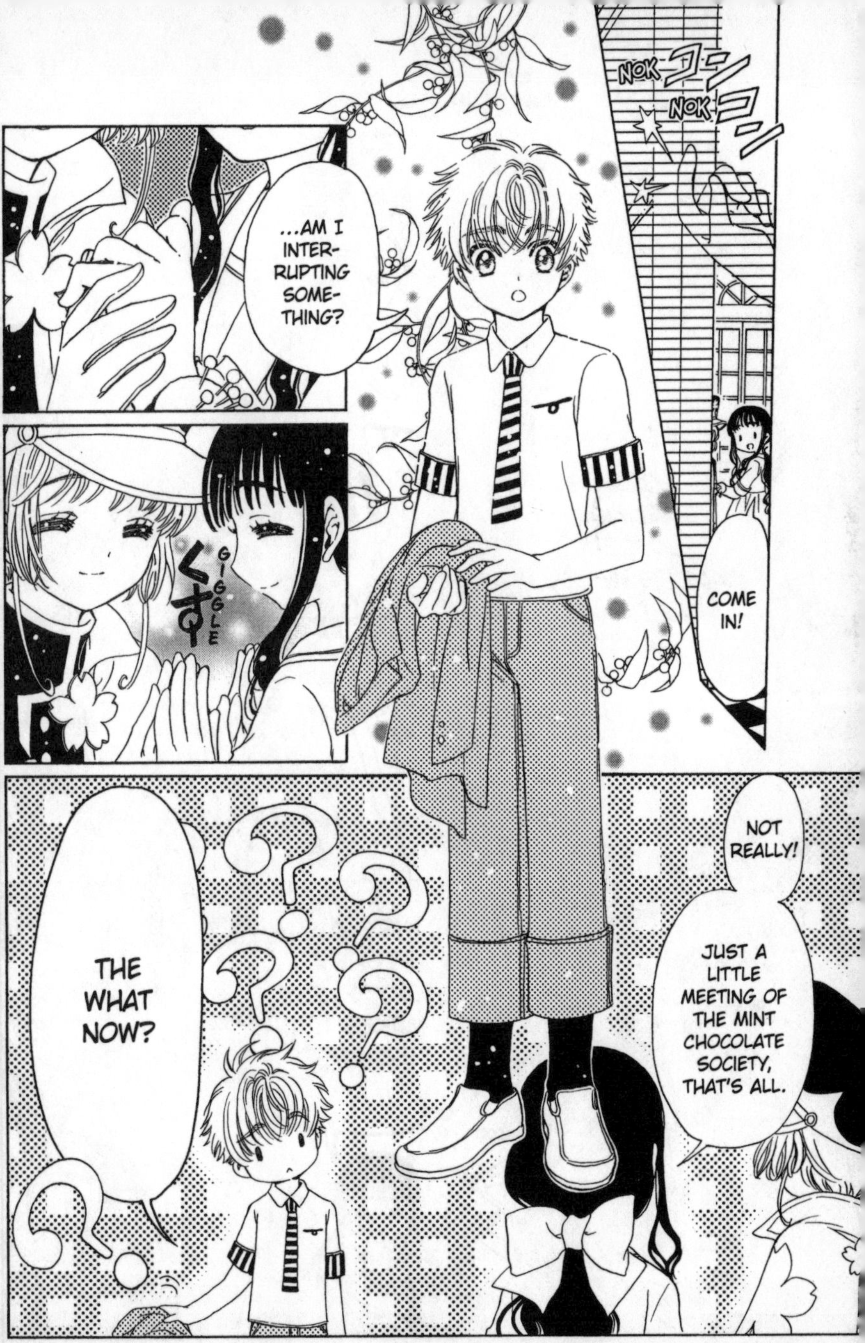
NOK NOK
COME IN!
...AM I INTERRUPTING SOMETHING?
GIGGLE
NOT REALLY!
JUST A LITTLE MEETING OF THE MINT CHOCOLATE SOCIETY, THAT'S ALL.
THE WHAT NOW?

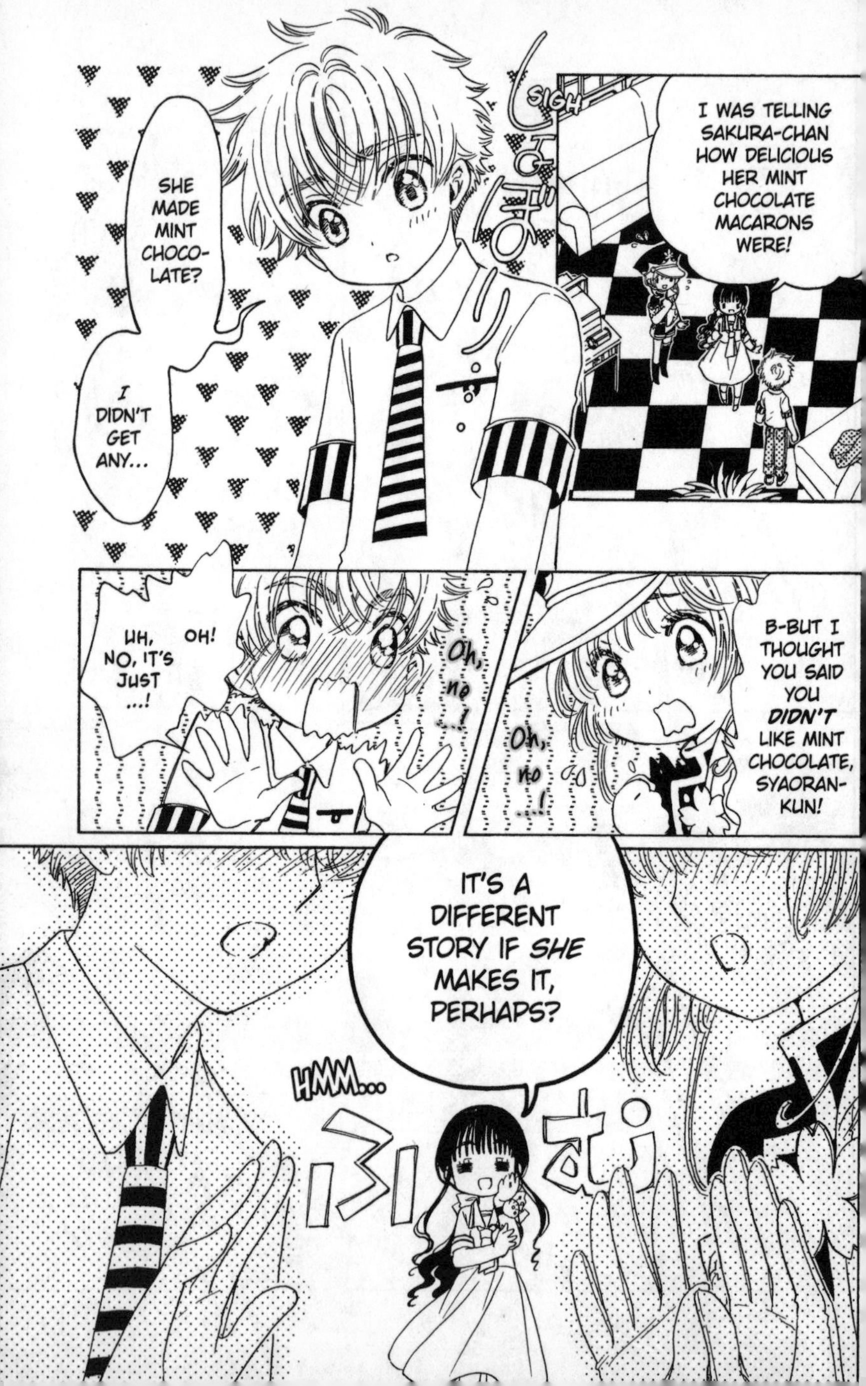
I WAS TELLING SAKURA-CHAN HOW DELICIOUS HER MINT CHOCOLATE MACARONS WERE!
SIGH
SHE MADE MINT CHOCO-LATE?
I DIDN'T GET ANY...
B-BUT I THOUGHT YOU SAID YOU *DIDN'T* LIKE MINT CHOCOLATE, SYAORAN-KUN!
Oh, no...!
Oh, no...!
UH, NO, IT'S JUST ...!
OH!
IT'S A DIFFERENT STORY IF *SHE* MAKES IT, PERHAPS?
HMM...

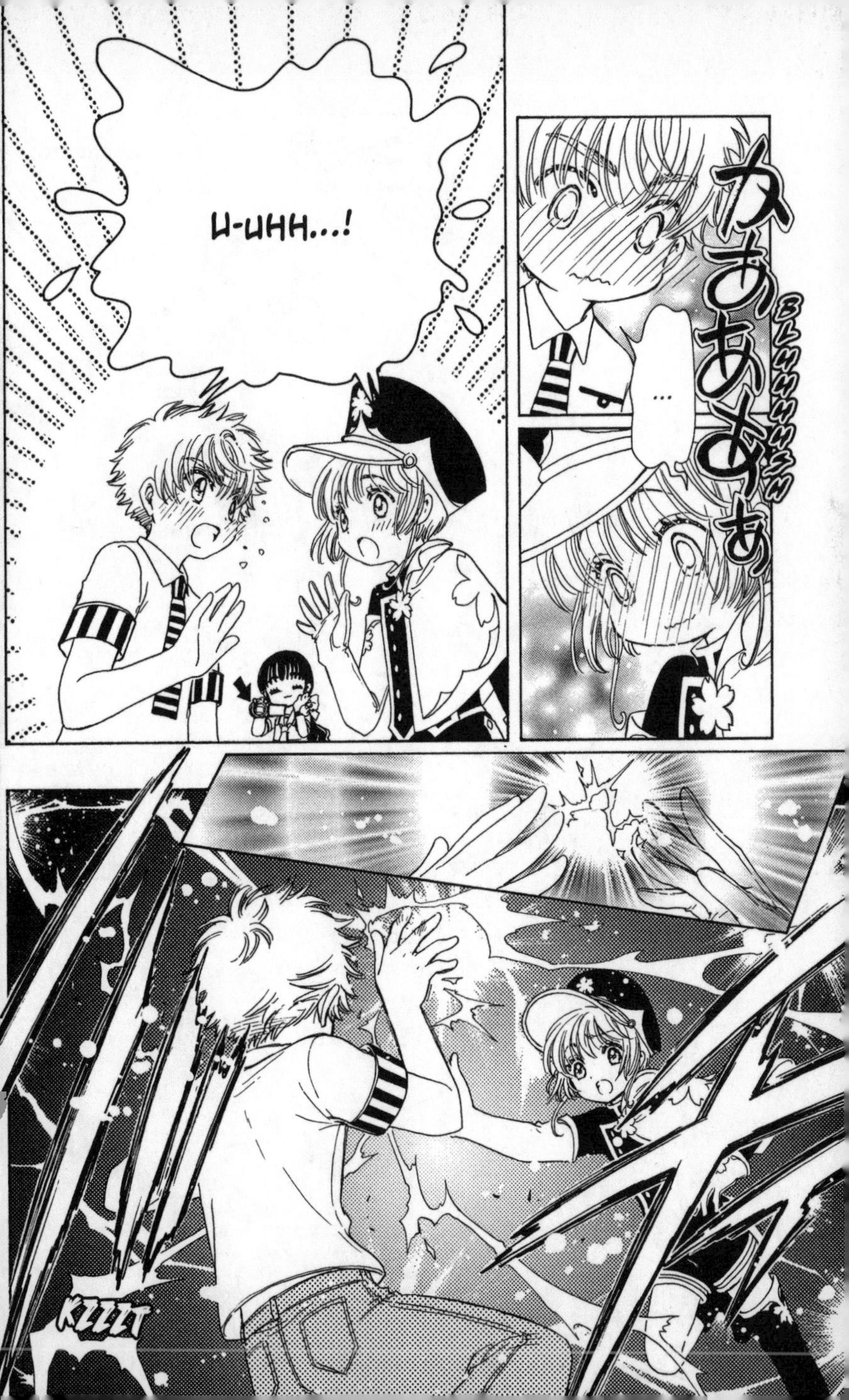
かあああああ
...
U-UHH...!
KZZZT

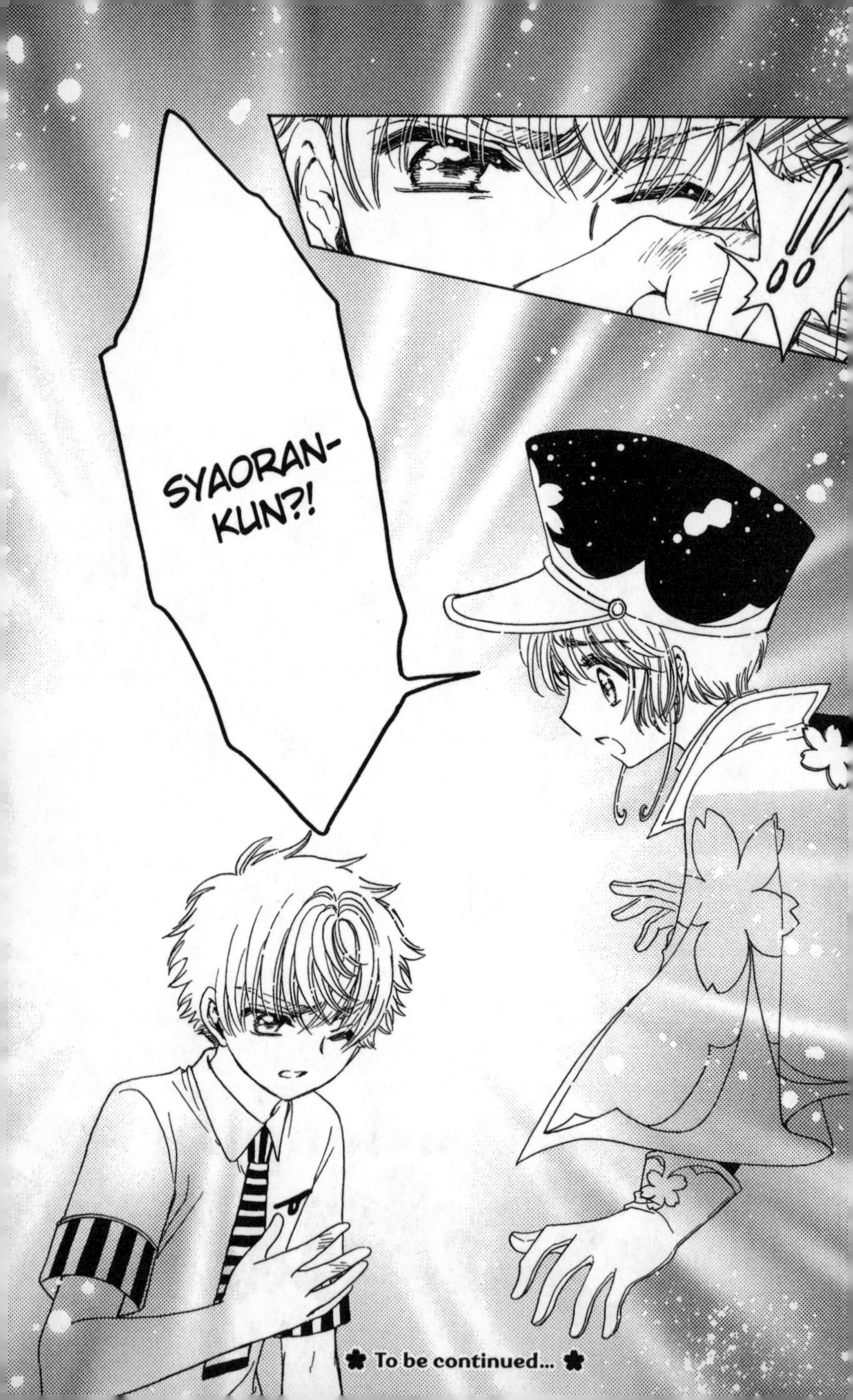
!!
SYAORAN-KUN?!
To be continued...

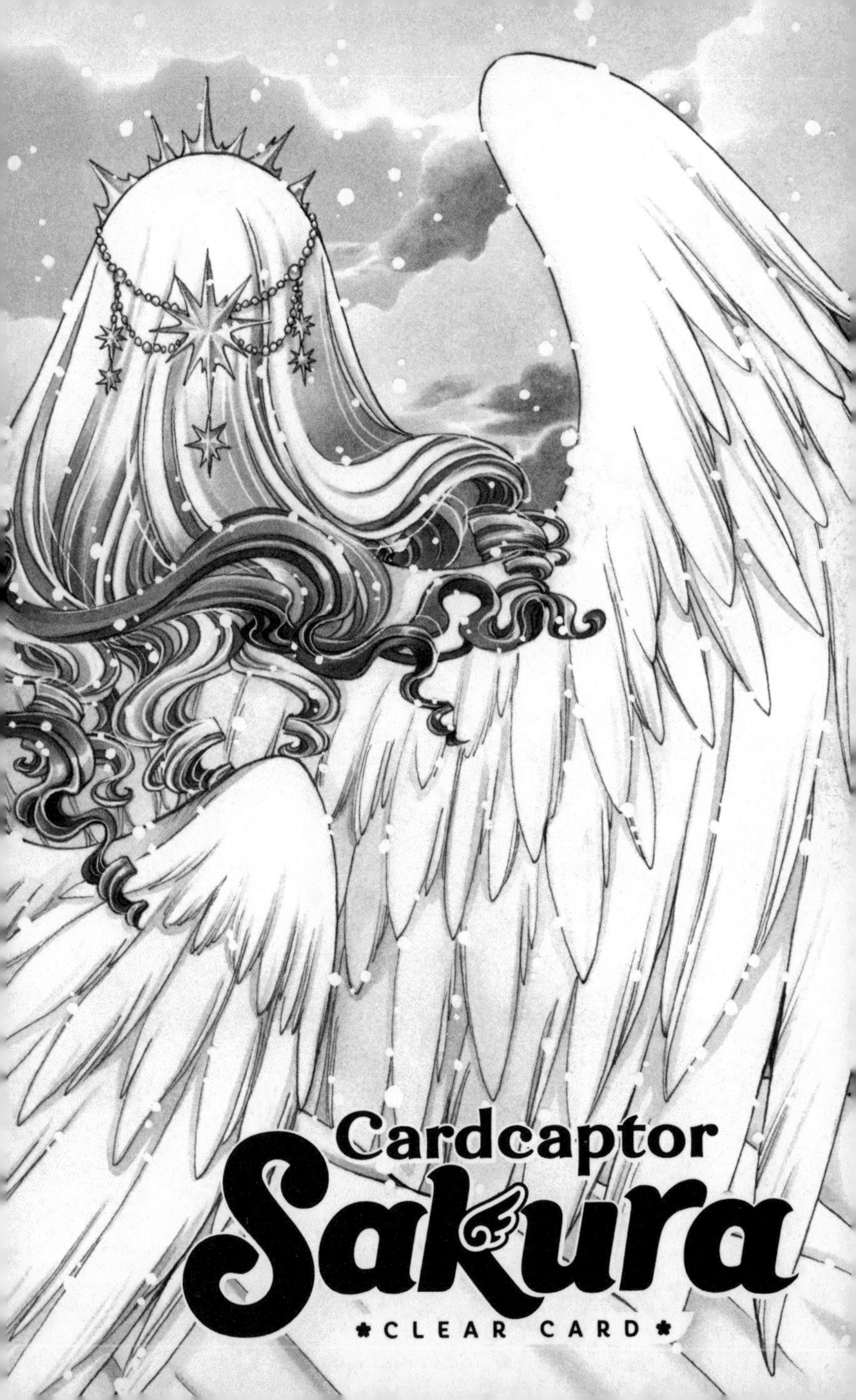
Cardcaptor
Sakura
CLEAR CARD

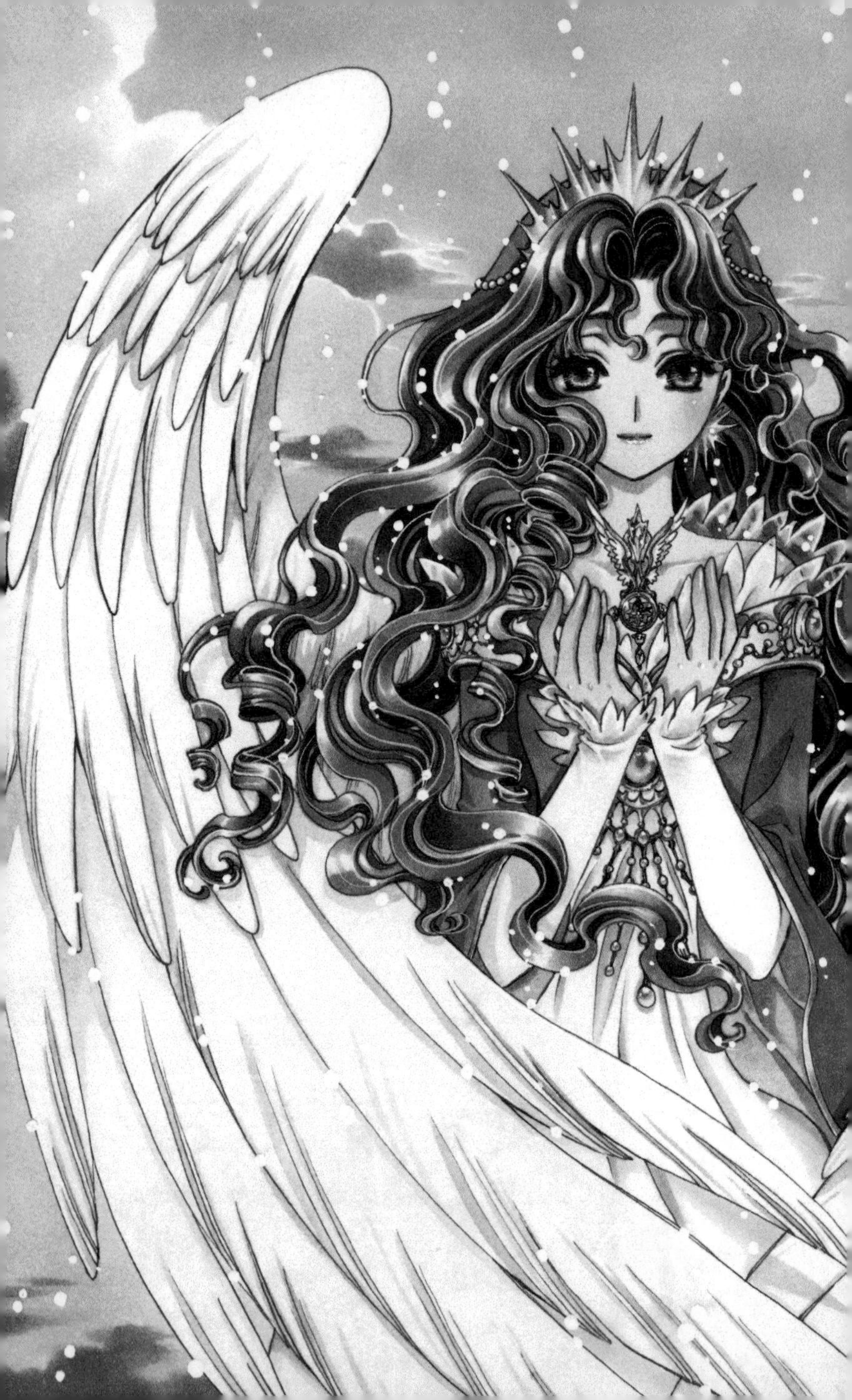

Cardcaptor Sakura

CLEAR CARD

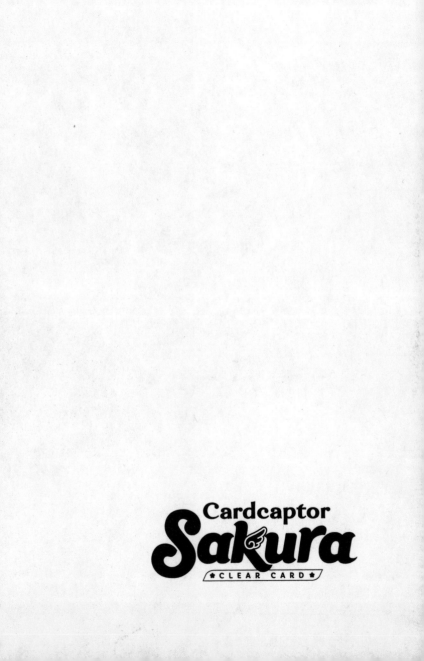

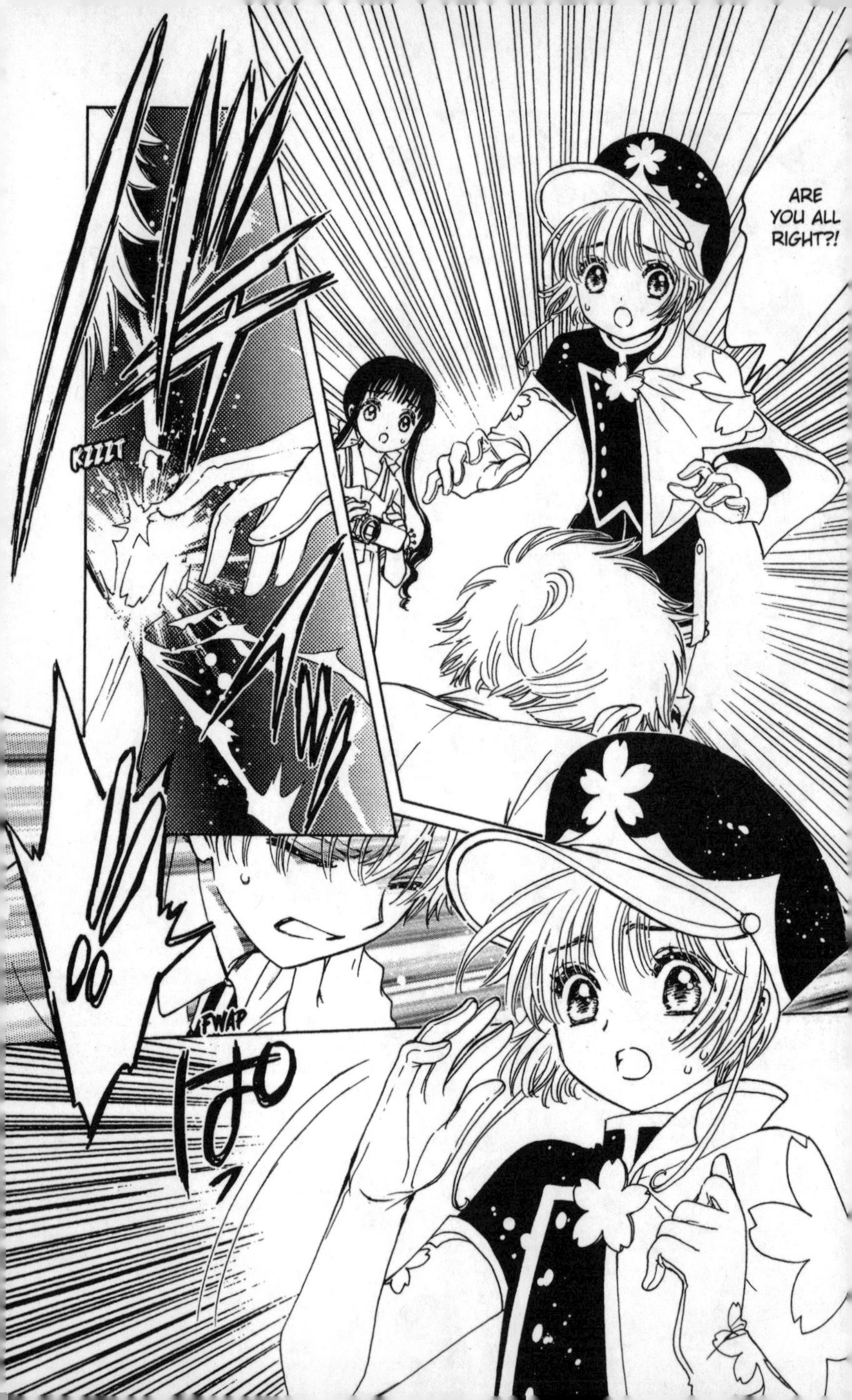
ARE YOU ALL RIGHT?!
KZZZT
FWAP
ぱっ

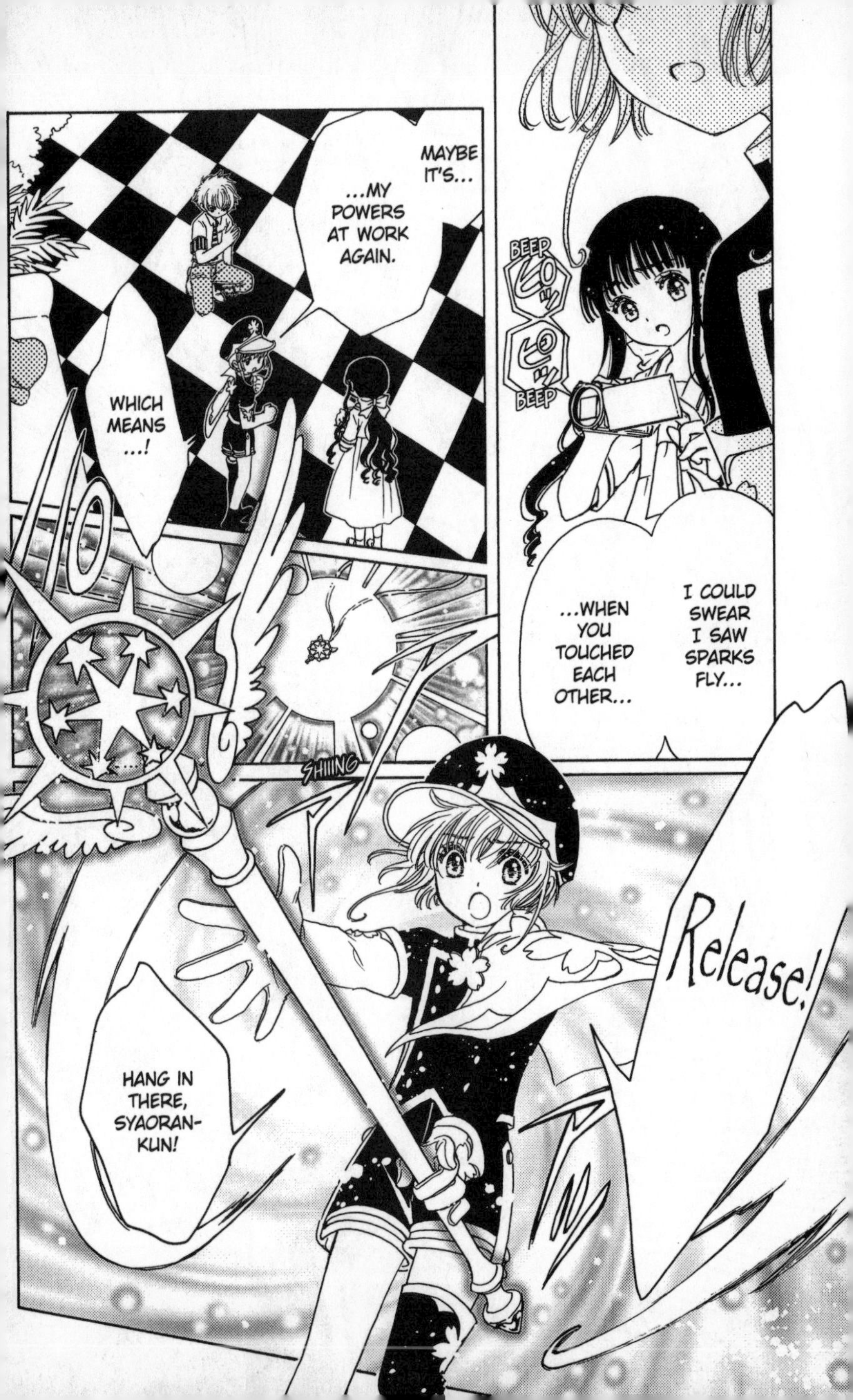

BEEP
BEEP
I COULD SWEAR I SAW SPARKS FLY...
...WHEN YOU TOUCHED EACH OTHER...
MAYBE IT'S...
...MY POWERS AT WORK AGAIN.
WHICH MEANS ...!
SHIIING
Release!
HANG IN THERE, SYAORAN-KUN!

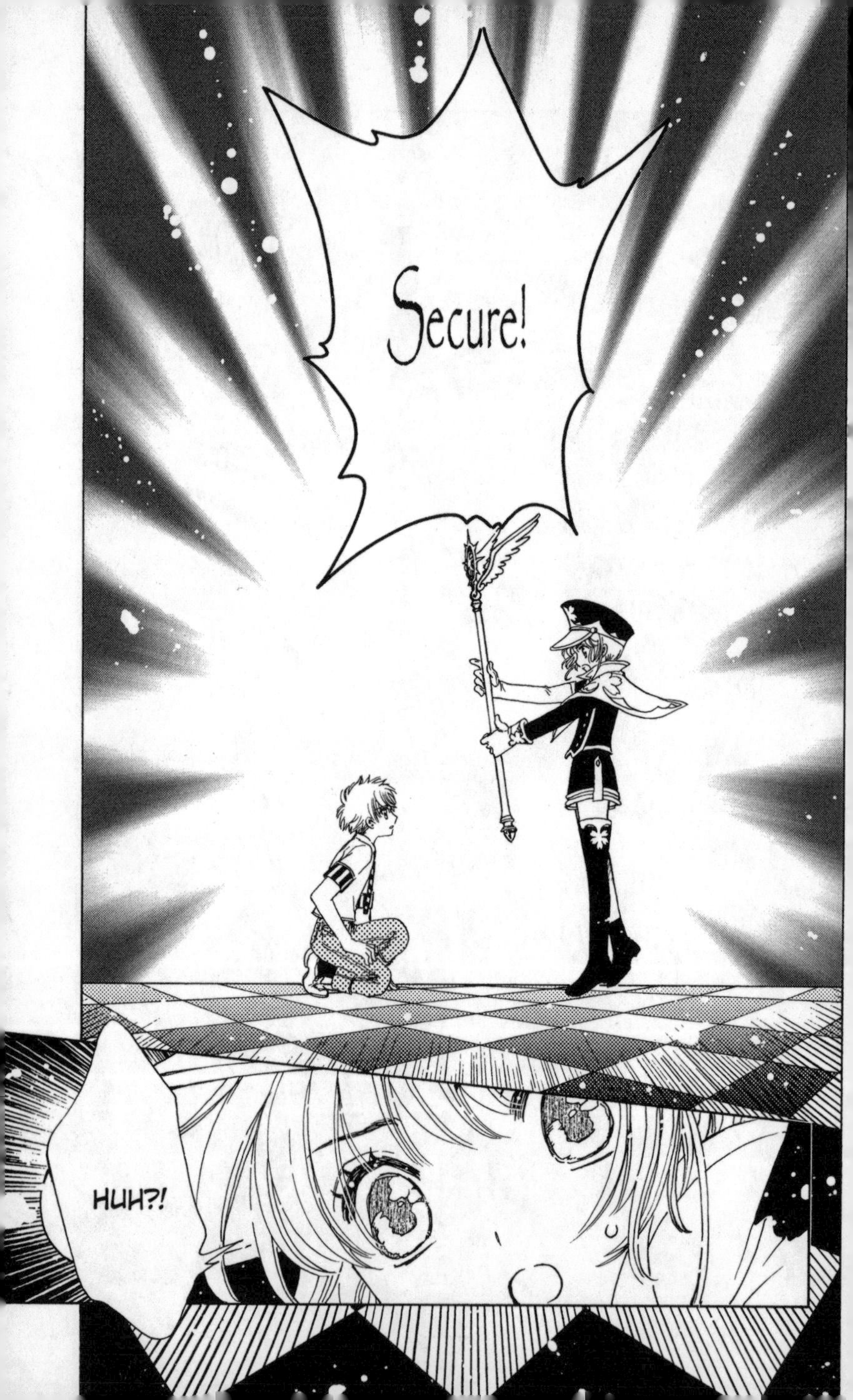
Secure!
HUH?!

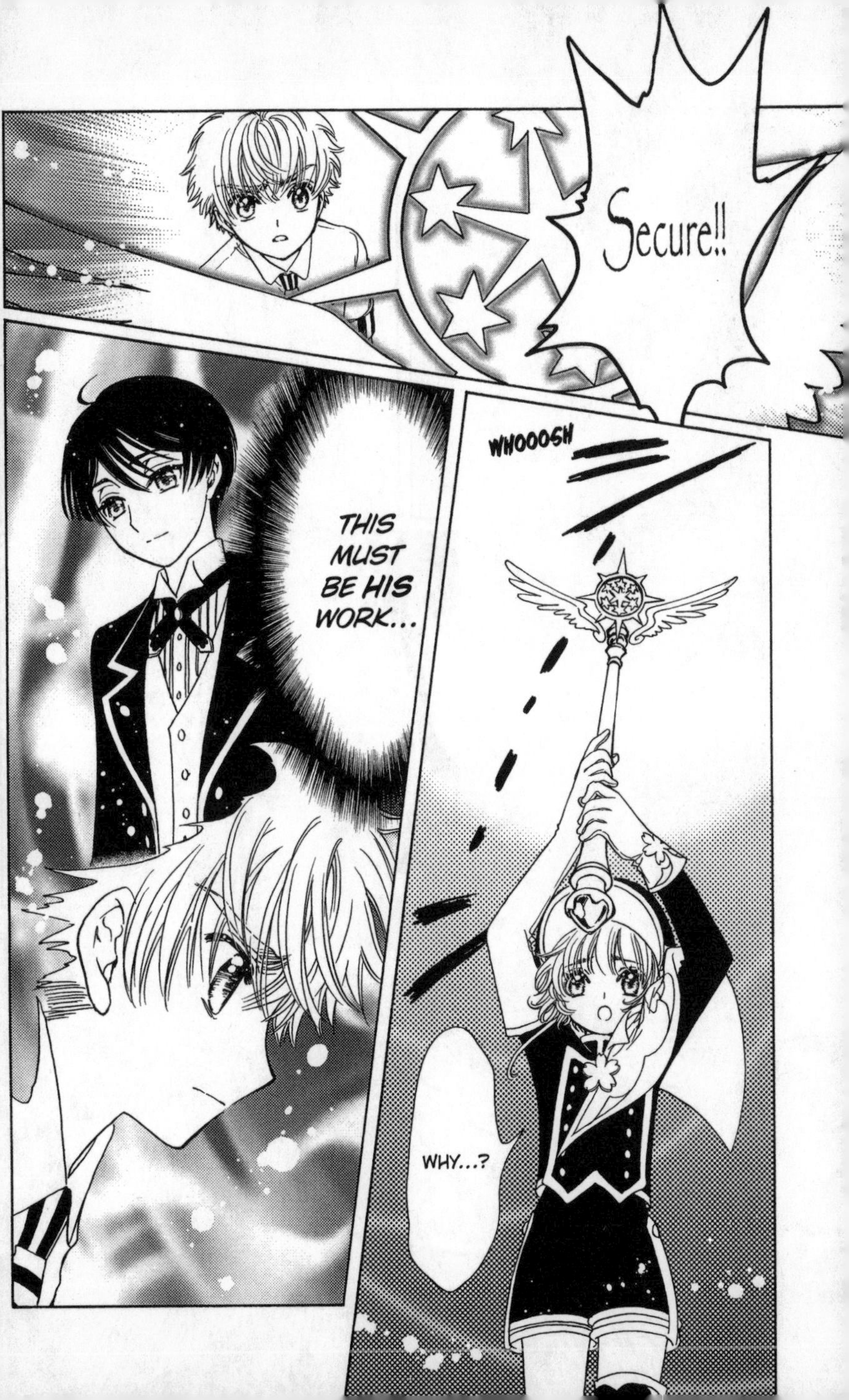
Secure!!
WHOOOSH
WHY...?
THIS MUST BE HIS WORK...

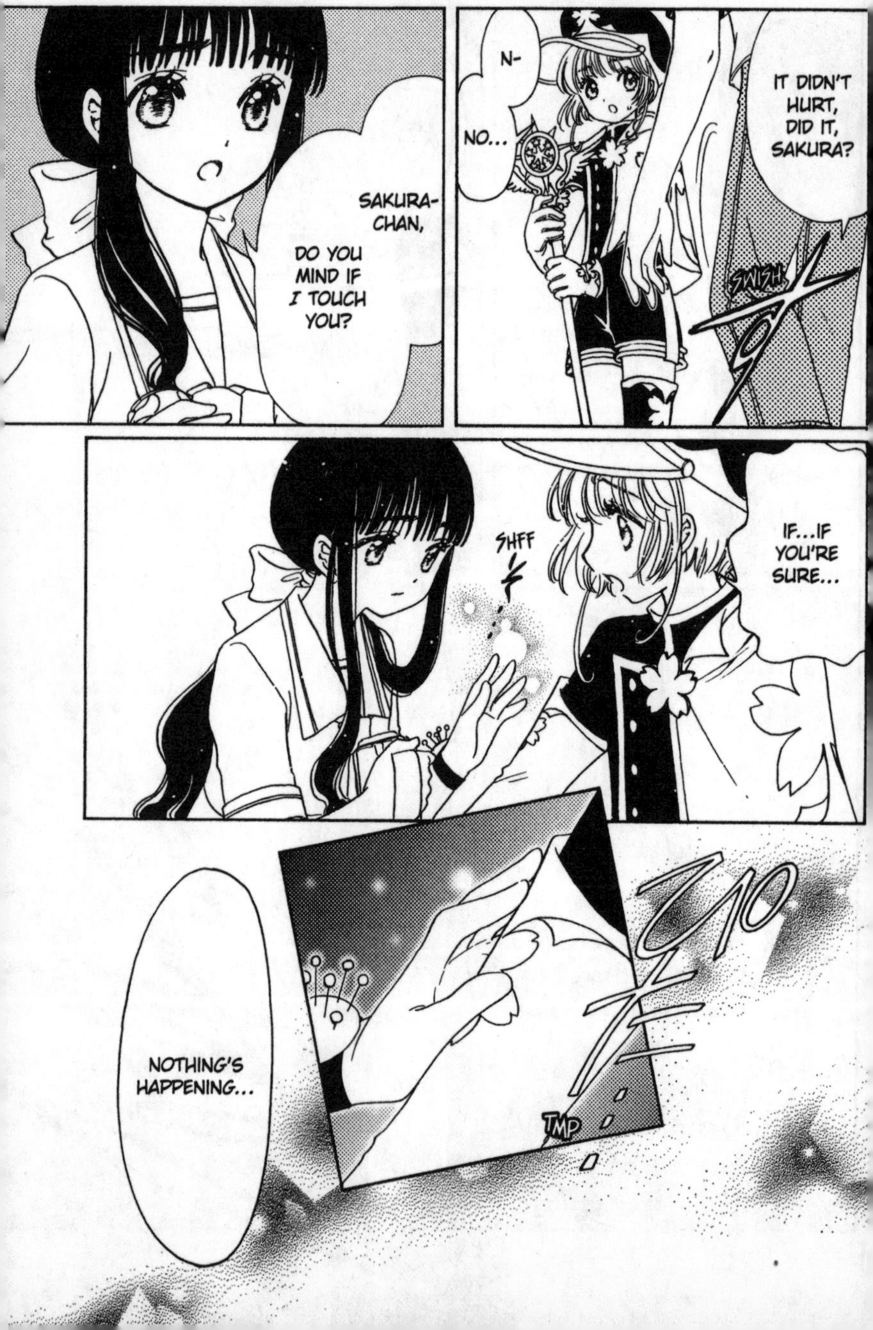
IT DIDN'T HURT, DID IT, SAKURA?
SWISH
N-
NO...
SAKURA-CHAN,
DO YOU MIND IF I TOUCH YOU?
IF...IF YOU'RE SURE...
SHFF
TMP
NOTHING'S HAPPENING...

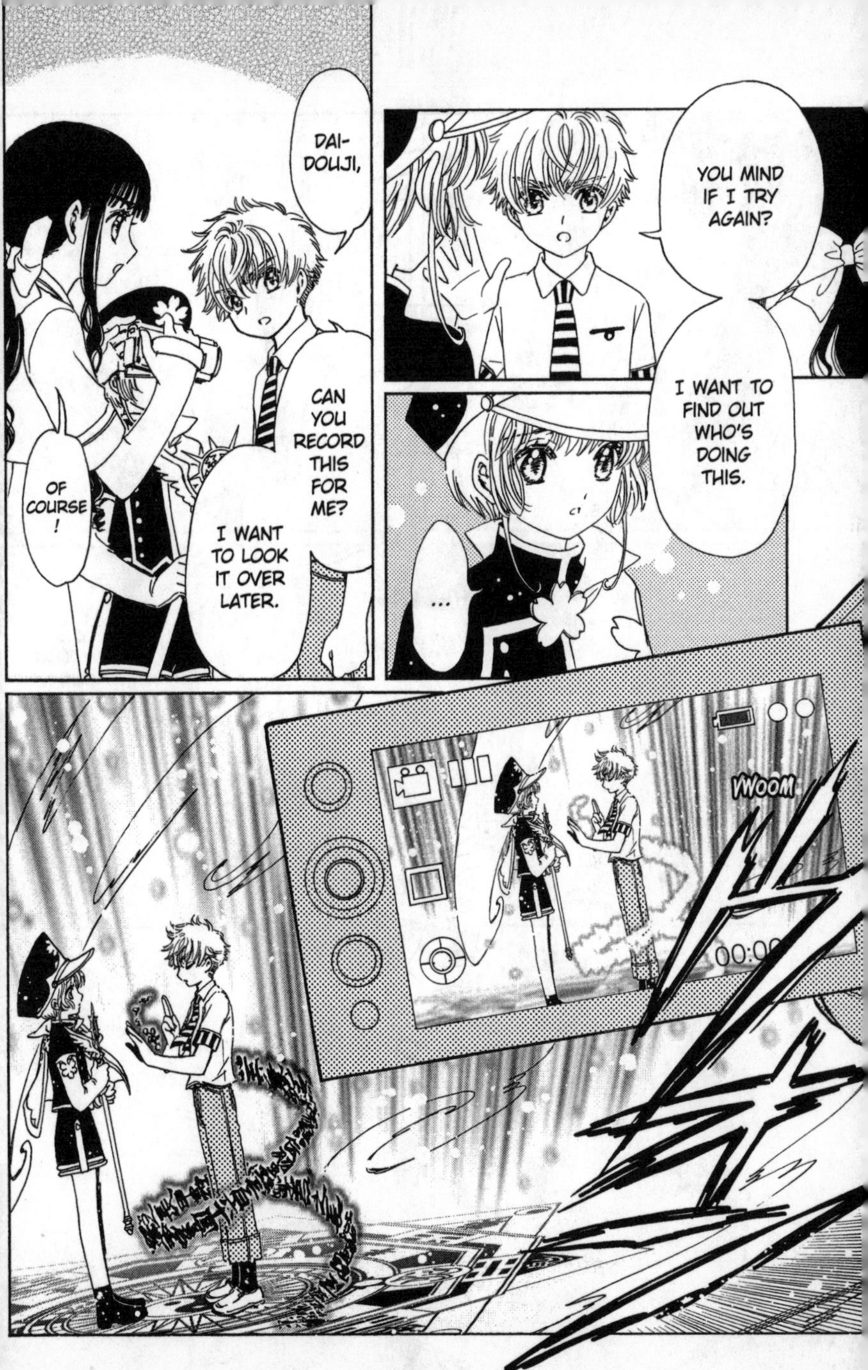
YOU MIND IF I TRY AGAIN?
I WANT TO FIND OUT WHO'S DOING THIS.
...
DAI-DOUJI,
CAN YOU RECORD THIS FOR ME?
I WANT TO LOOK IT OVER LATER.
OF COURSE!
VWOOM

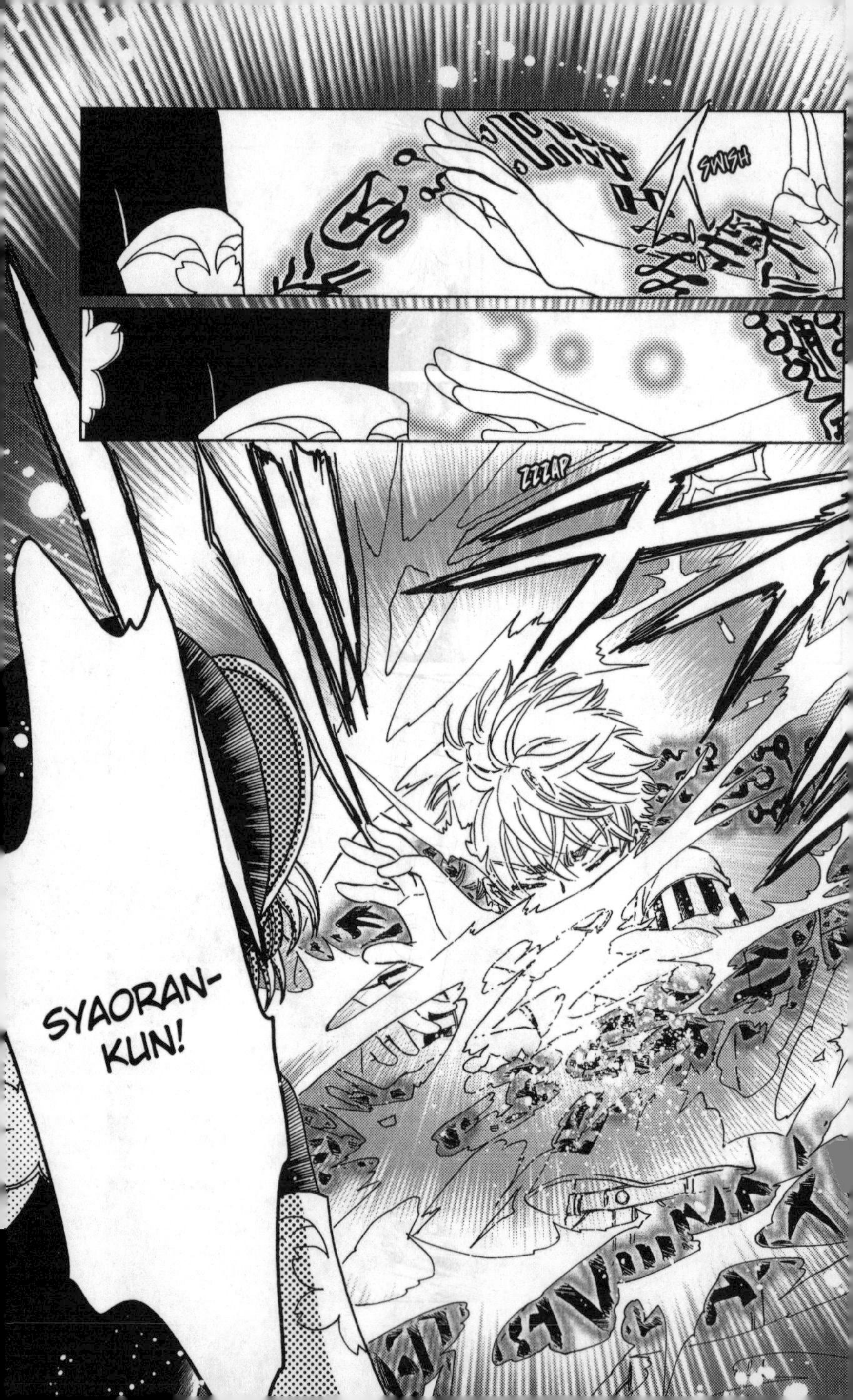
SWISH
ZZZAP
SYAORAN-KUN!

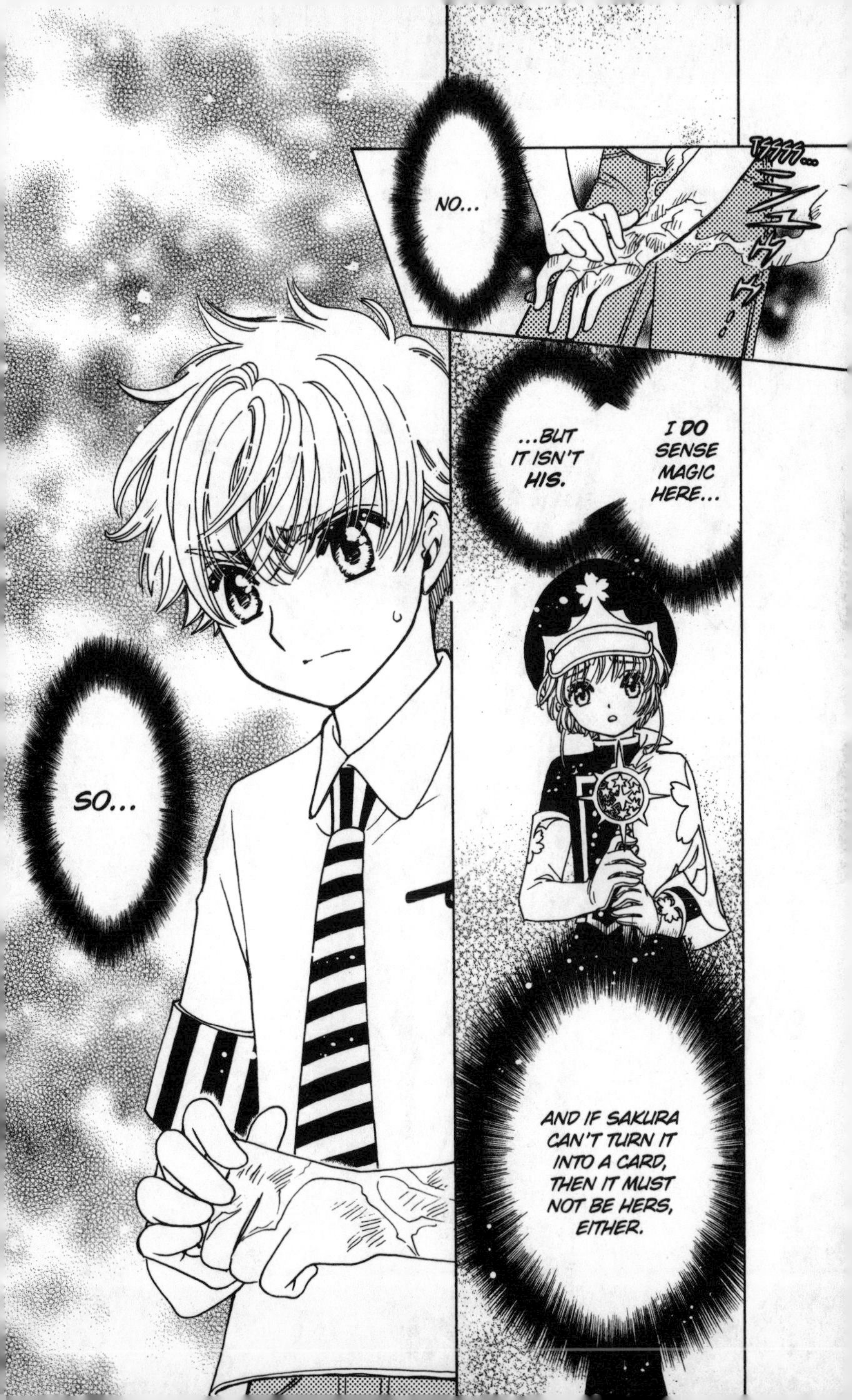
TSSSS...
NO...
I DO SENSE MAGIC HERE...
...BUT IT ISN'T HIS.
AND IF SAKURA CAN'T TURN IT INTO A CARD, THEN IT MUST NOT BE HERS, EITHER.
SO...

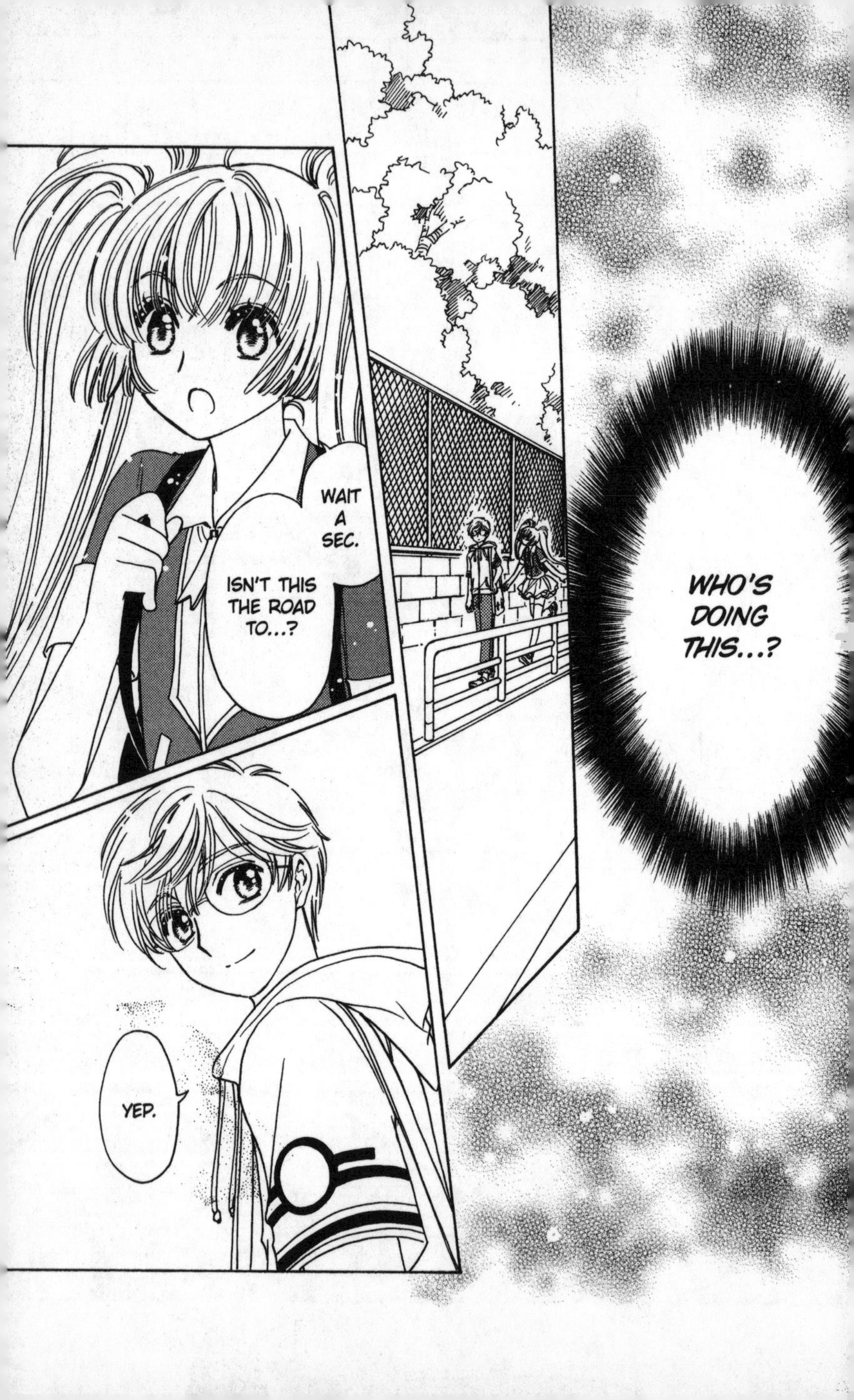
WHO'S DOING THIS...?
WAIT A SEC.
ISN'T THIS THE ROAD TO...?
YEP.

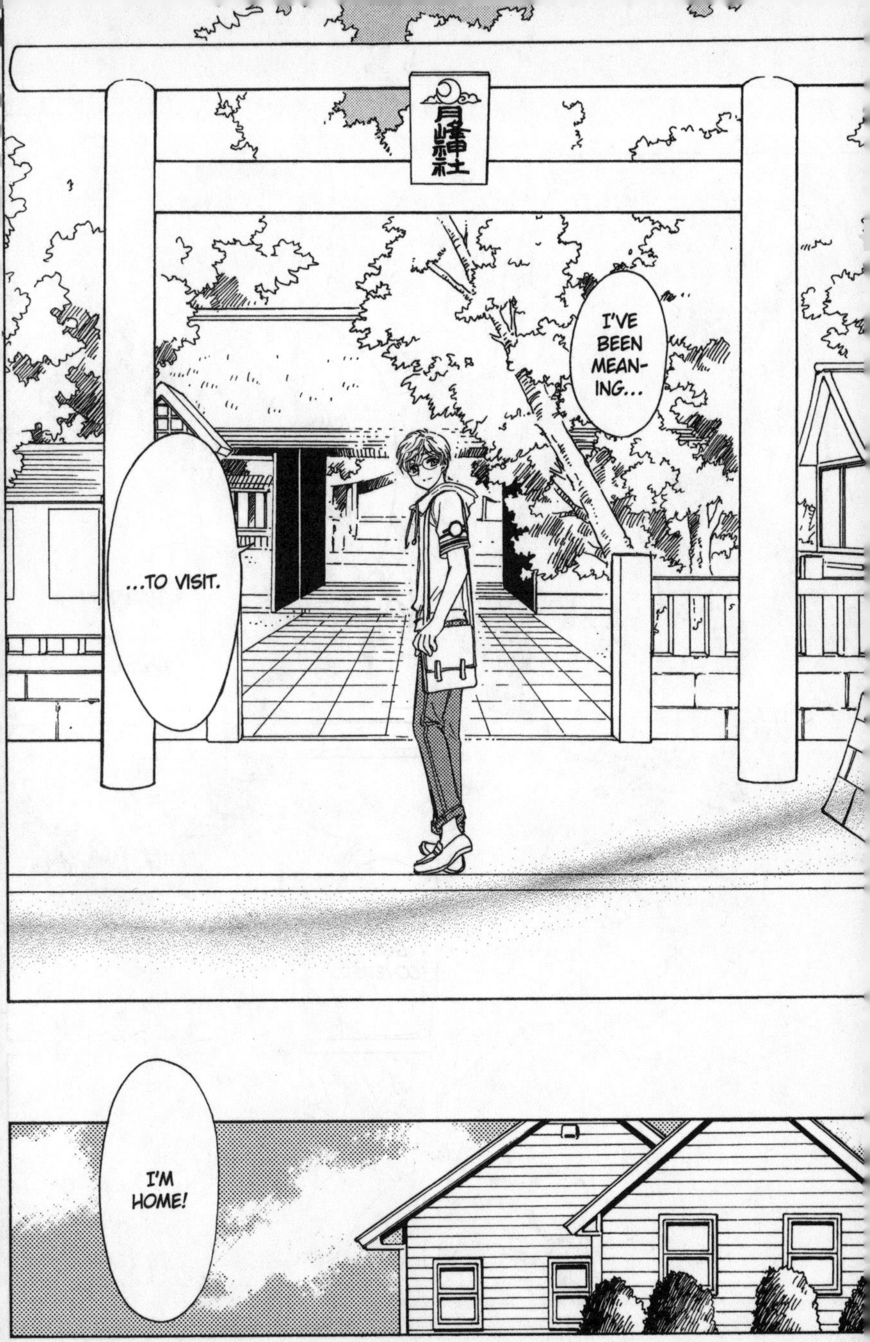
月峰神社
I'VE BEEN MEANING...
...TO VISIT.
I'M HOME!

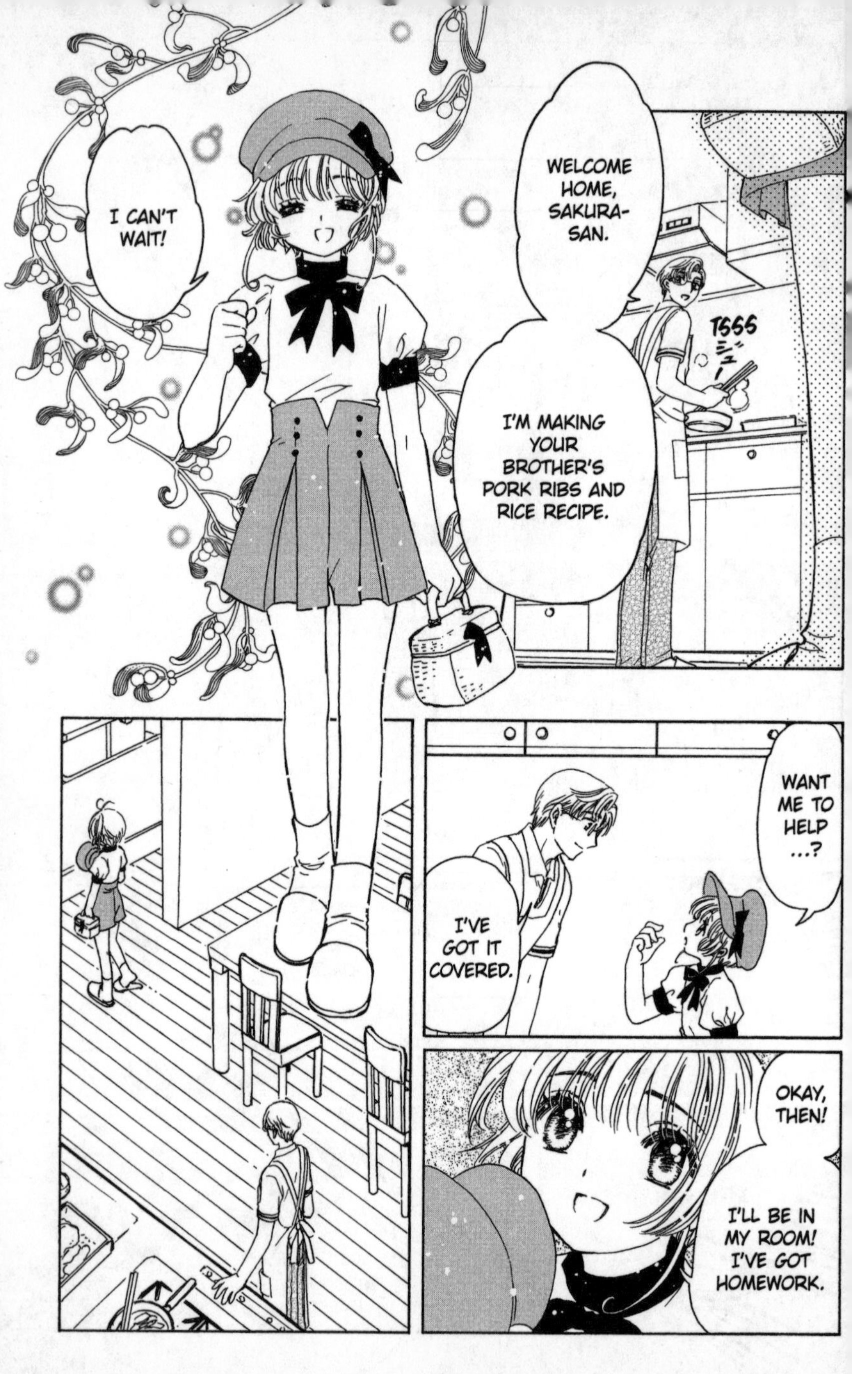
WELCOME HOME, SAKURA-SAN.
I'M MAKING YOUR BROTHER'S PORK RIBS AND RICE RECIPE.
TSSS
I CAN'T WAIT!
WANT ME TO HELP ...?
I'VE GOT IT COVERED.
OKAY, THEN!
I'LL BE IN MY ROOM! I'VE GOT HOMEWORK.

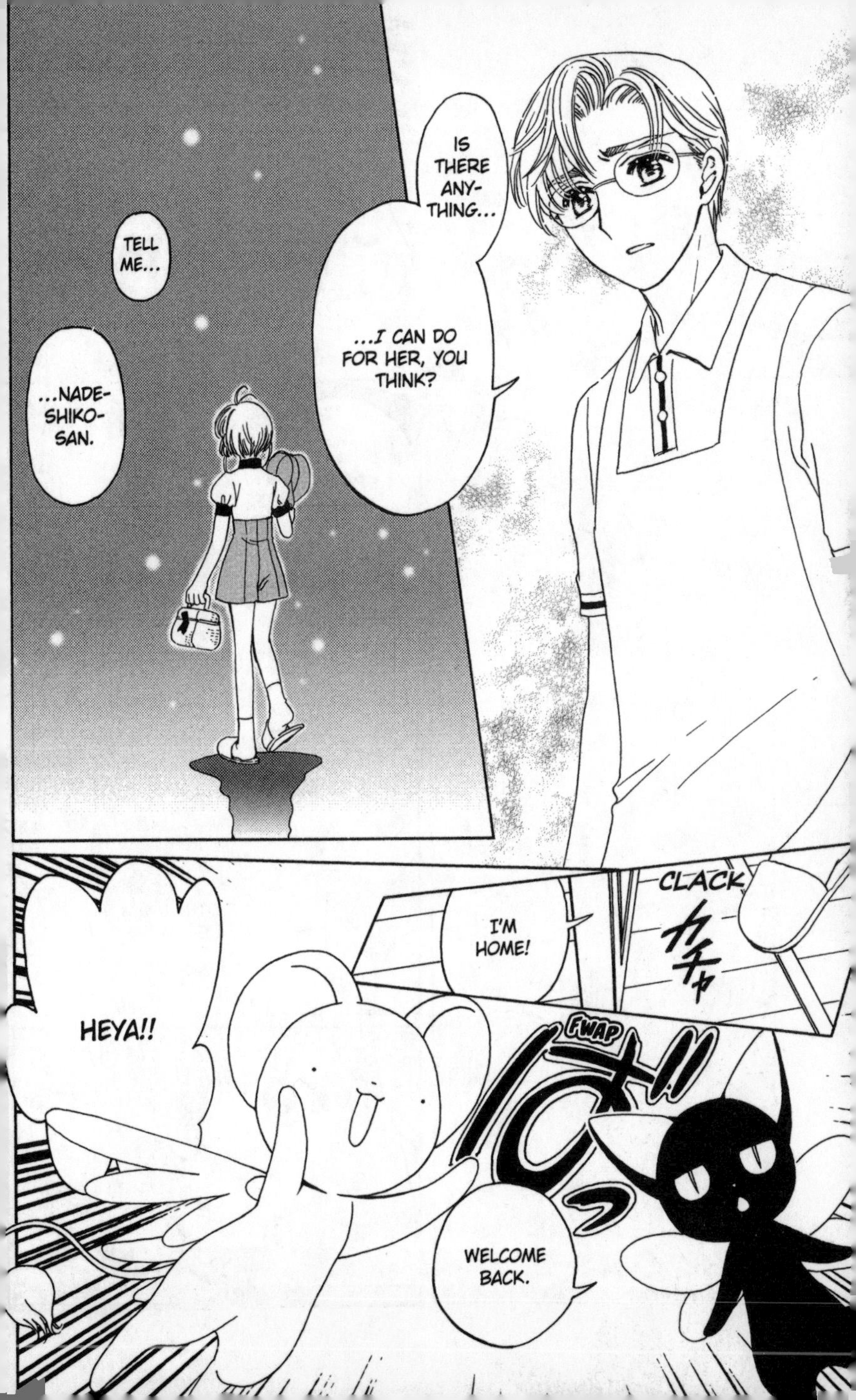
IS THERE ANYTHING...
...I CAN DO FOR HER, YOU THINK?
TELL ME...
...NADESHIKO-SAN.
CLACK
I'M HOME!
FWAP
HEYA!!
WELCOME BACK.

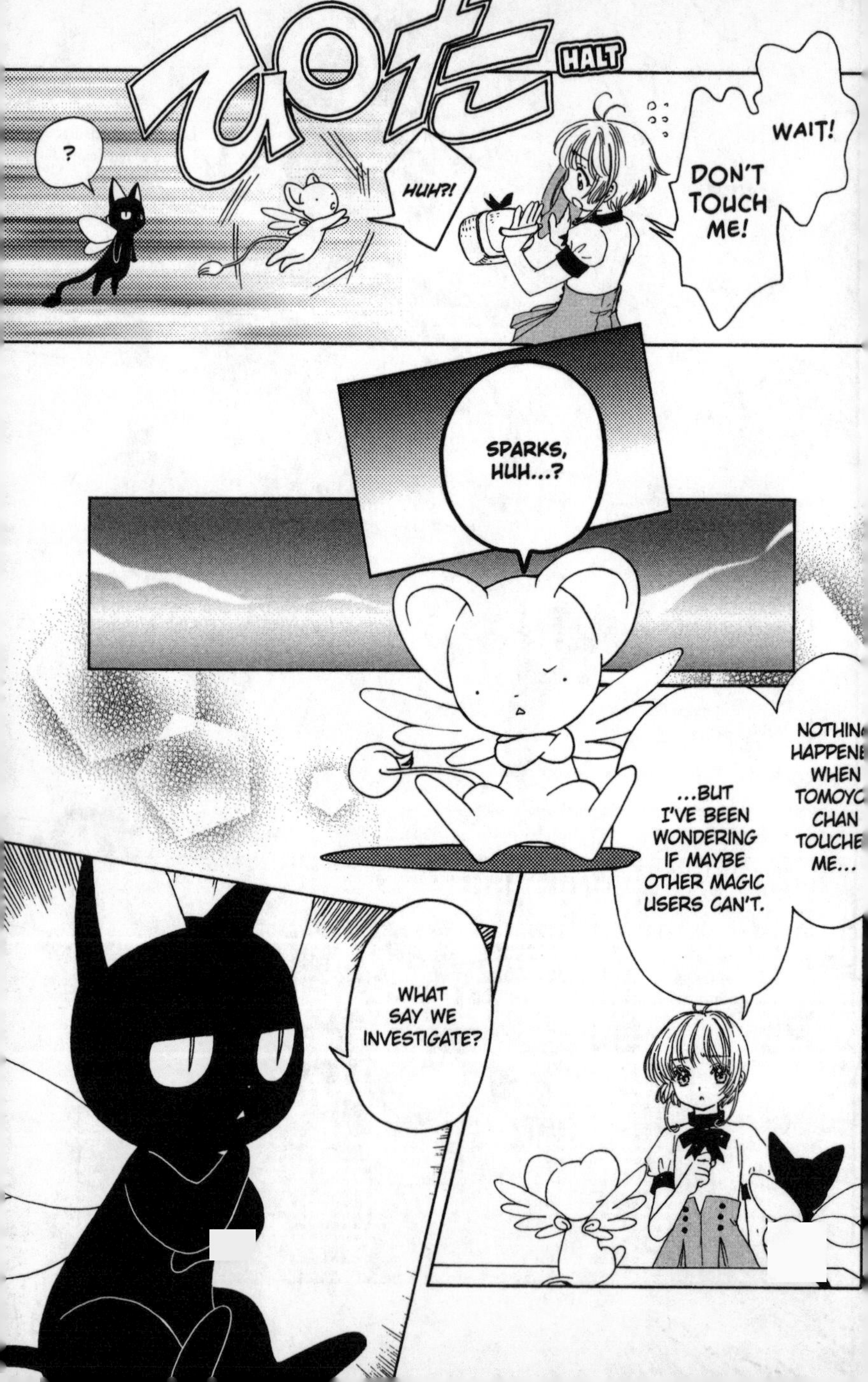
WAIT!
DON'T TOUCH ME!
HALT
HUH?!
?
SPARKS, HUH...?
NOTHIN HAPPENE WHEN TOMOYO CHAN TOUCHE ME...
...BUT I'VE BEEN WONDERING IF MAYBE OTHER MAGIC USERS CAN'T.
WHAT SAY WE INVESTIGATE?

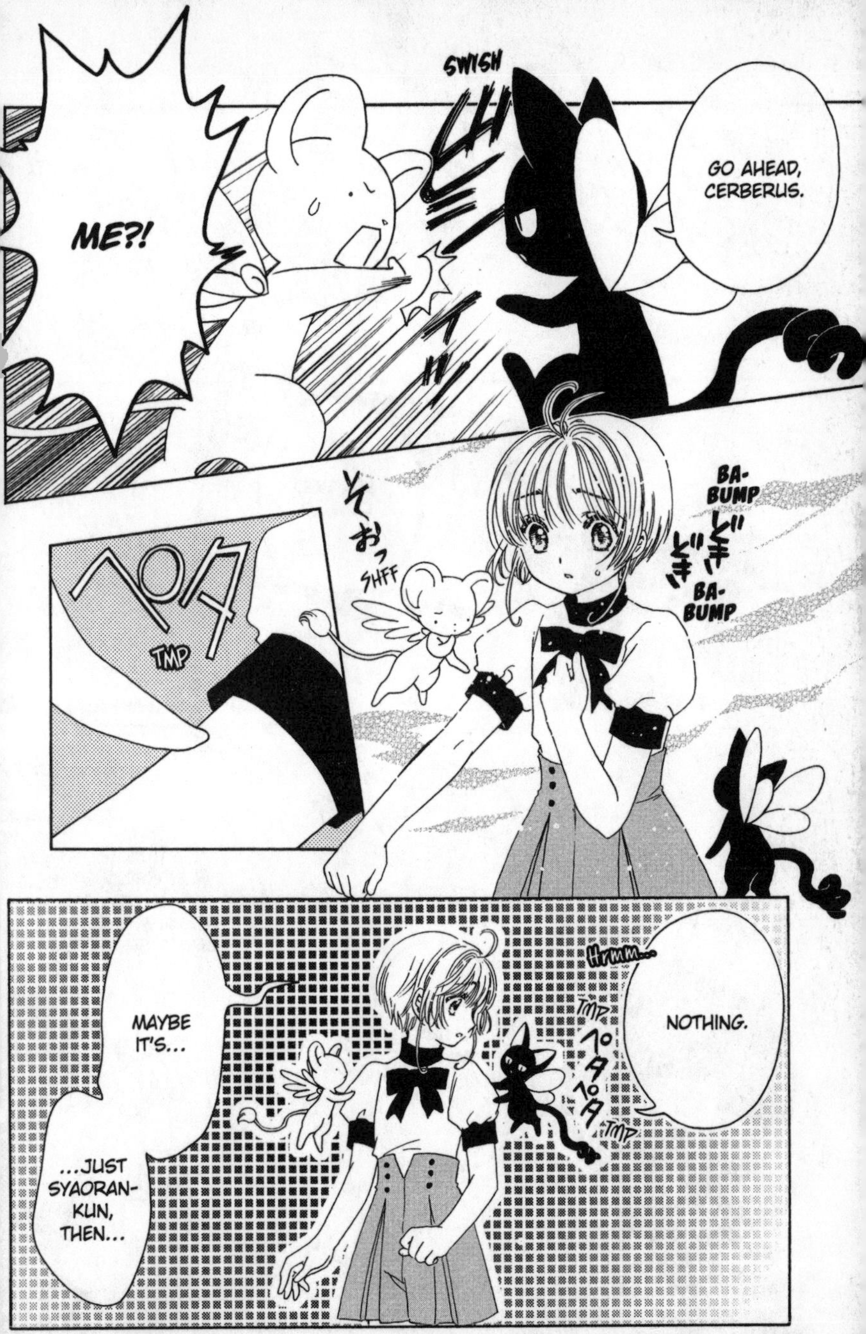

GO AHEAD, CERBERUS.
SWISH
ME?!
BA-BUMP
BA-BUMP
SHFF
TMP
Hrmm...
NOTHING.
TMP
TMP
MAYBE IT'S...
...JUST SYAORAN-KUN, THEN...

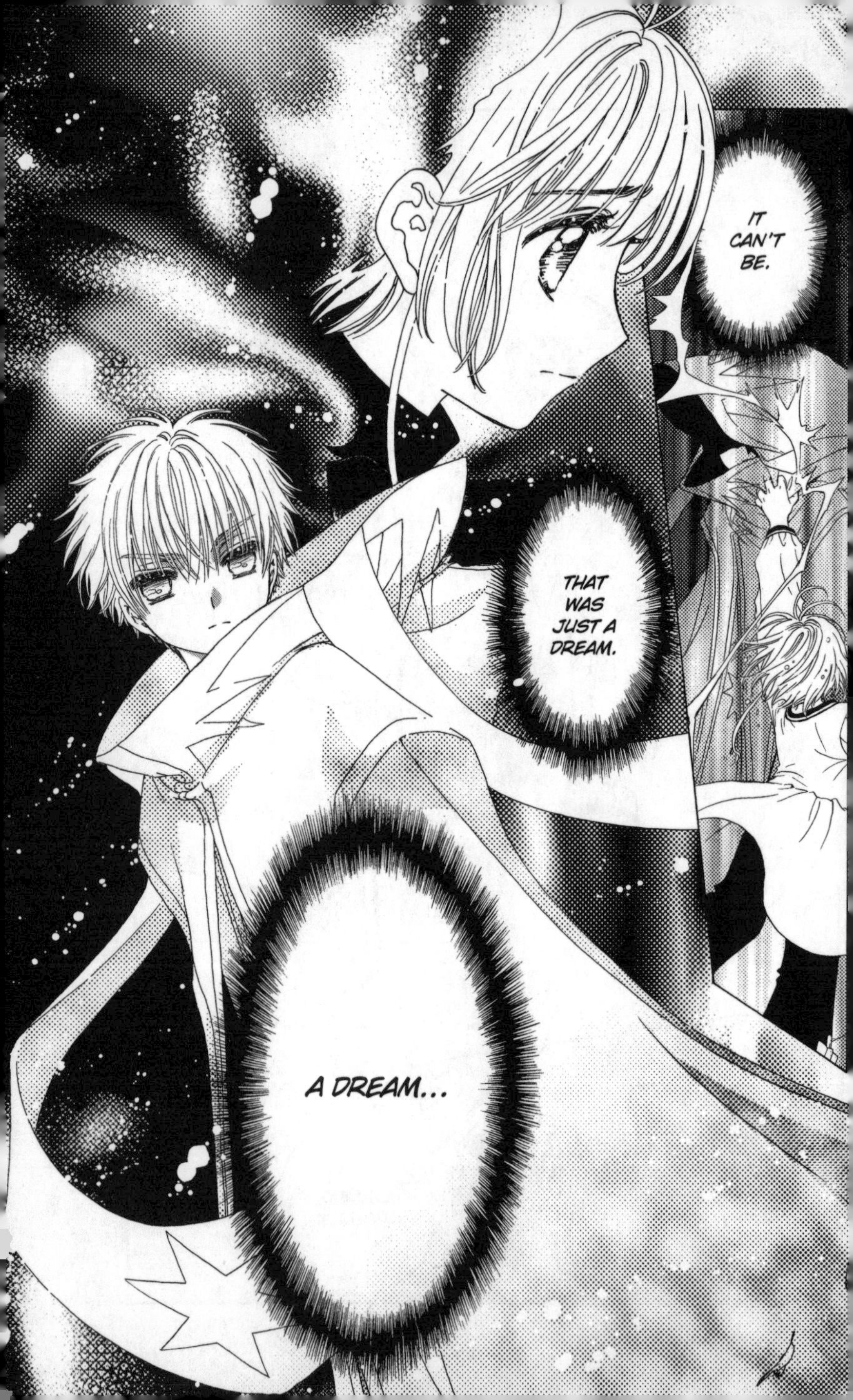
IT CAN'T BE.
THAT WAS JUST A DREAM.
A DREAM...

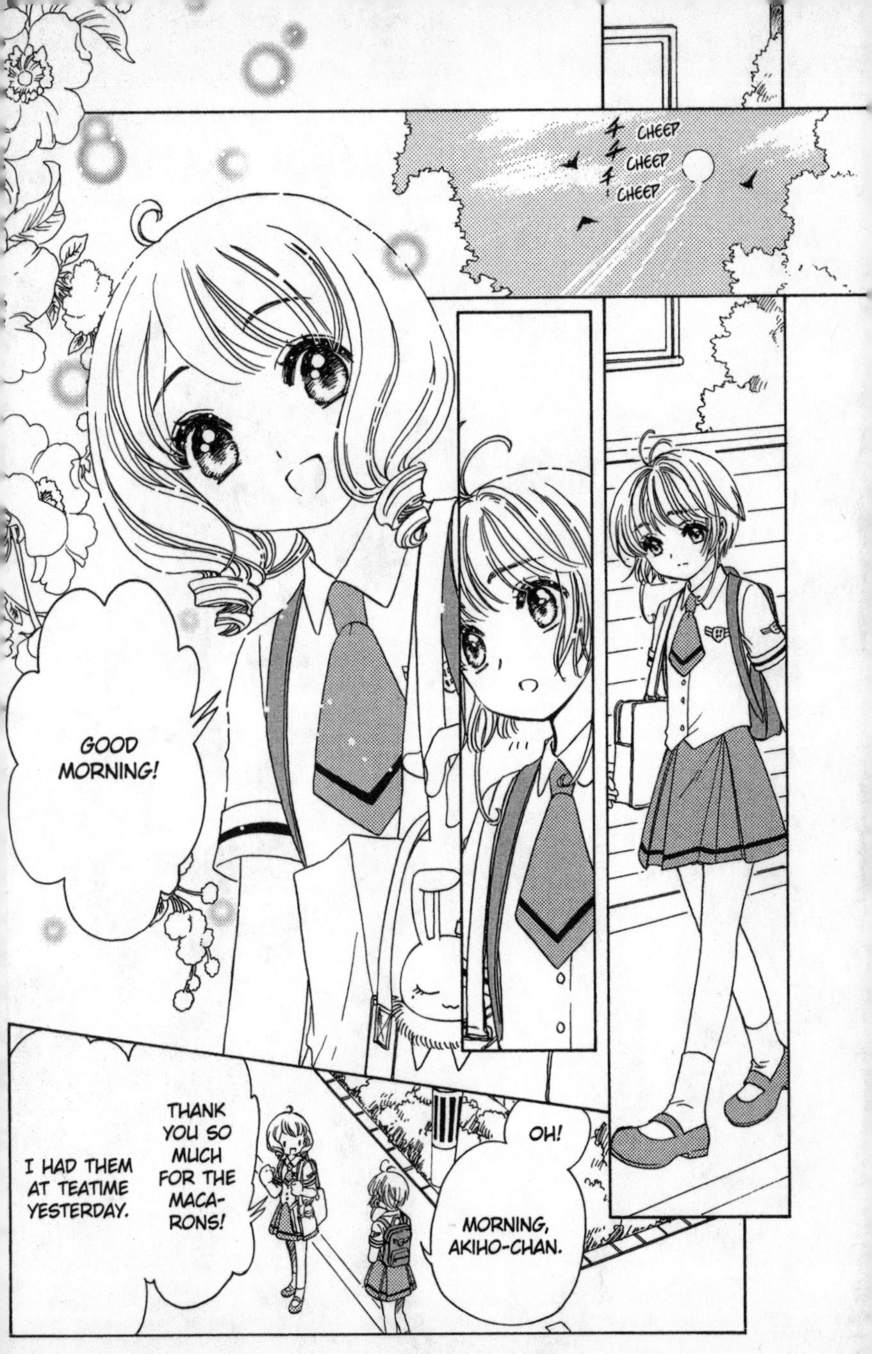
チ チ チ
CHEEP
CHEEP
CHEEP
GOOD MORNING!
OH!
MORNING, AKIHO-CHAN.
THANK YOU SO MUCH FOR THE MACA-RONS!
I HAD THEM AT TEATIME YESTERDAY.

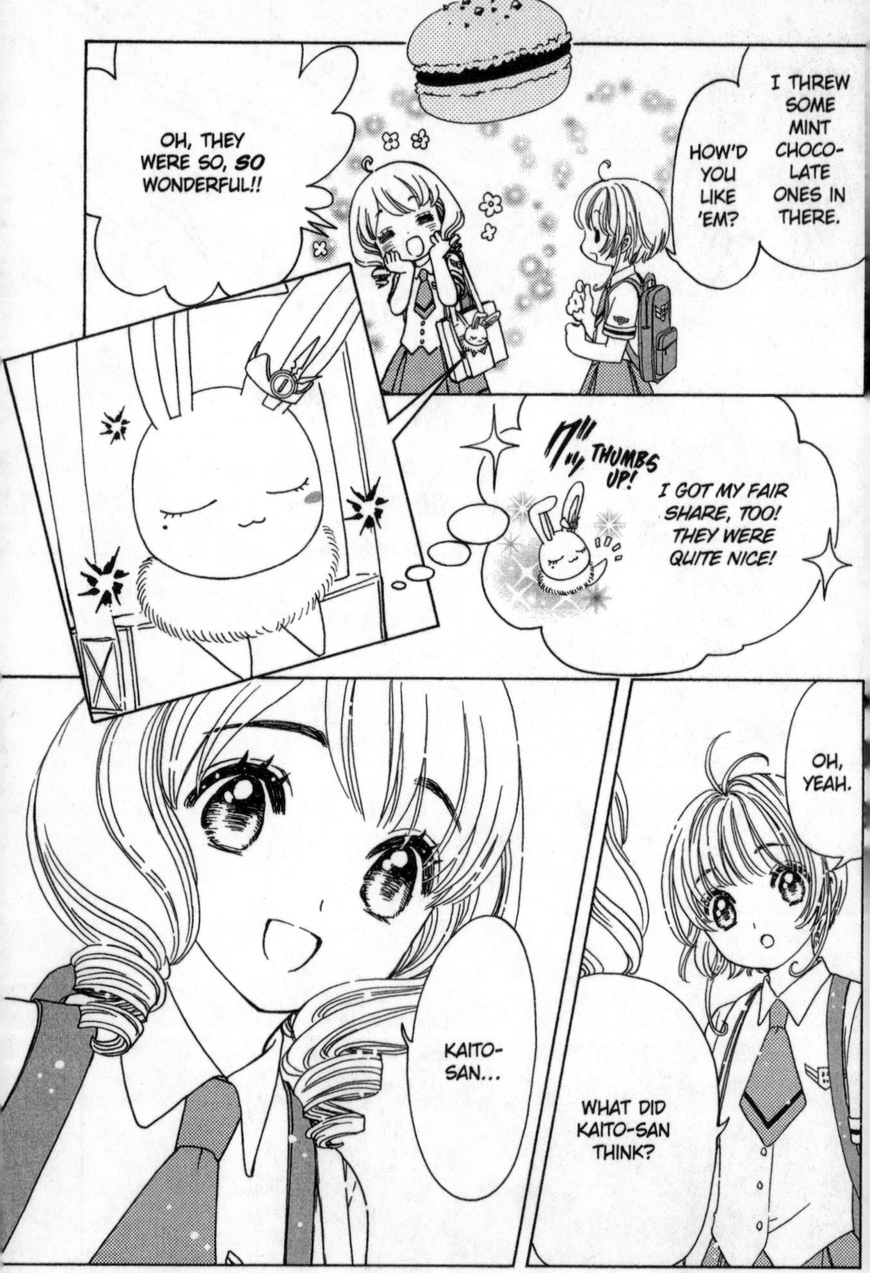
I THREW SOME MINT CHOCOLATE ONES IN THERE.
HOW'D YOU LIKE 'EM?
OH, THEY WERE SO, SO WONDERFUL!!
THUMBS UP!
I GOT MY FAIR SHARE, TOO! THEY WERE QUITE NICE!
OH, YEAH.
WHAT DID KAITO-SAN THINK?
KAITO-SAN...

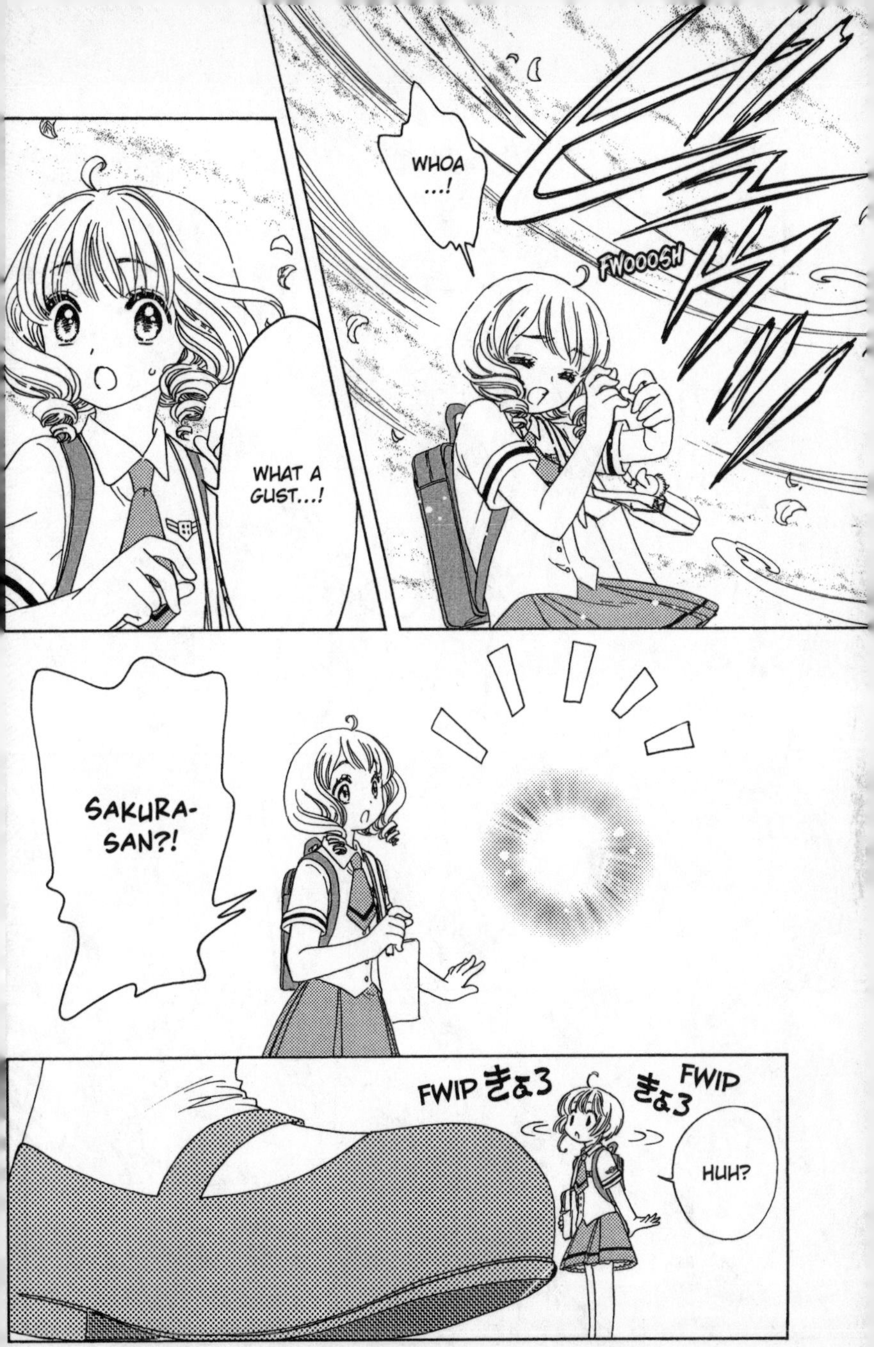
WHOA ...!
FWOOOSH
WHAT A GUST...!
SAKURA-SAN?!
FWIP きょろ
FWIP きょろ
HUH?

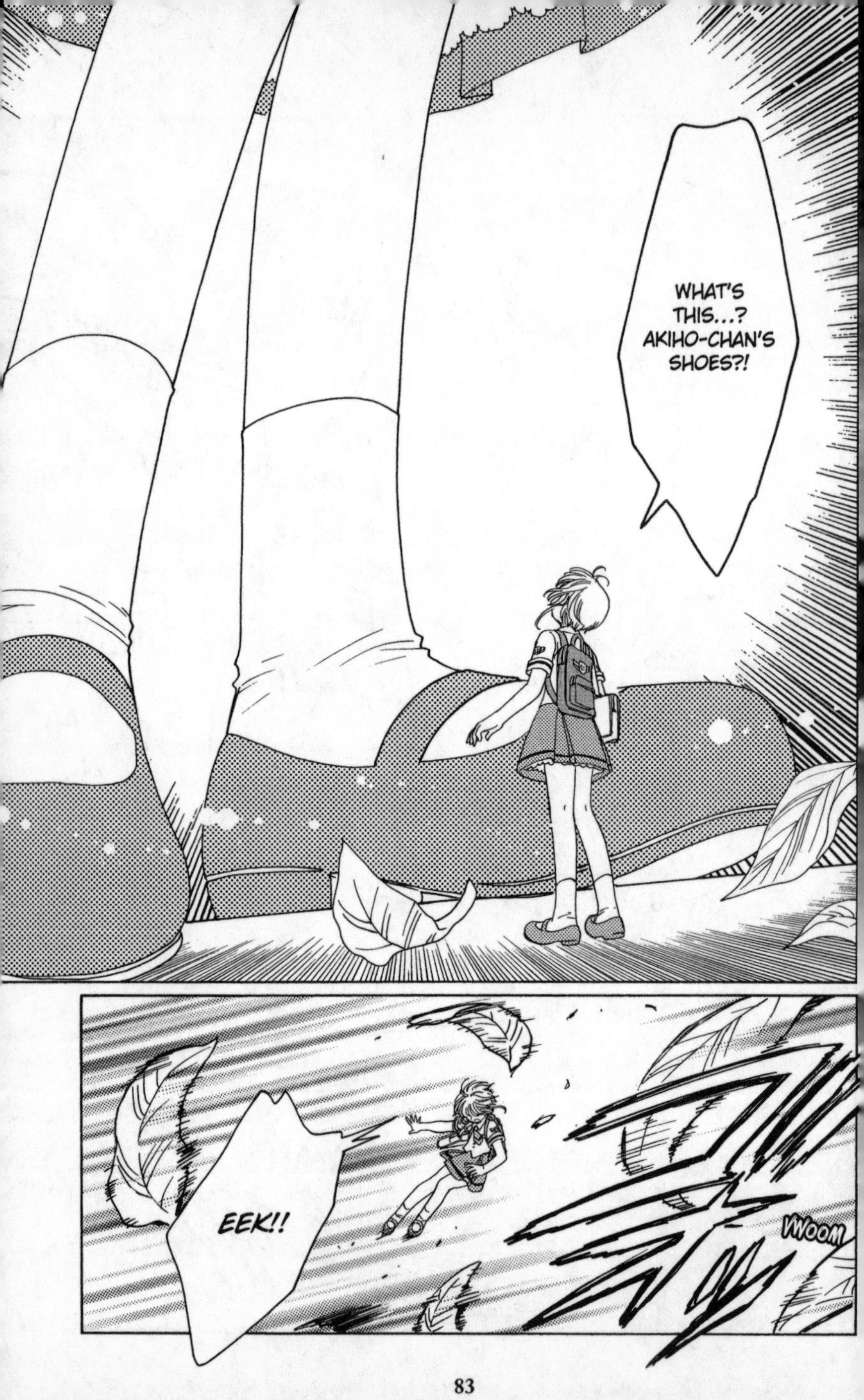
WHAT'S THIS...? AKIHO-CHAN'S SHOES?!
VWOOM
EEK!!

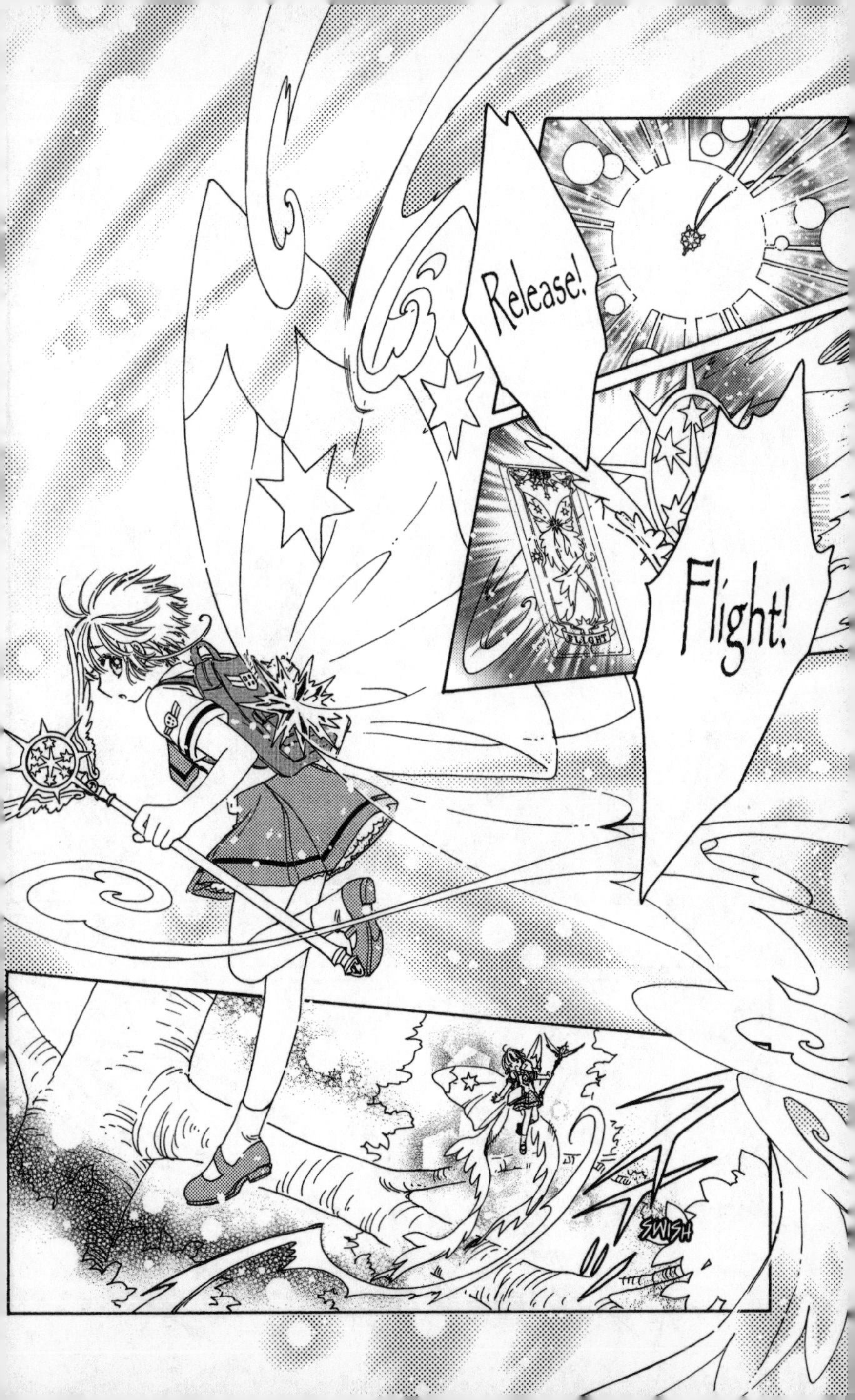
Release!
Flight!
FLIGHT
SWISH

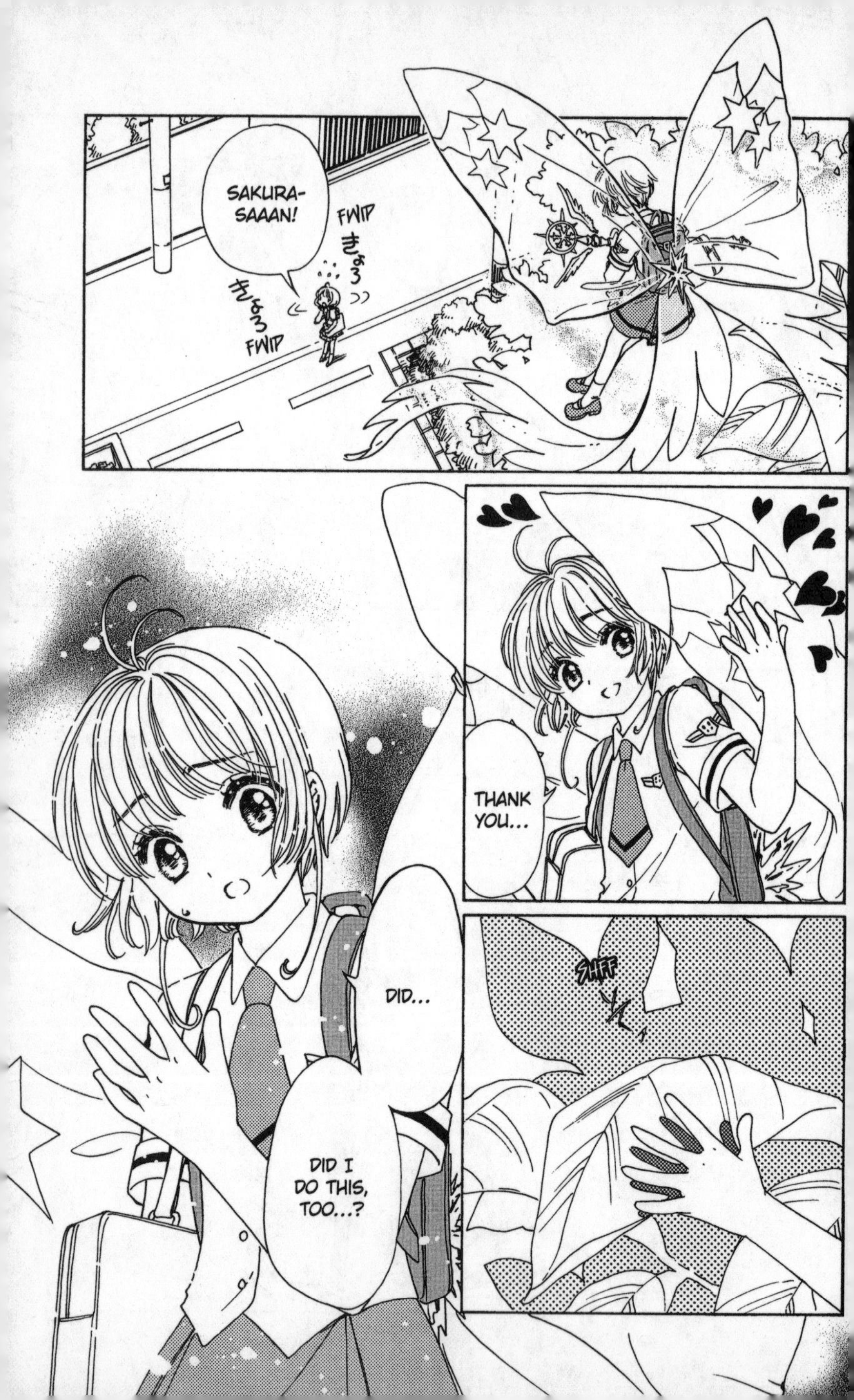
SAKURA-SAAAN!
FWIP
きょろ
きょろ
FWIP
THANK YOU...
SHFF
DID...
DID I DO THIS, TOO...?

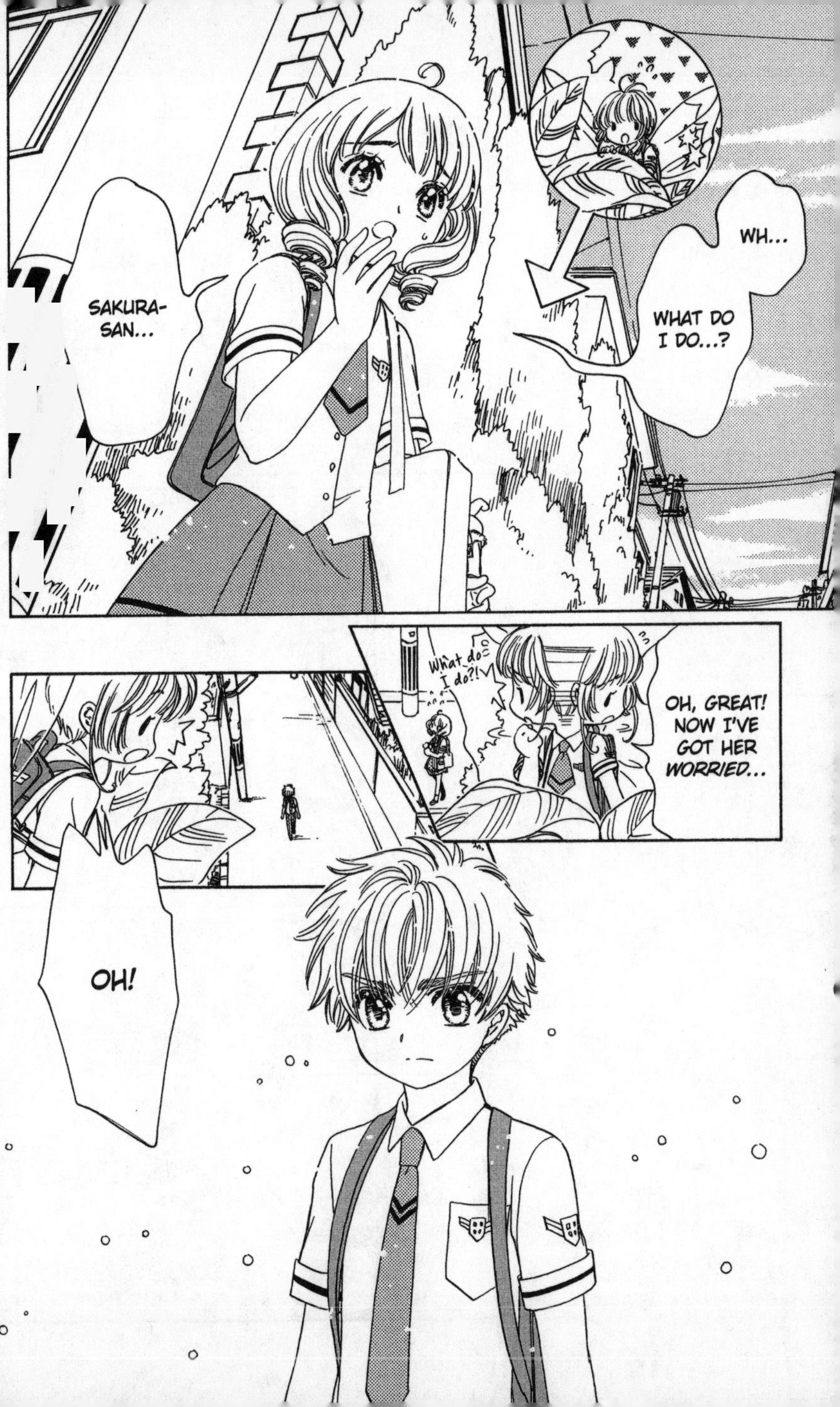
WH...
WHAT DO I DO...?
SAKURA-SAN...
OH, GREAT! NOW I'VE GOT HER WORRIED...
What do I do?!
OH!

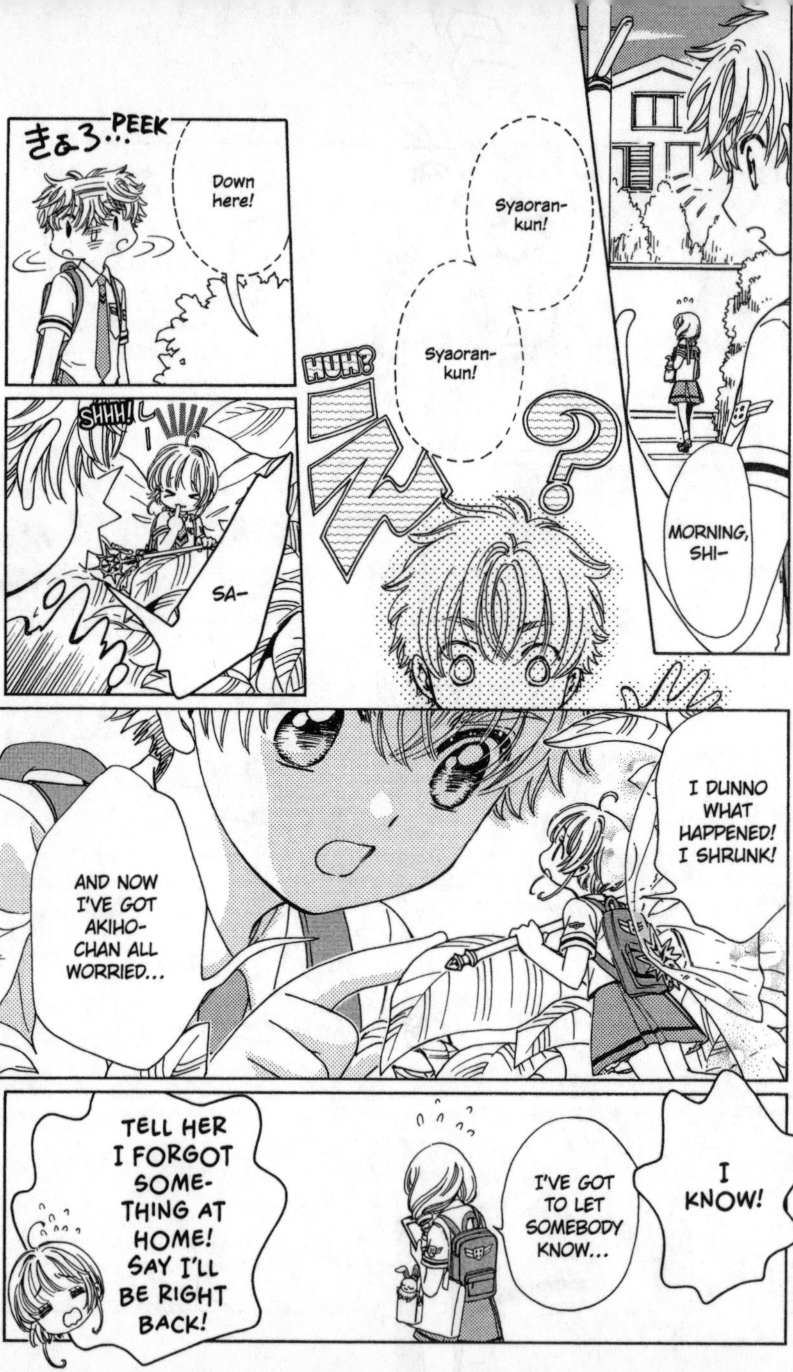
MORNING, SHI-
Syaoran-kun!
Syaoran-kun!
HUH?
きょろ…PEEK
Down here!
SHHH!
SA-
I DUNNO WHAT HAPPENED! I SHRUNK!
AND NOW I'VE GOT AKIHO-CHAN ALL WORRIED...
I KNOW!
I'VE GOT TO LET SOMEBODY KNOW...
TELL HER I FORGOT SOME-THING AT HOME! SAY I'LL BE RIGHT BACK!

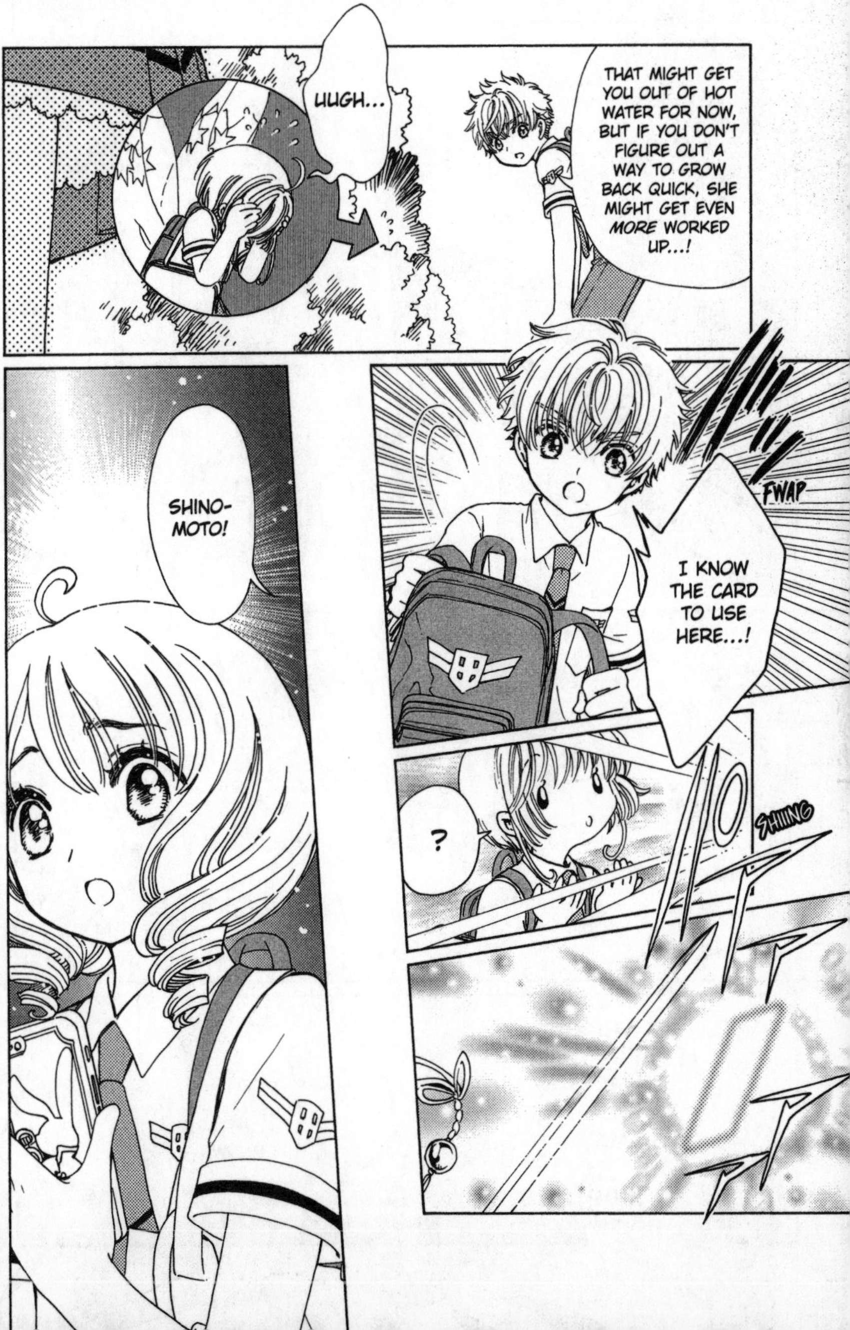
THAT MIGHT GET YOU OUT OF HOT WATER FOR NOW, BUT IF YOU DON'T FIGURE OUT A WAY TO GROW BACK QUICK, SHE MIGHT GET EVEN *MORE* WORKED UP...!
UUGH...
FWAP
I KNOW THE CARD TO USE HERE...!
?
SHIIING
SHINO-MOTO!

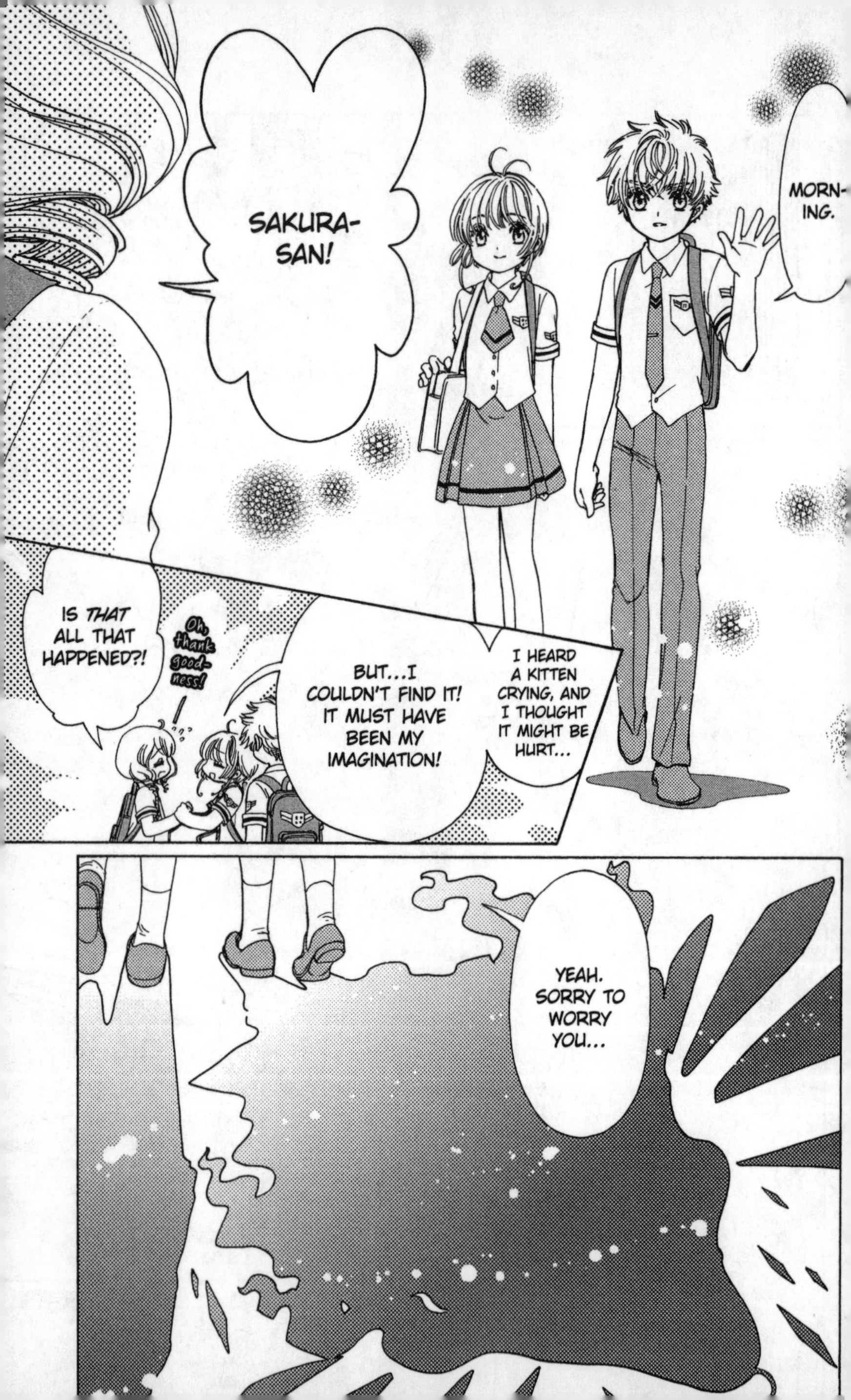
MORNING.
SAKURA-SAN!
I HEARD A KITTEN CRYING, AND I THOUGHT IT MIGHT BE HURT...
BUT...I COULDN'T FIND IT! IT MUST HAVE BEEN MY IMAGINATION!
Oh, thank goodness!
IS THAT ALL THAT HAPPENED?!
YEAH. SORRY TO WORRY YOU...

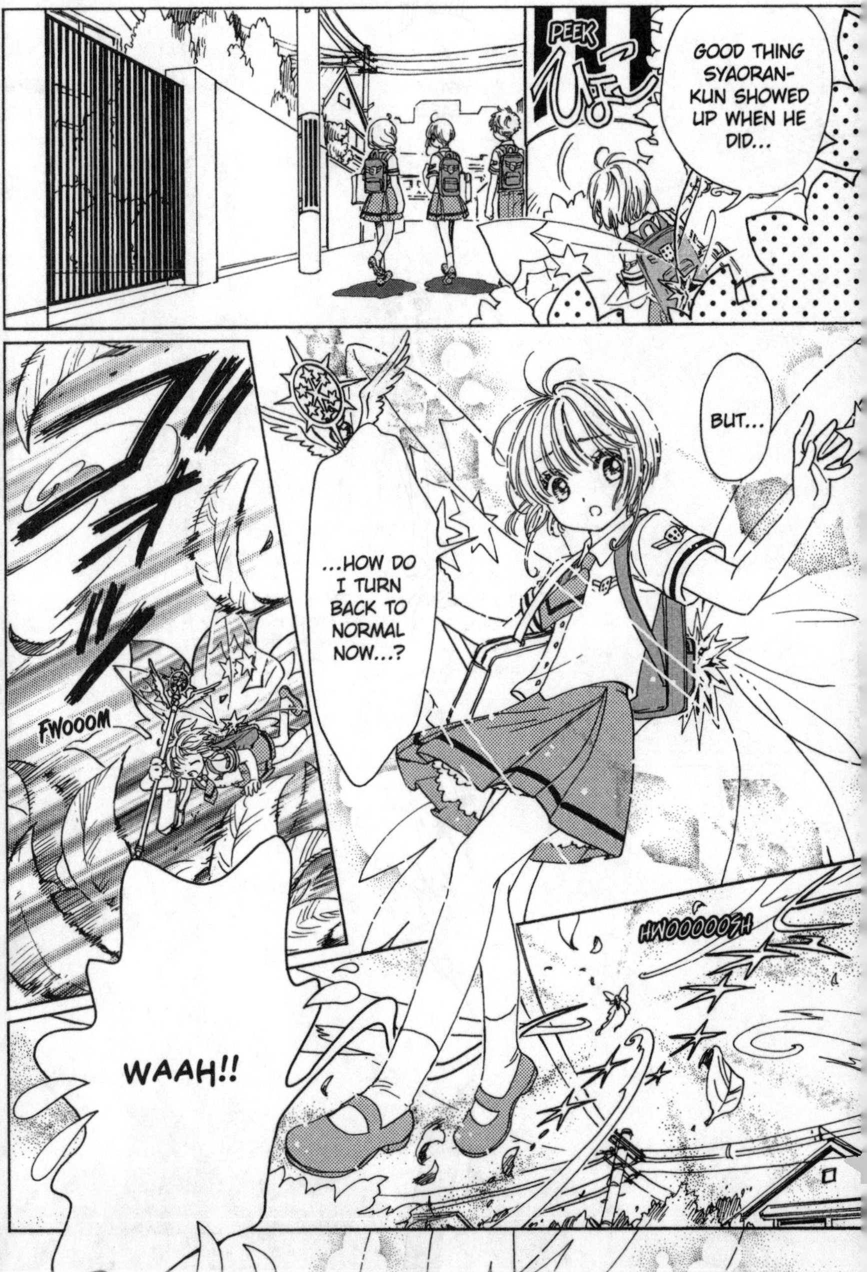
GOOD THING SYAORAN-KUN SHOWED UP WHEN HE DID...
PEEK
BUT...
...HOW DO I TURN BACK TO NORMAL NOW...?
WHOOOOOSH
FWOOOM
WAAH!!

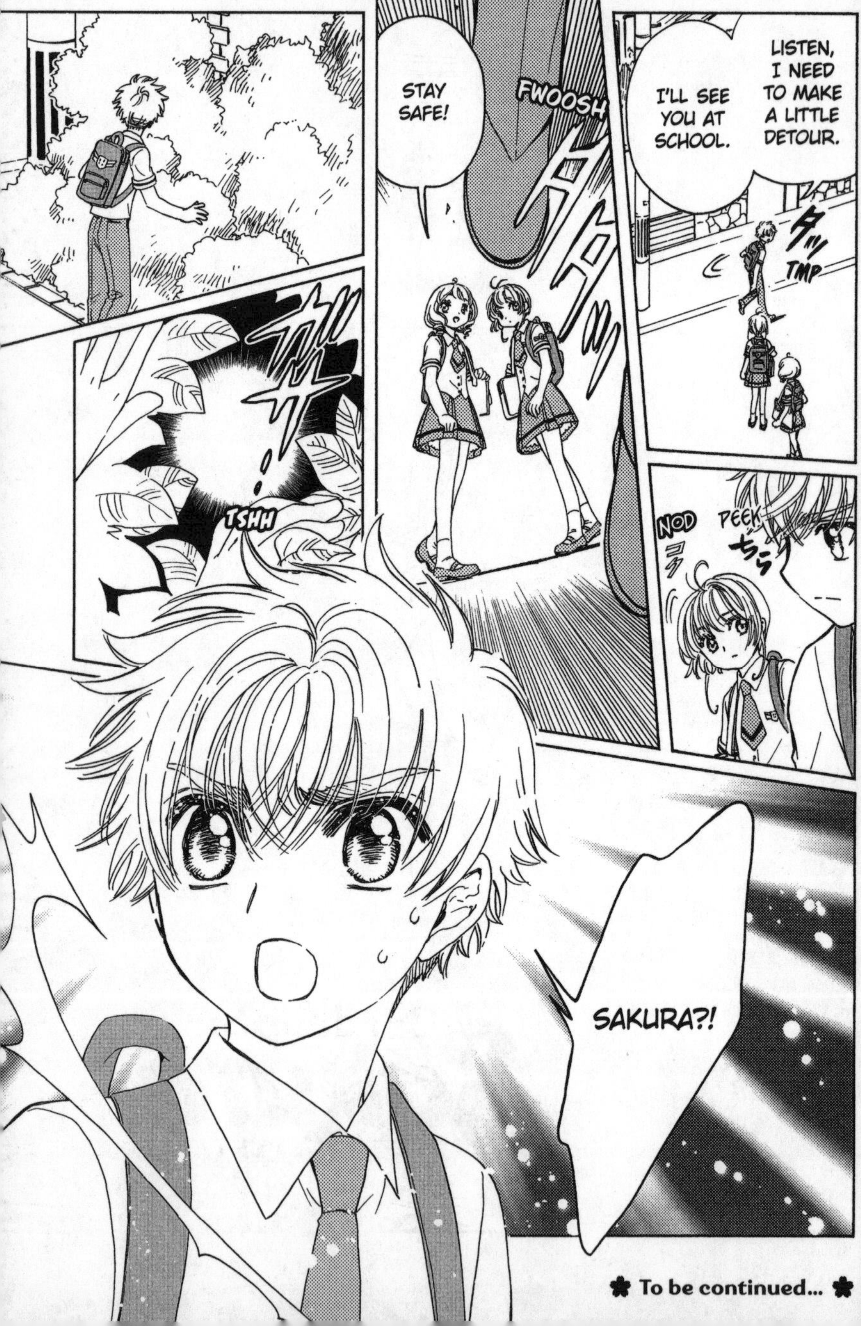
LISTEN, I NEED TO MAKE A LITTLE DETOUR.
I'LL SEE YOU AT SCHOOL.
TMP
NOD
PEEK
FWOOSH
STAY SAFE!
TSHH
SAKURA?!

To be continued...

Cardcaptor
Sakura
CLEAR CARD

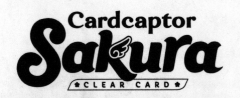

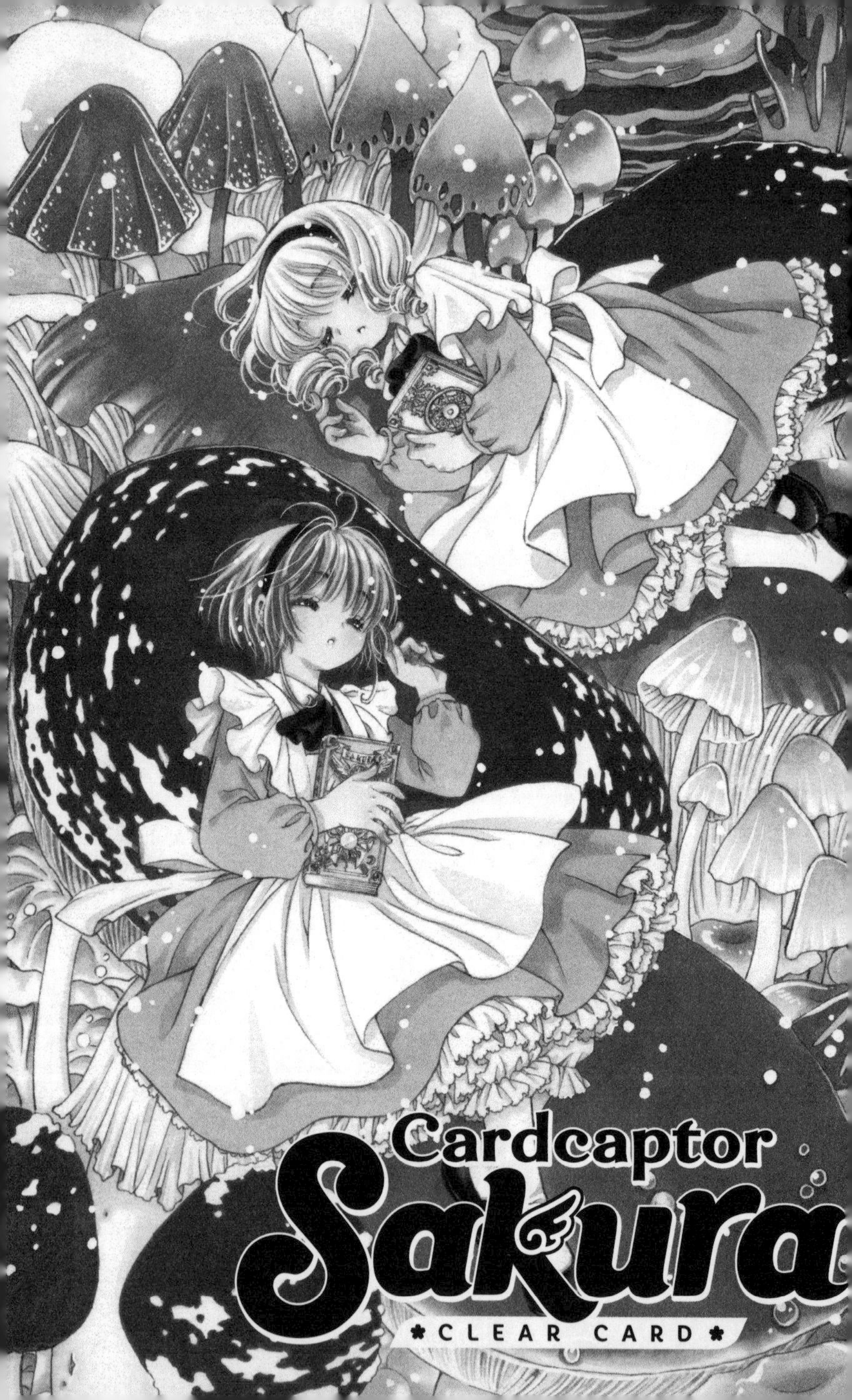
Cardcaptor
Sakura
CLEAR CARD

Cardcaptor Sakura

CLEAR CARD

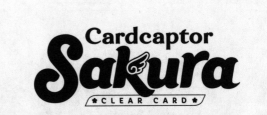

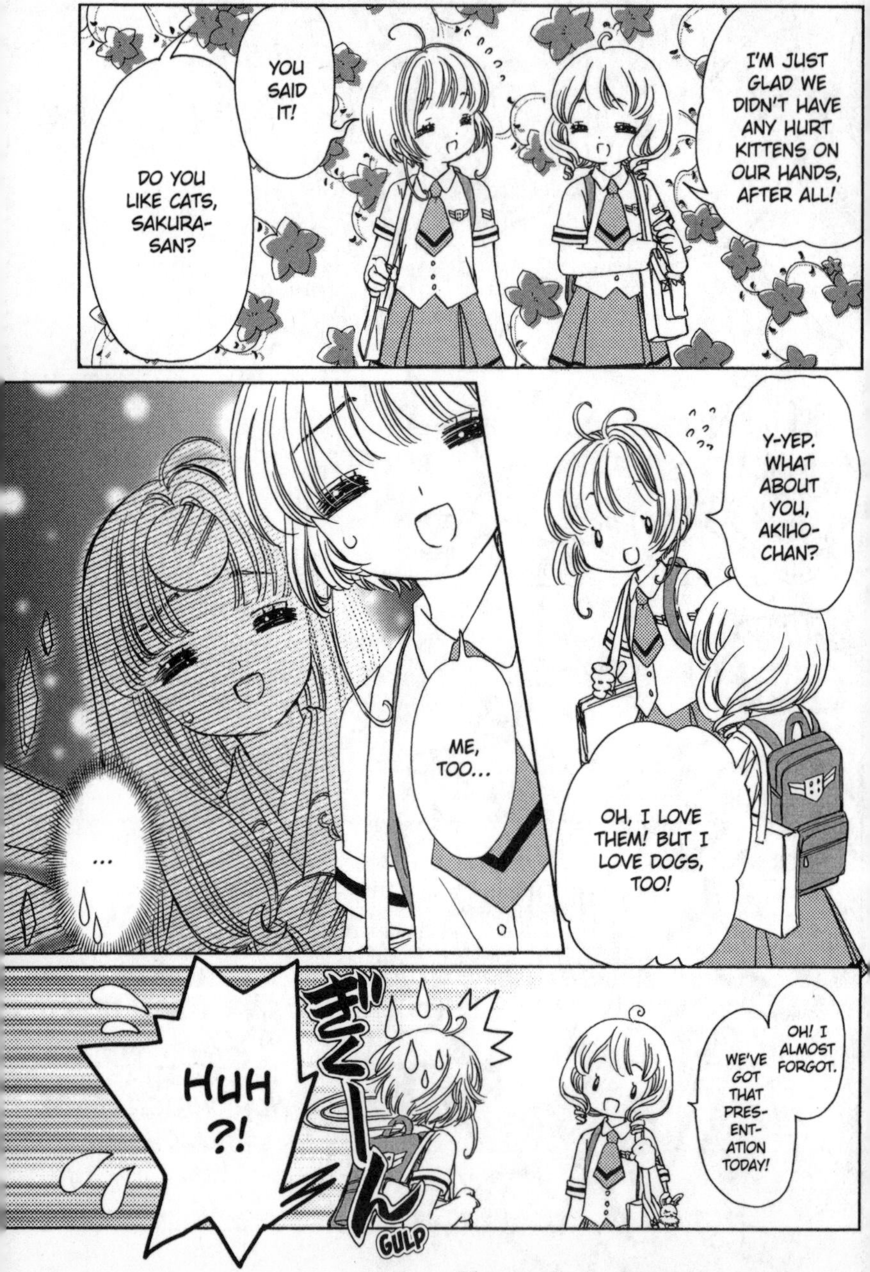
I'M JUST GLAD WE DIDN'T HAVE ANY HURT KITTENS ON OUR HANDS, AFTER ALL!
YOU SAID IT!
DO YOU LIKE CATS, SAKURA-SAN?
Y-YEP. WHAT ABOUT YOU, AKIHO-CHAN?
OH, I LOVE THEM! BUT I LOVE DOGS, TOO!
ME, TOO...
...
OH! I ALMOST FORGOT.
WE'VE GOT THAT PRES-ENT-ATION TODAY!
ぎくーん
GULP
HUH ?!

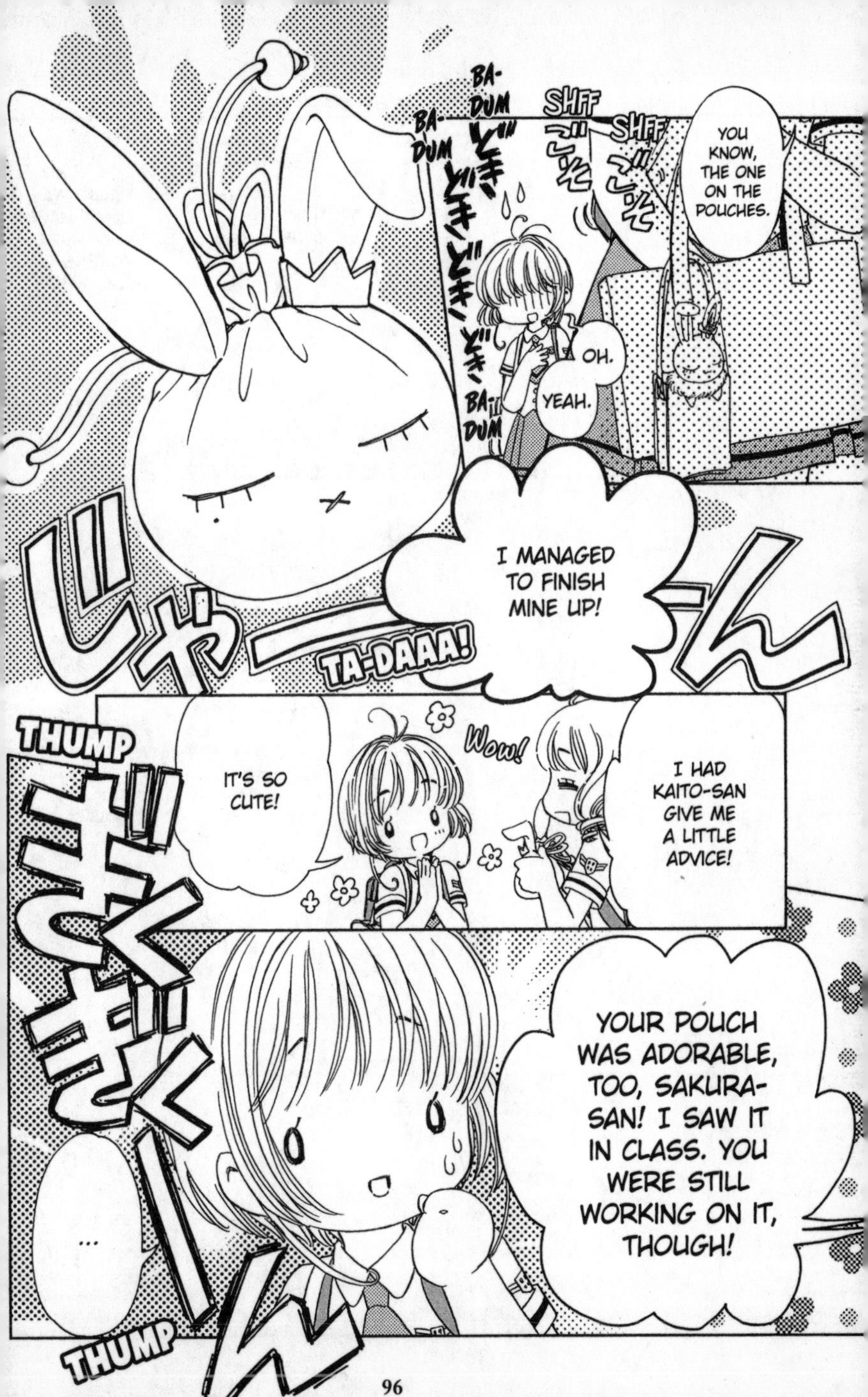
SHFF
SHFF
YOU KNOW, THE ONE ON THE POUCHES.
BA-DUM
BA-DUM
OH.
YEAH.
BA-DUM
I MANAGED TO FINISH MINE UP!
TA-DAAA!
I HAD KAITO-SAN GIVE ME A LITTLE ADVICE!
WOW!
IT'S SO CUTE!
THUMP
YOUR POUCH WAS ADORABLE, TOO, SAKURA-SAN! I SAW IT IN CLASS. YOU WERE STILL WORKING ON IT, THOUGH!
...
THUMP

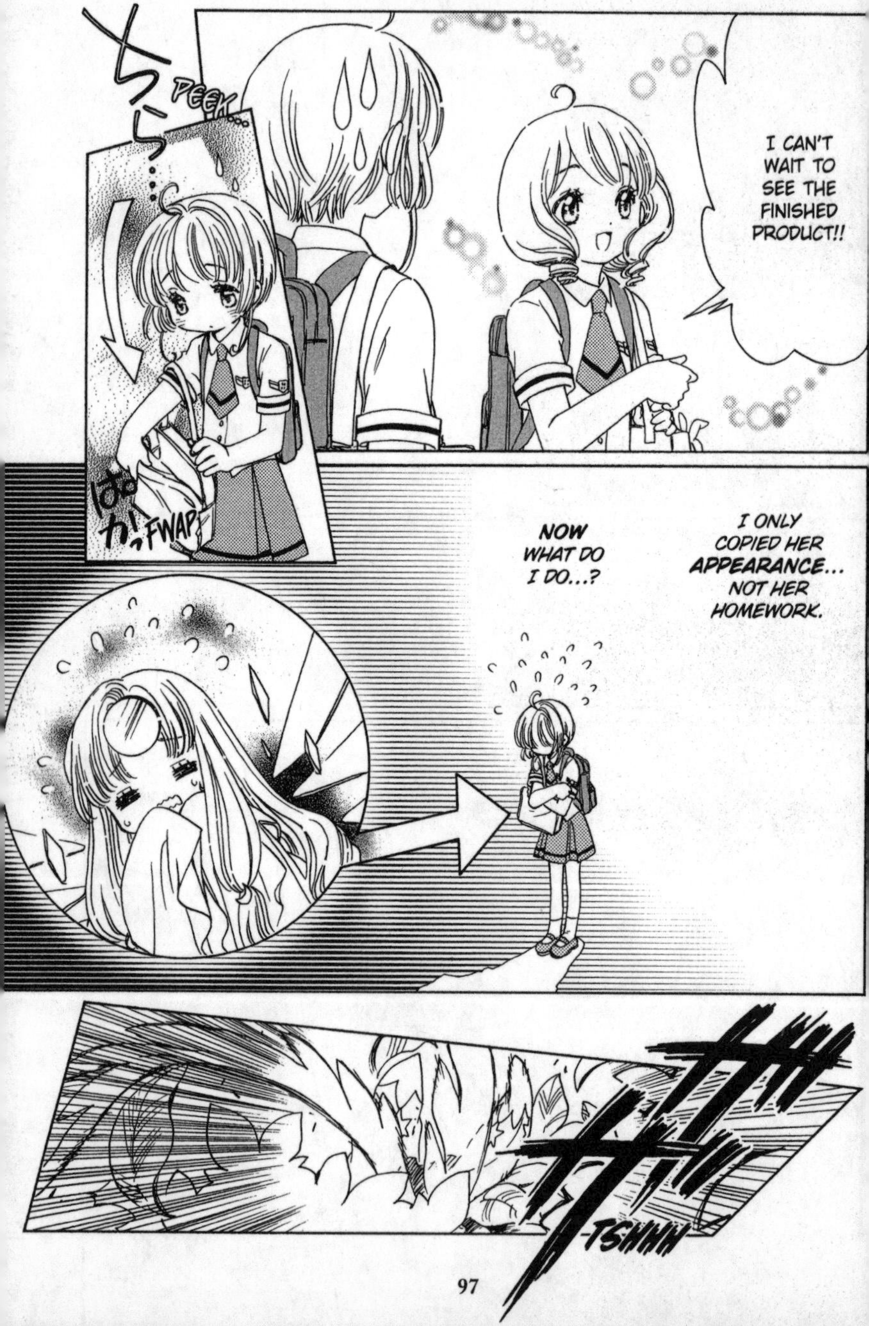
I CAN'T WAIT TO SEE THE FINISHED PRODUCT!!
ちら〜
PEEK...
ぱか!
FWAP
I ONLY COPIED HER APPEARANCE... NOT HER HOMEWORK.
NOW WHAT DO I DO...?
TSHHH

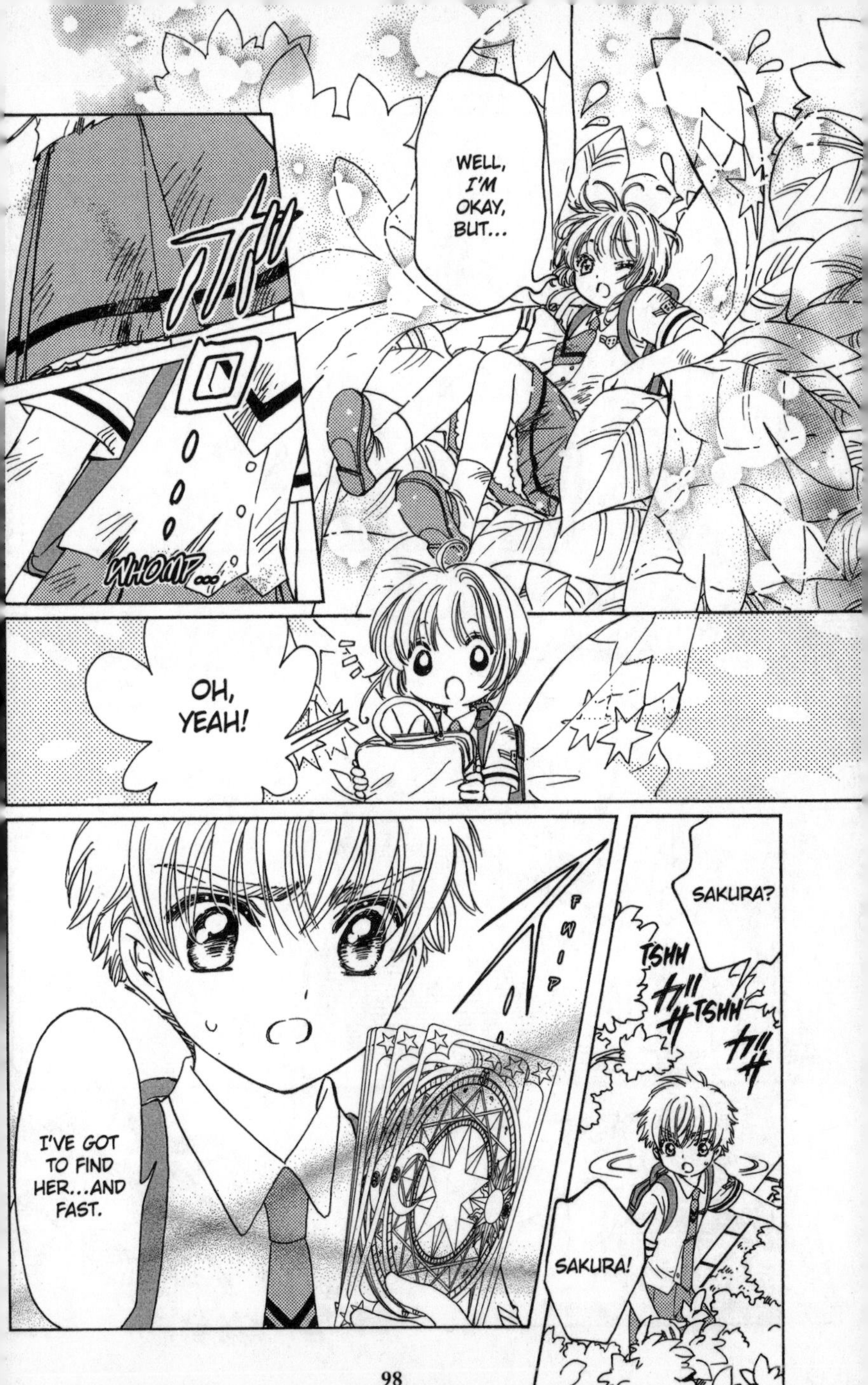
WELL, I'M OKAY, BUT...
WHOMP...
OH, YEAH!
SAKURA?
TSHH
TSHH
SAKURA!
FWIP
I'VE GOT TO FIND HER...AND FAST.

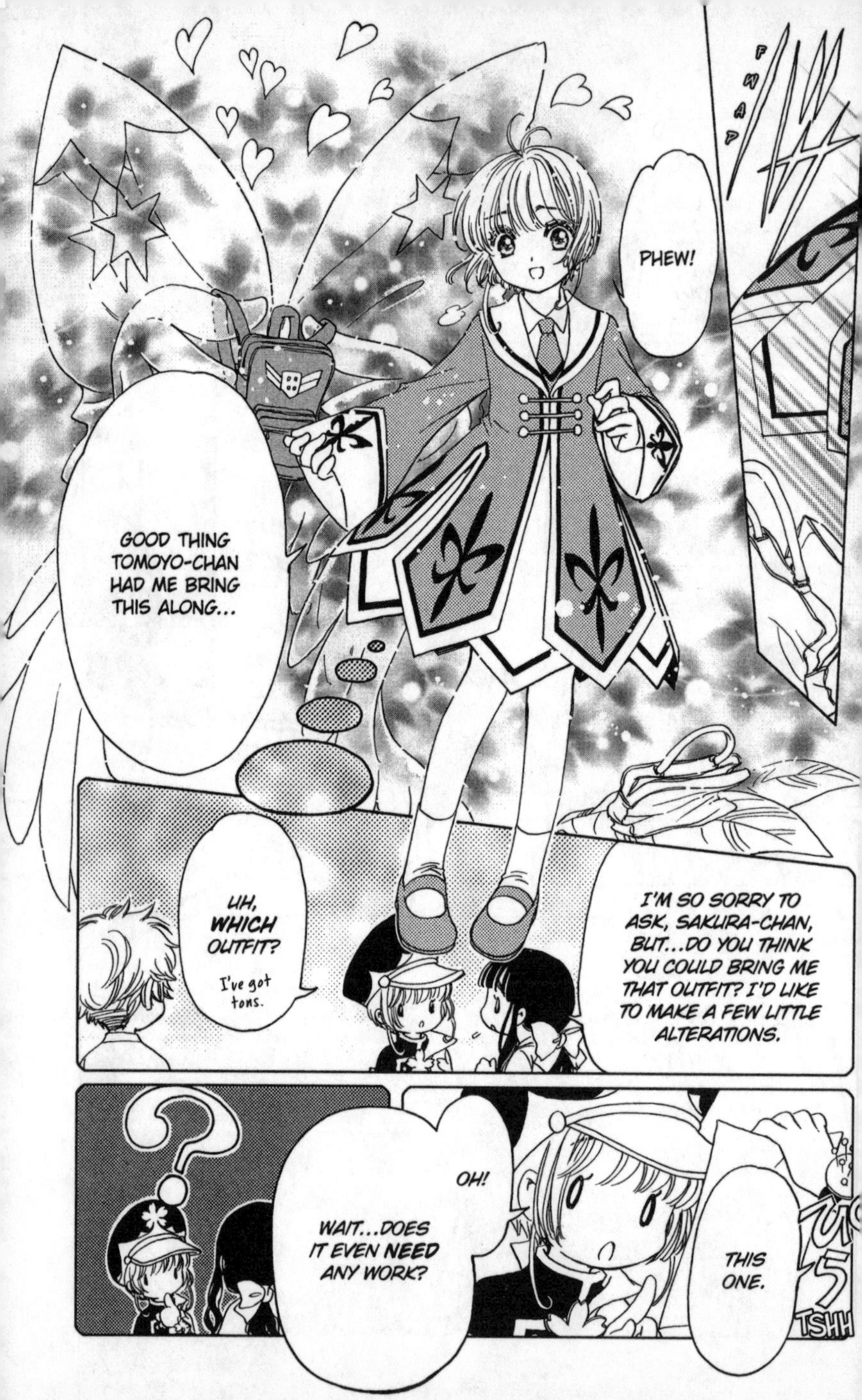
FWAP
PHEW!
GOOD THING TOMOYO-CHAN HAD ME BRING THIS ALONG...
I'M SO SORRY TO ASK, SAKURA-CHAN, BUT...DO YOU THINK YOU COULD BRING ME THAT OUTFIT? I'D LIKE TO MAKE A FEW LITTLE ALTERATIONS.
UH, WHICH OUTFIT?
I've got tons.
THIS ONE.
TSHH
OH!
WAIT...DOES IT EVEN NEED ANY WORK?

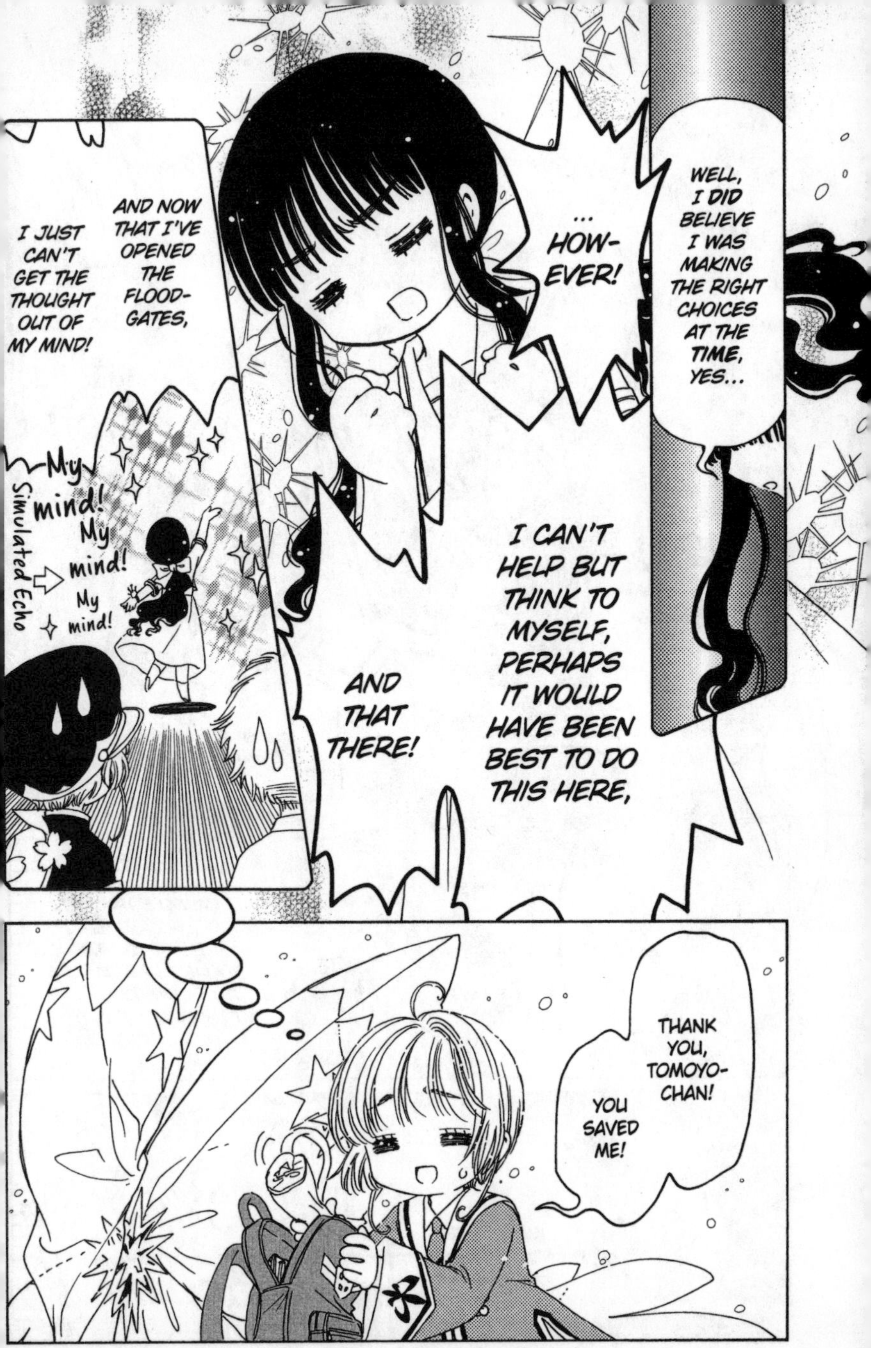
WELL, I DID BELIEVE I WAS MAKING THE RIGHT CHOICES AT THE TIME, YES...
... HOW-EVER!
I CAN'T HELP BUT THINK TO MYSELF, PERHAPS IT WOULD HAVE BEEN BEST TO DO THIS HERE,
AND THAT THERE!
AND NOW THAT I'VE OPENED THE FLOOD-GATES,
I JUST CAN'T GET THE THOUGHT OUT OF MY MIND!
My mind! My mind! My mind! My mind!
Simulated Echo
THANK YOU, TOMOYO-CHAN!
YOU SAVED ME!

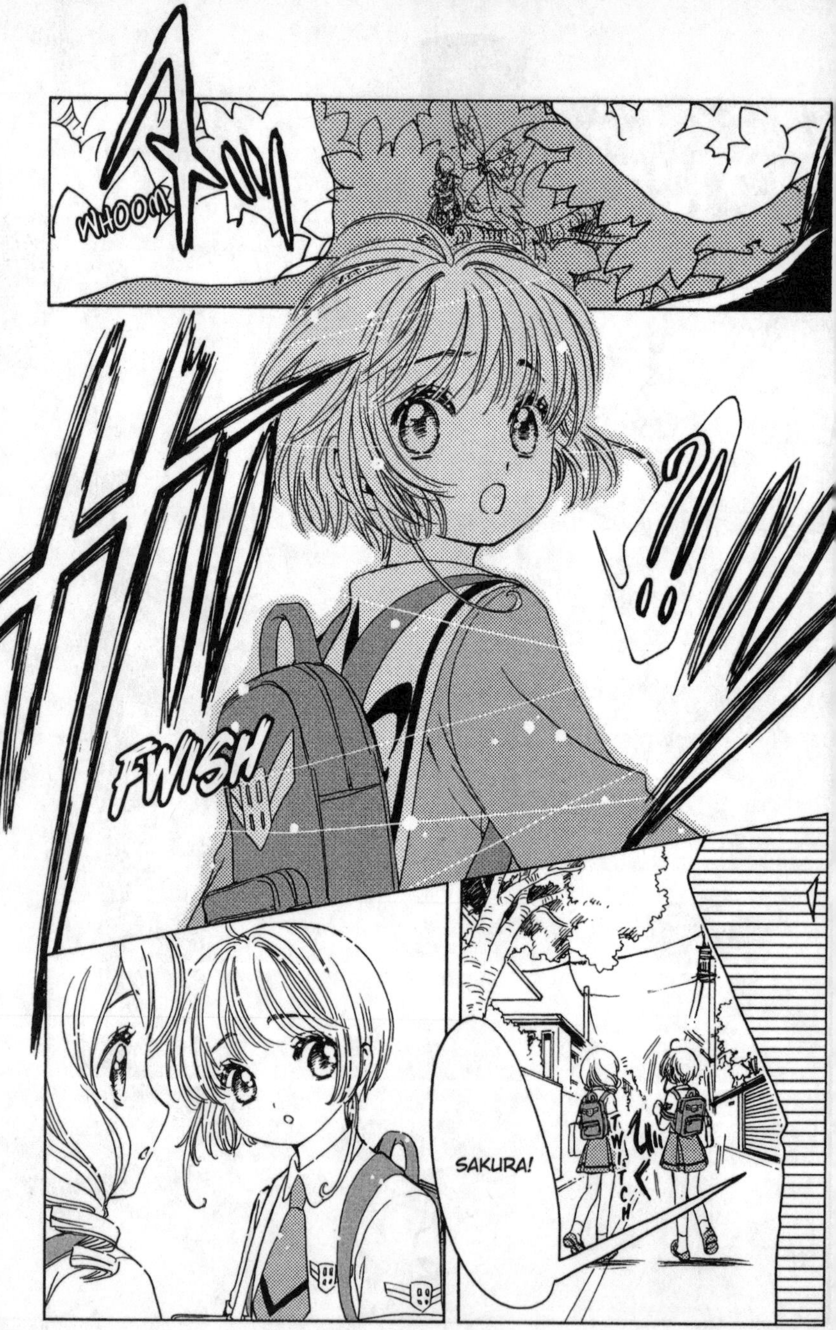
WHOOM
?!!
FWISH
SAKURA!
TWITCH

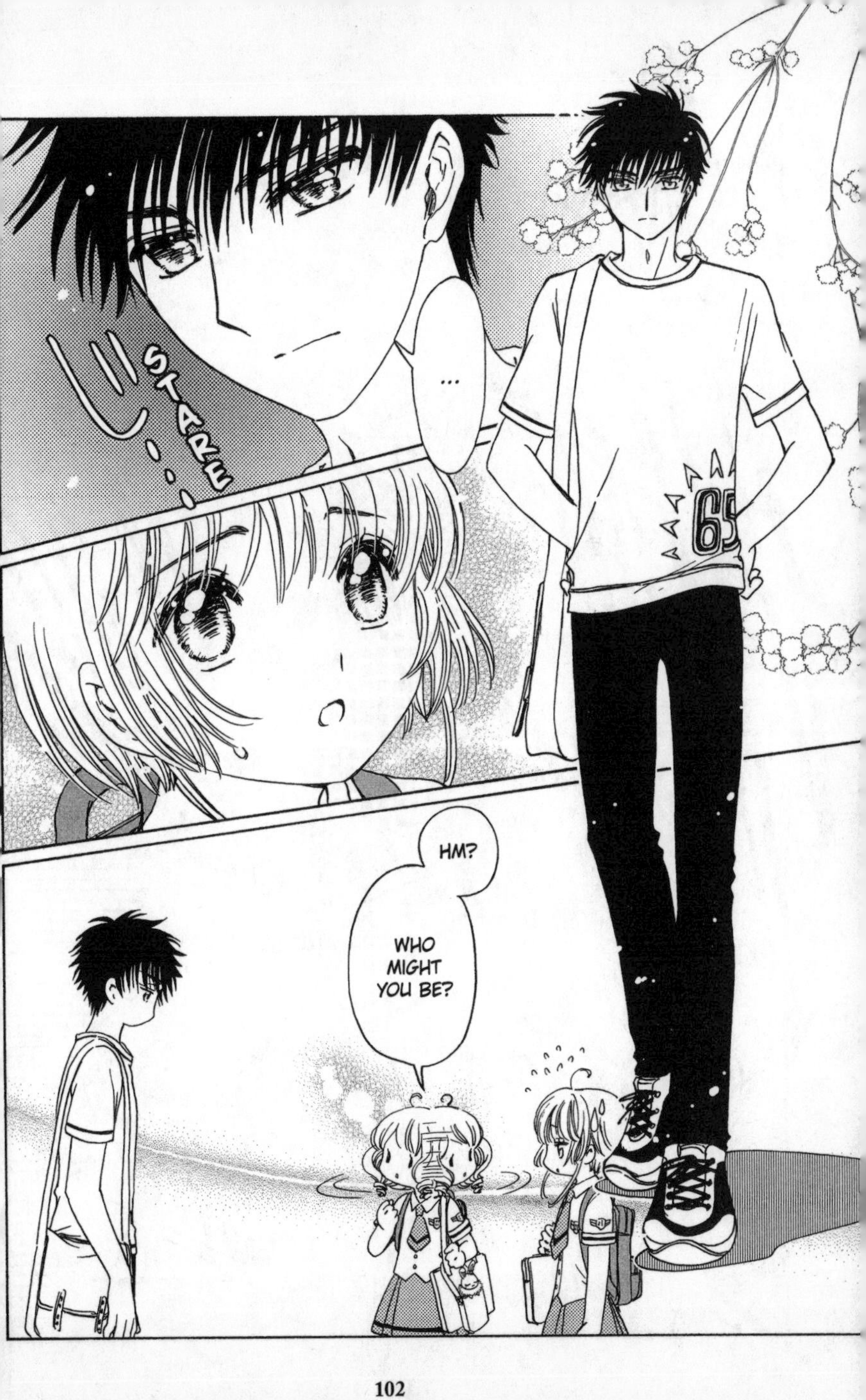
...
STARE
HM?
WHO MIGHT YOU BE?

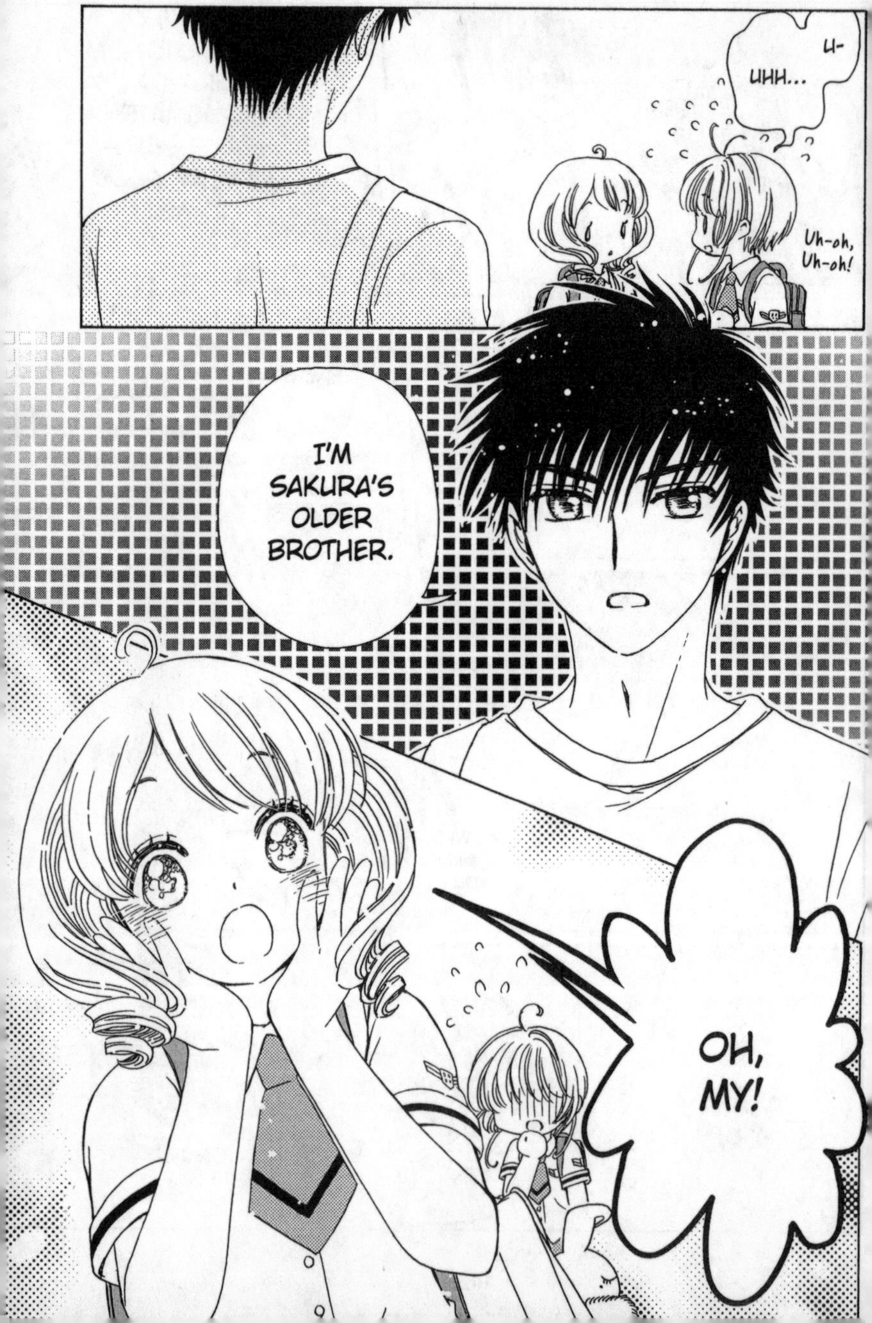
U-
UHH...
Uh-oh,
Uh-oh!
I'M SAKURA'S OLDER BROTHER.
OH, MY!

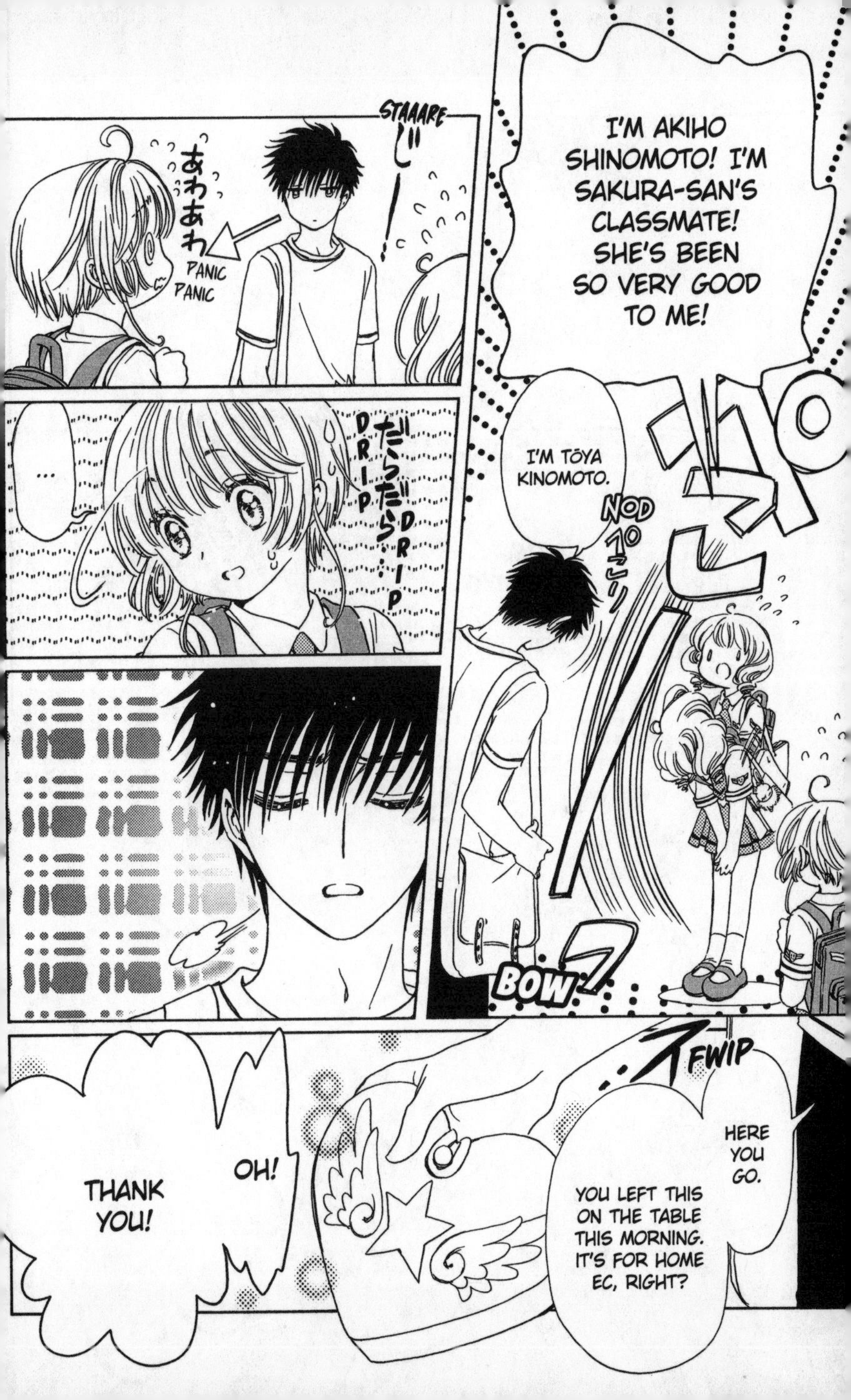

I'M AKIHO SHINOMOTO! I'M SAKURA-SAN'S CLASSMATE! SHE'S BEEN SO VERY GOOD TO ME!
I'M TŌYA KINOMOTO.
NOD
BOW
STAAARE
じー
あわあわ
PANIC PANIC
...
だらだら
DRIP DRIP
FWIP
HERE YOU GO.
YOU LEFT THIS ON THE TABLE THIS MORNING. IT'S FOR HOME EC, RIGHT?
OH!
THANK YOU!

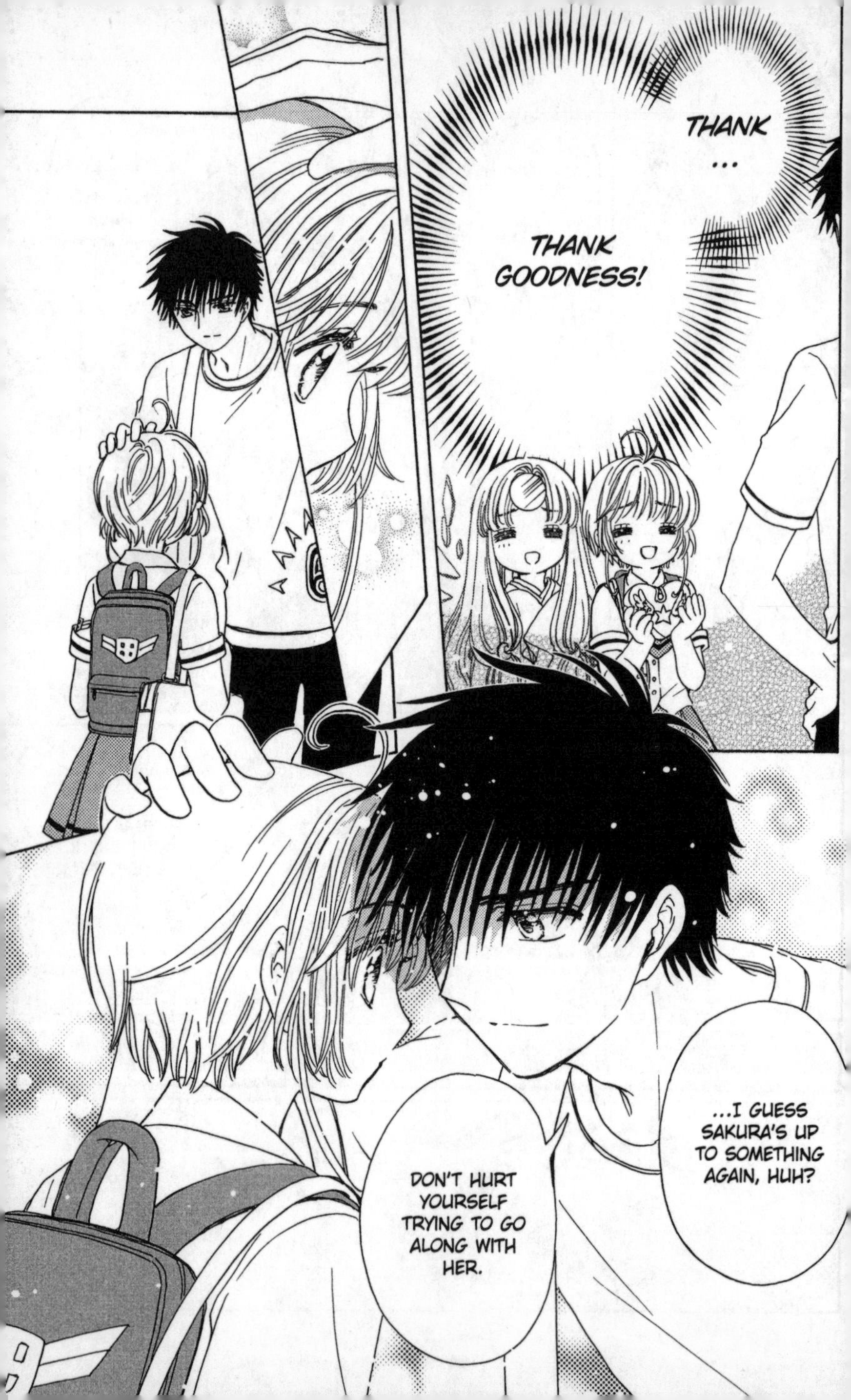
THANK ...
THANK GOODNESS!
...I GUESS SAKURA'S UP TO SOMETHING AGAIN, HUH?
DON'T HURT YOURSELF TRYING TO GO ALONG WITH HER.

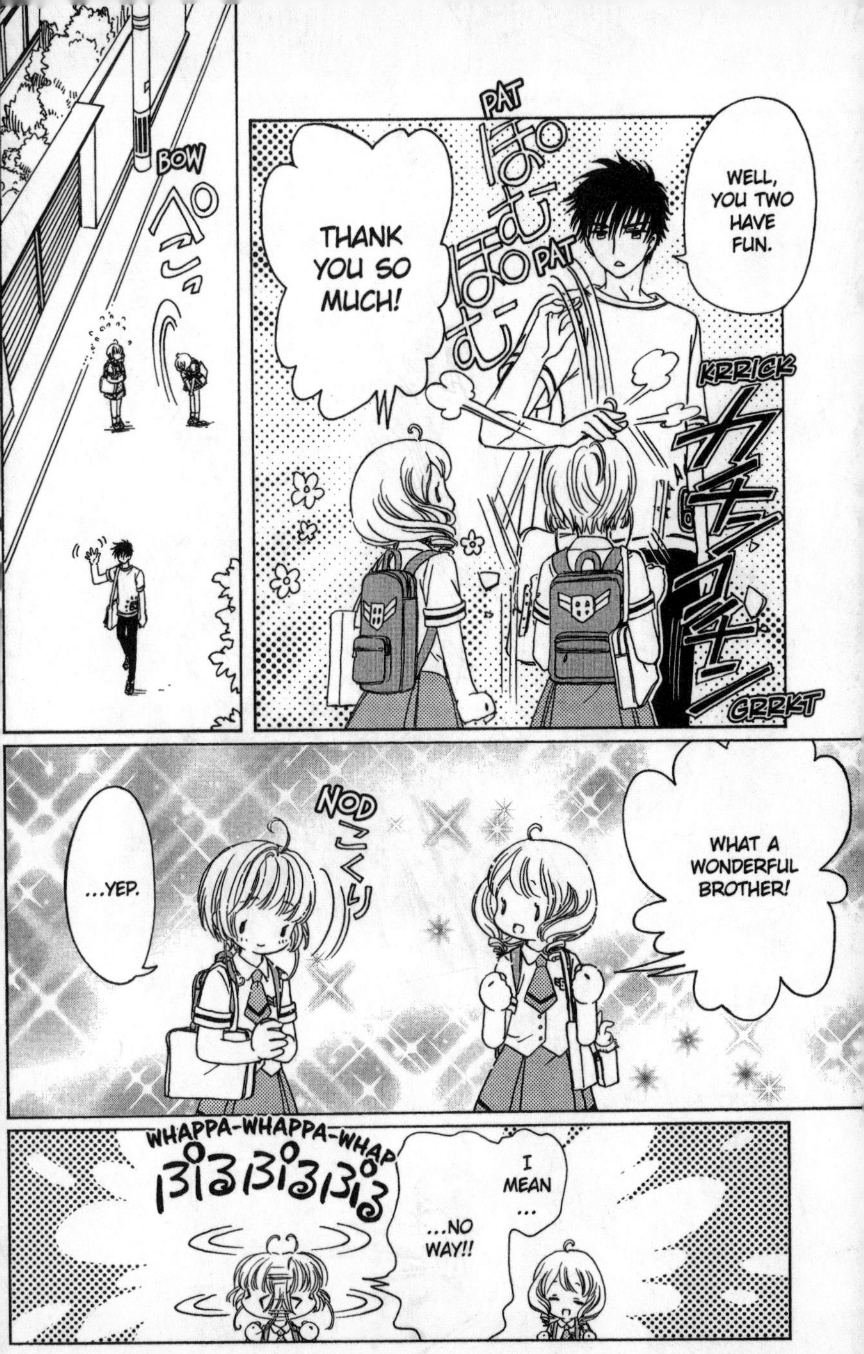
WELL, YOU TWO HAVE FUN.
PAT
PAT
THANK YOU SO MUCH!
KRRICK
GRRKT
BOW
WHAT A WONDERFUL BROTHER!
NOD
...YEP.
I MEAN ...
...NO WAY!!
WHAPPA-WHAPPA-WHAP

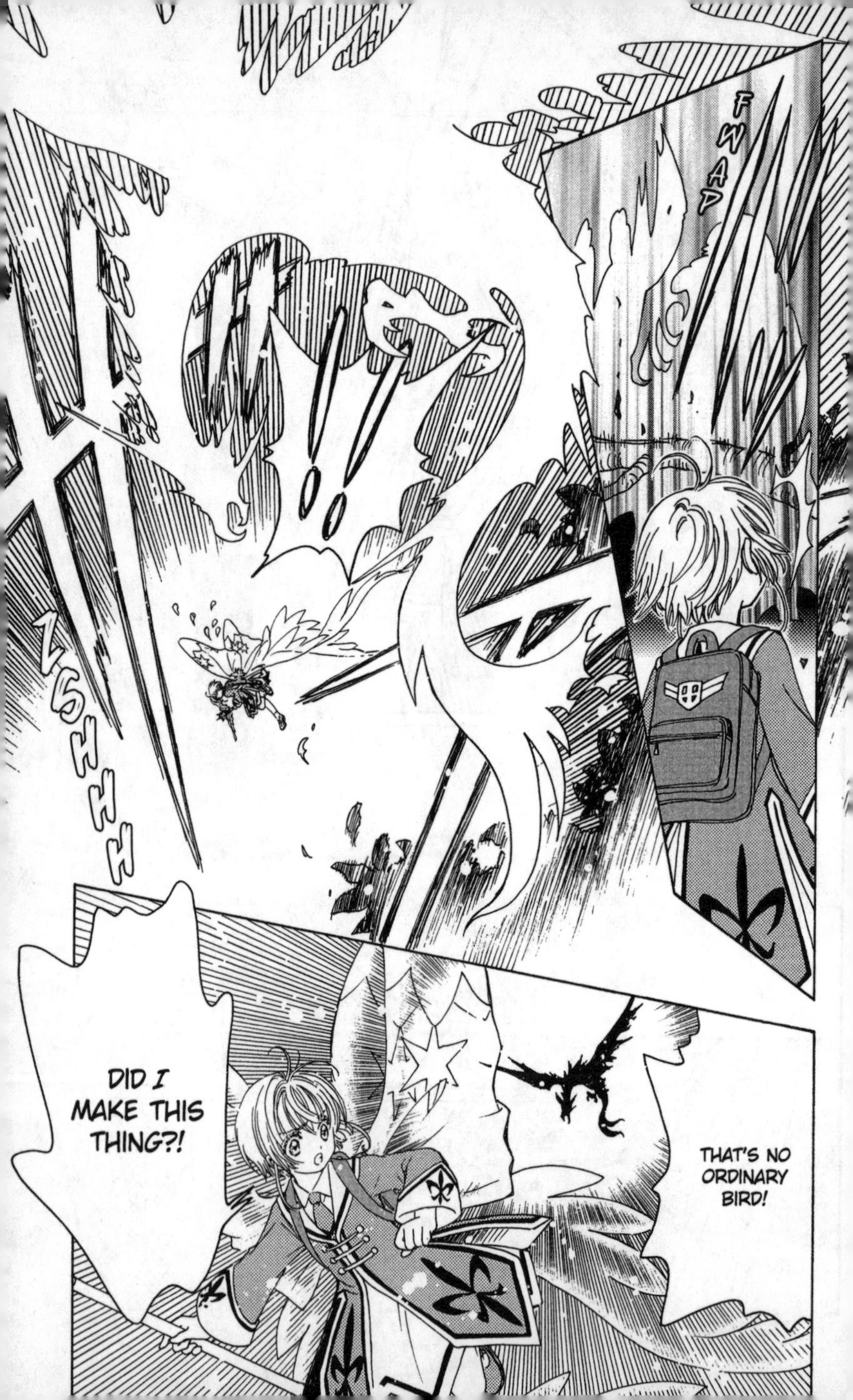
FWAP
!!
ZSHHHHH
THAT'S NO ORDINARY BIRD!
DID I MAKE THIS THING?!

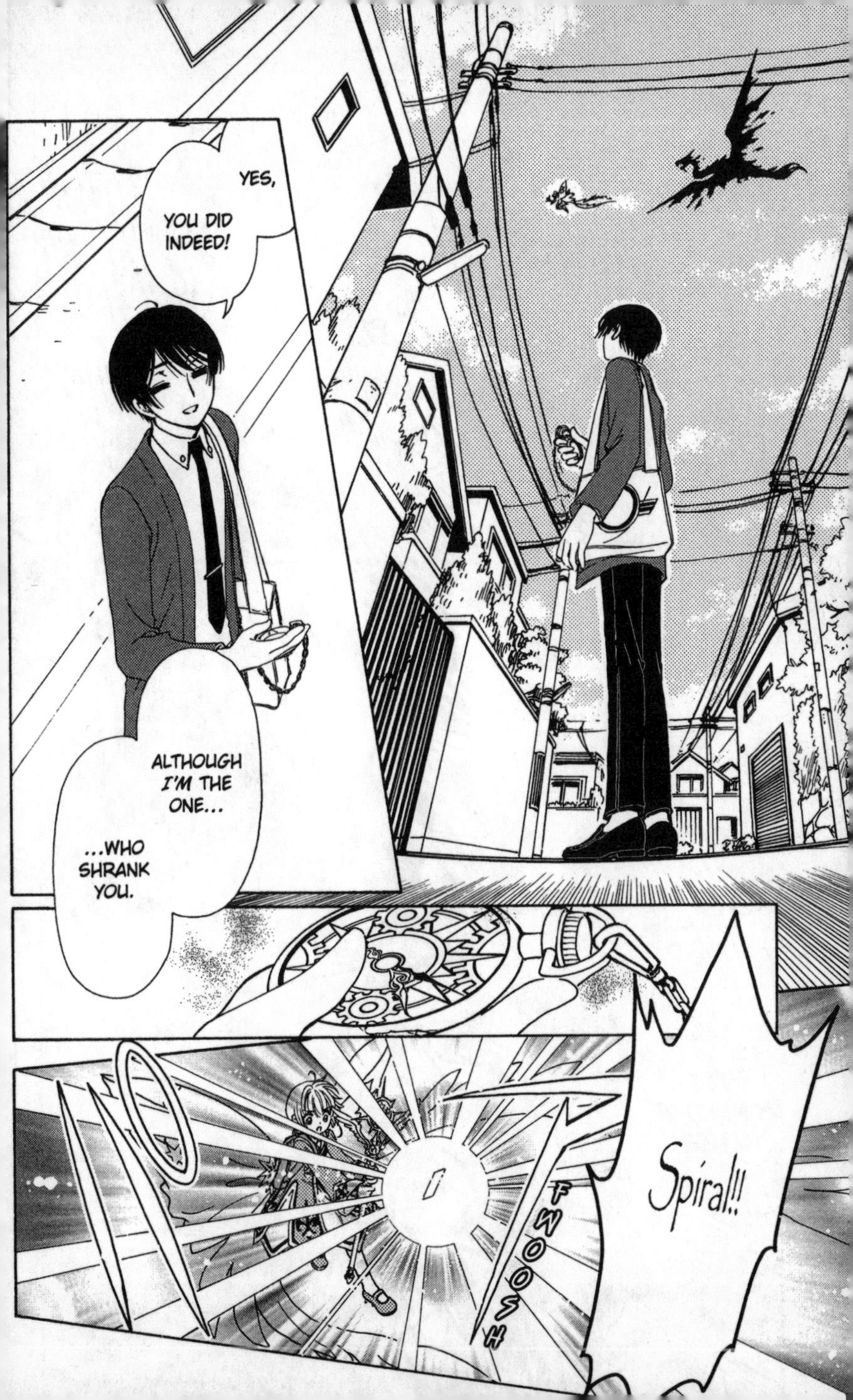
YES,
YOU DID INDEED!
ALTHOUGH I'M THE ONE...
...WHO SHRANK YOU.
Spiral!!
FWOOOSH

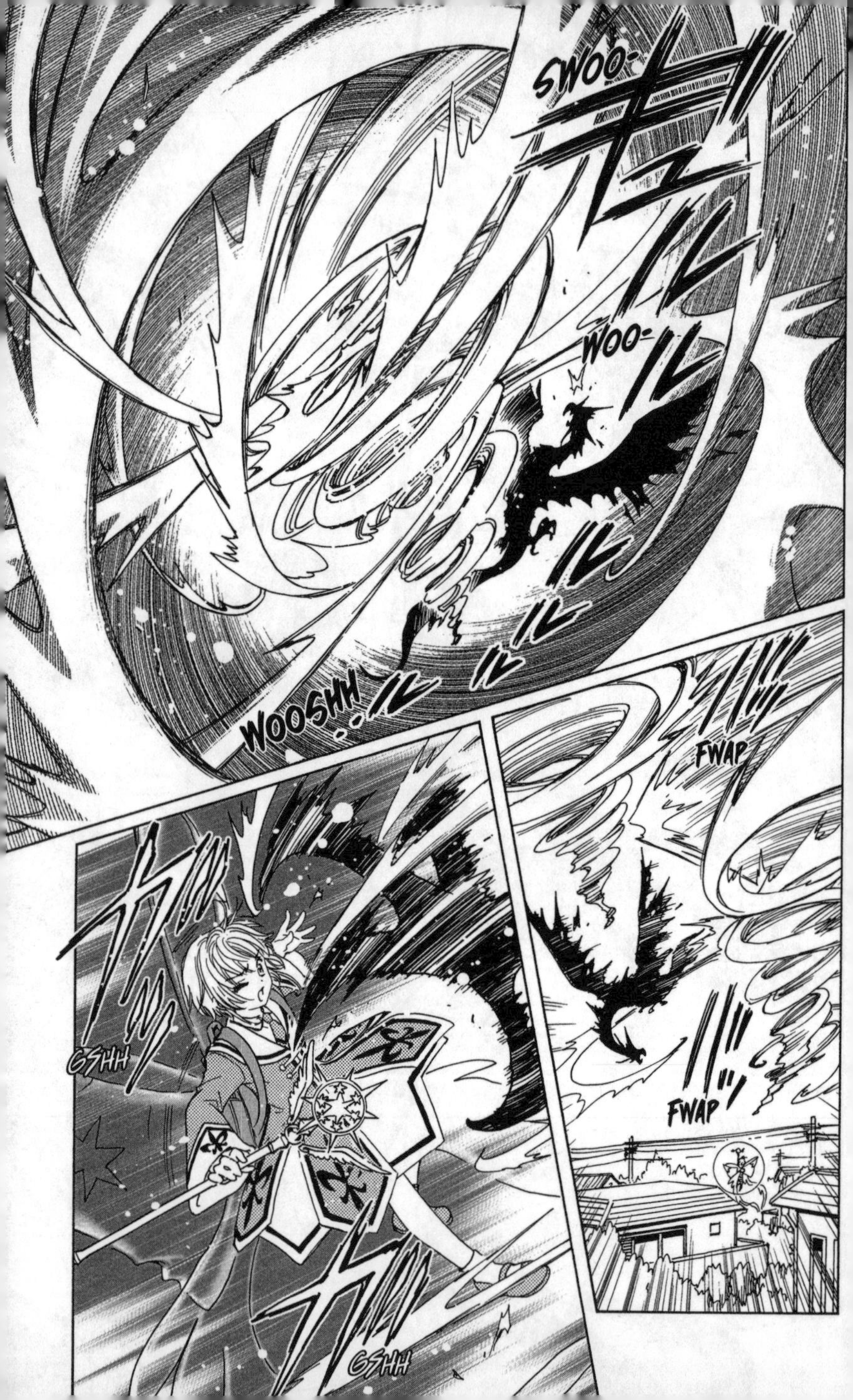

SWOO-
WOO-
WOOSHH
FWAP
FWAP
GSHH
GSHH

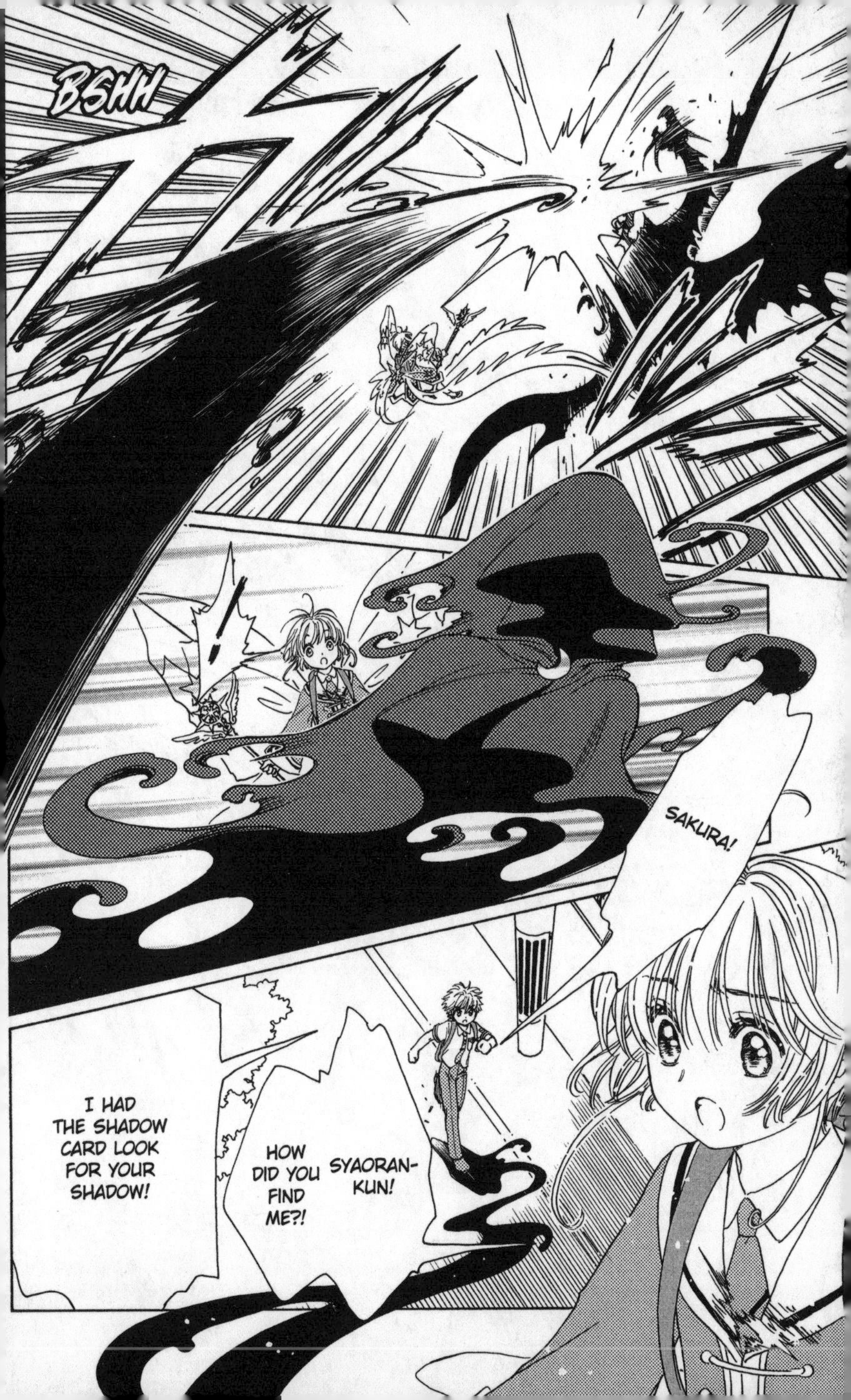
BSHH
SAKURA!
SYAORAN-KUN!
HOW DID YOU FIND ME?!
I HAD THE SHADOW CARD LOOK FOR YOUR SHADOW!

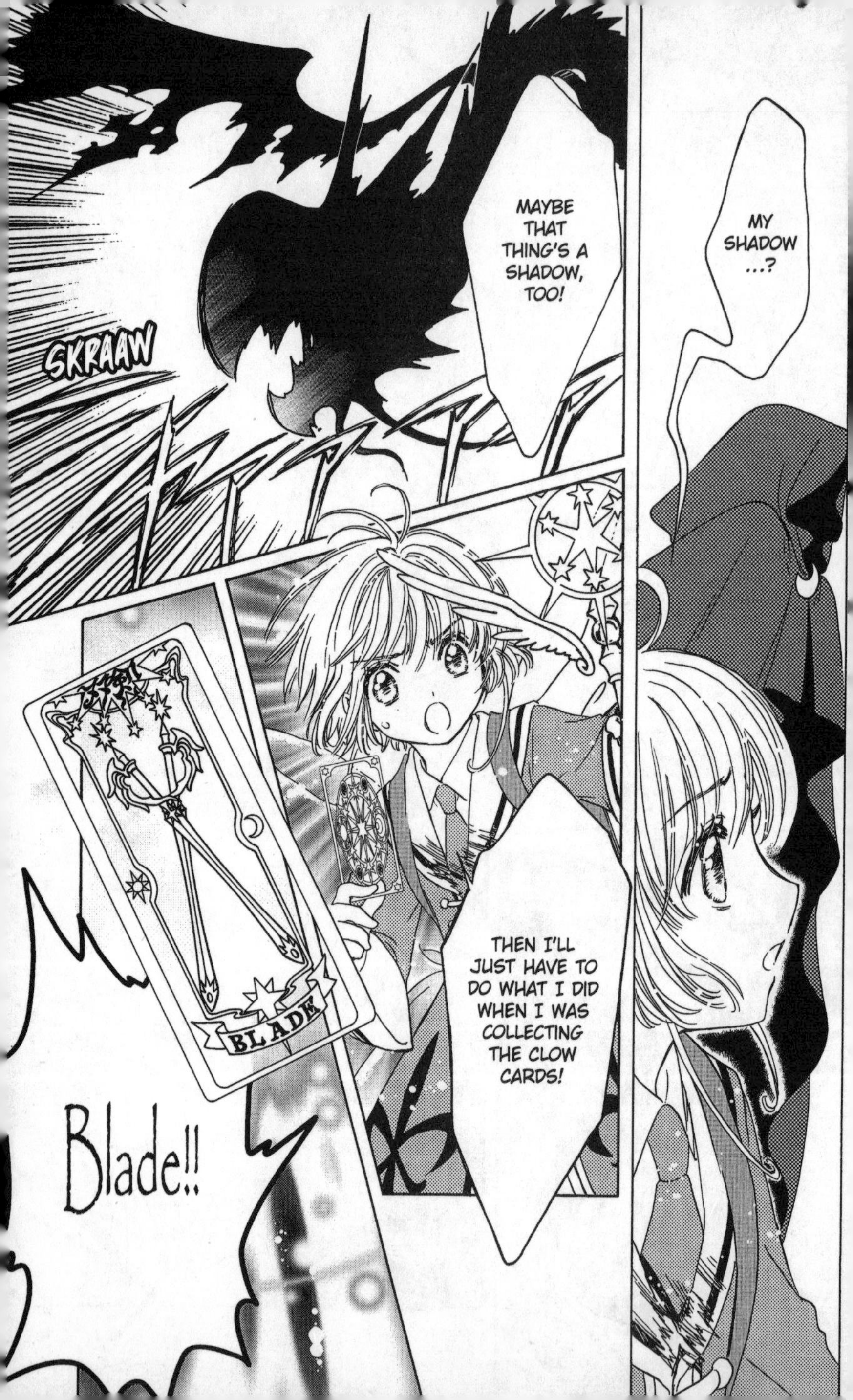
MY SHADOW ...?
MAYBE THAT THING'S A SHADOW, TOO!
SKRAAW
THEN I'LL JUST HAVE TO DO WHAT I DID WHEN I WAS COLLECTING THE CLOW CARDS!
BLADE
Blade!!

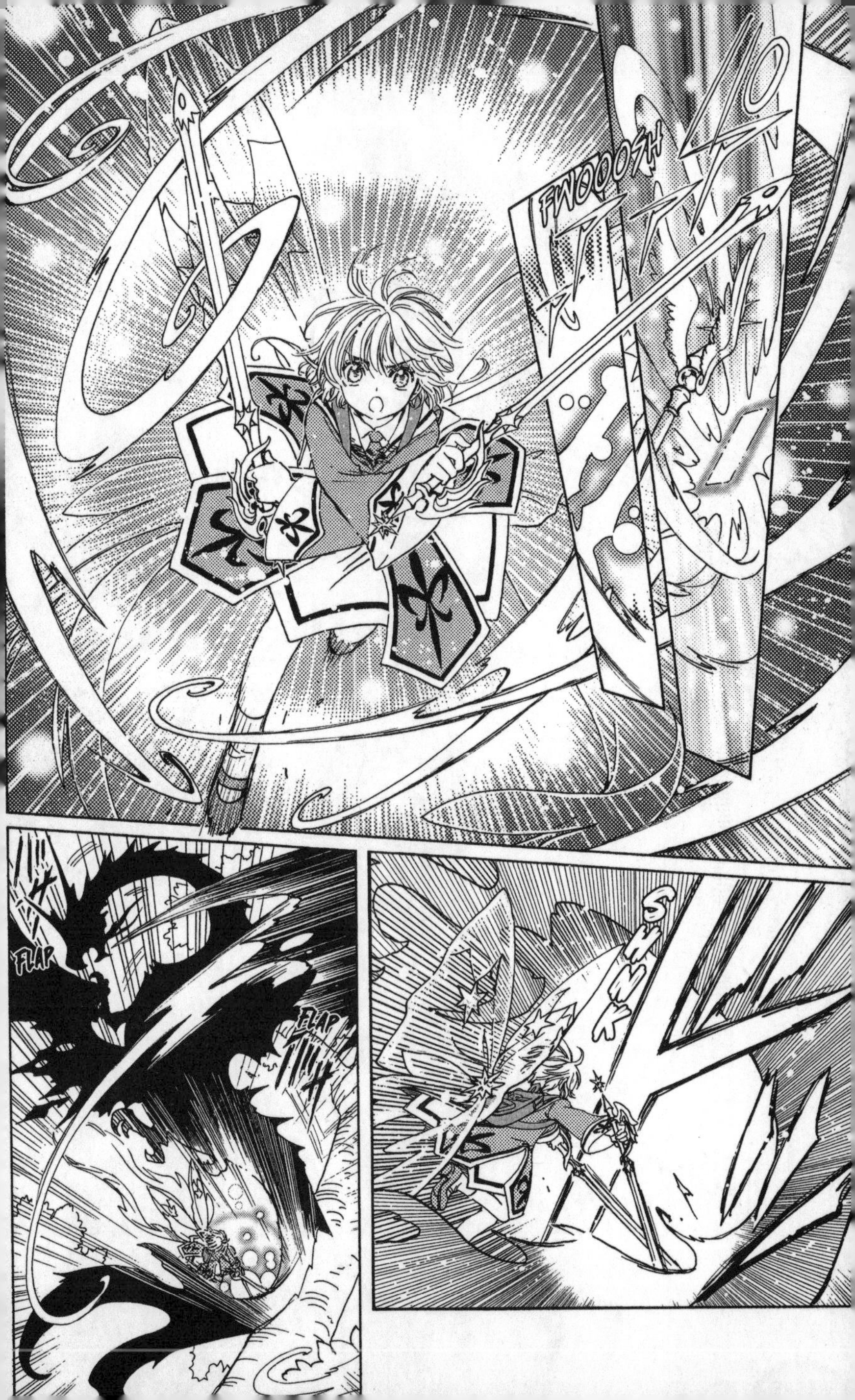
FWOOOSH
SHNK
FLAP
FLAP

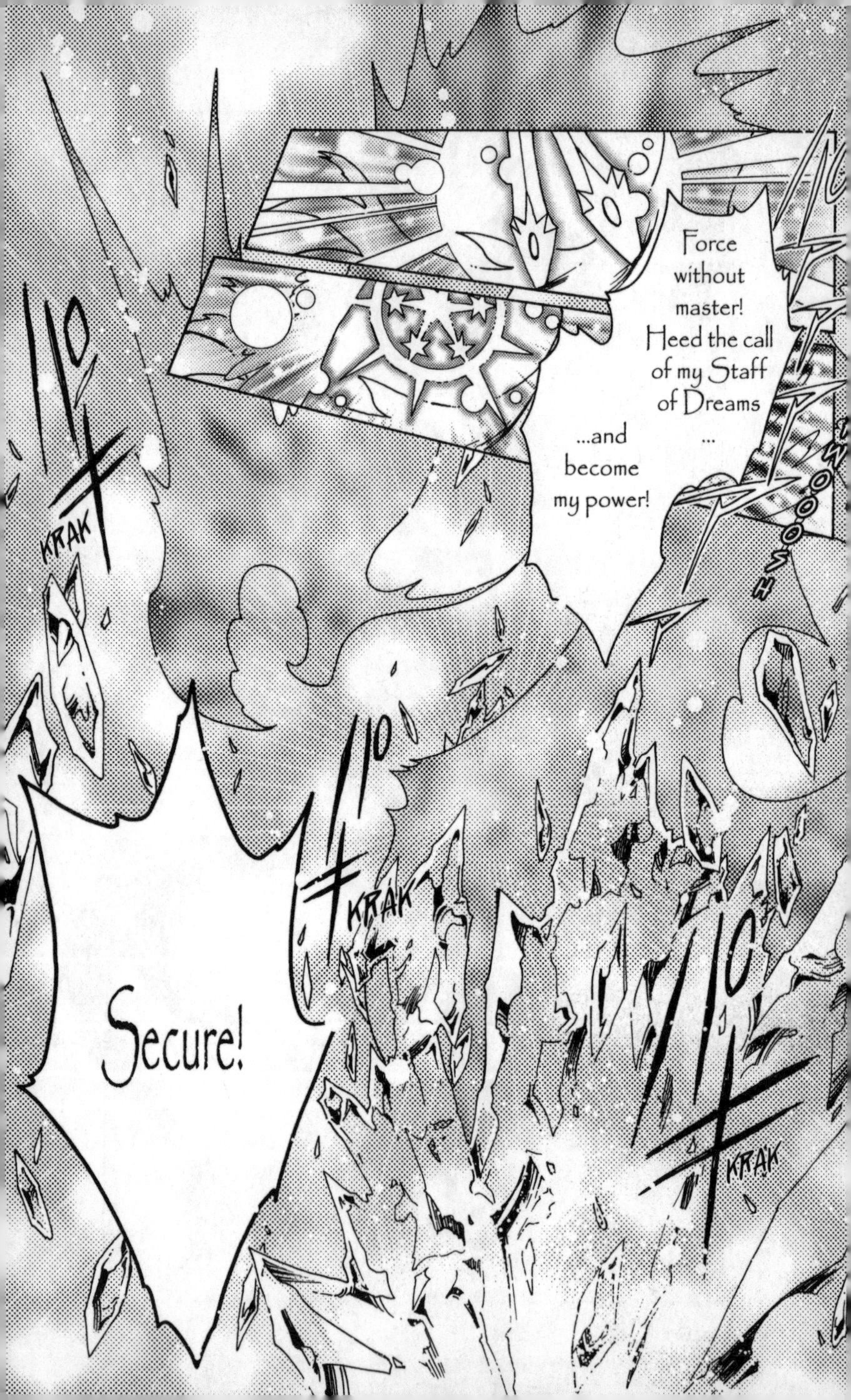
WOOOSH
Force without master! Heed the call of my Staff of Dreams ...
...and become my power!
KRAK
KRAK
KRAK
Secure!

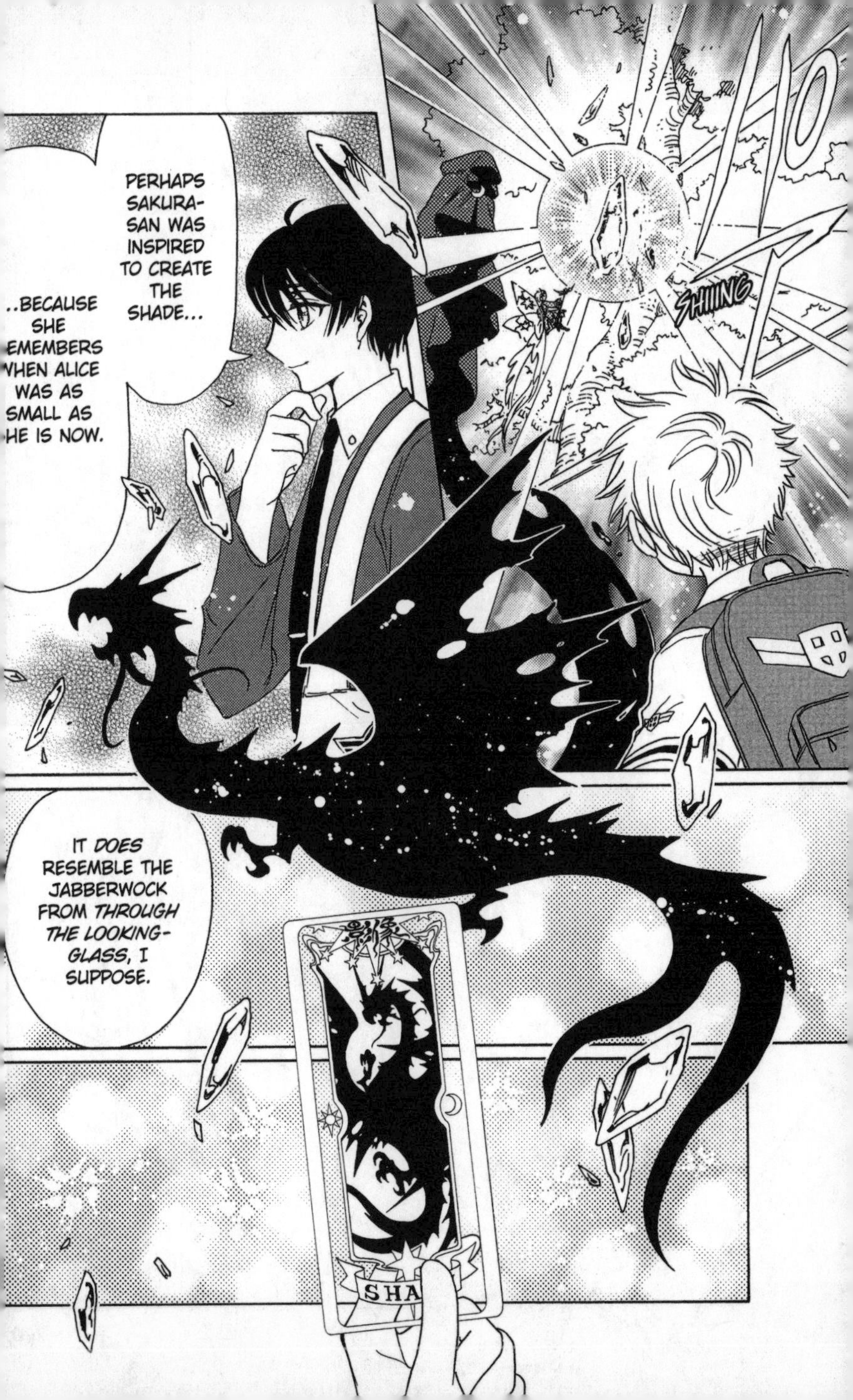
SHIIING
PERHAPS SAKURA-SAN WAS INSPIRED TO CREATE THE SHADE...
..BECAUSE SHE EMEMBERS VHEN ALICE WAS AS SMALL AS HE IS NOW.
IT DOES RESEMBLE THE JABBERWOCK FROM THROUGH THE LOOKING-GLASS, I SUPPOSE.
SHA

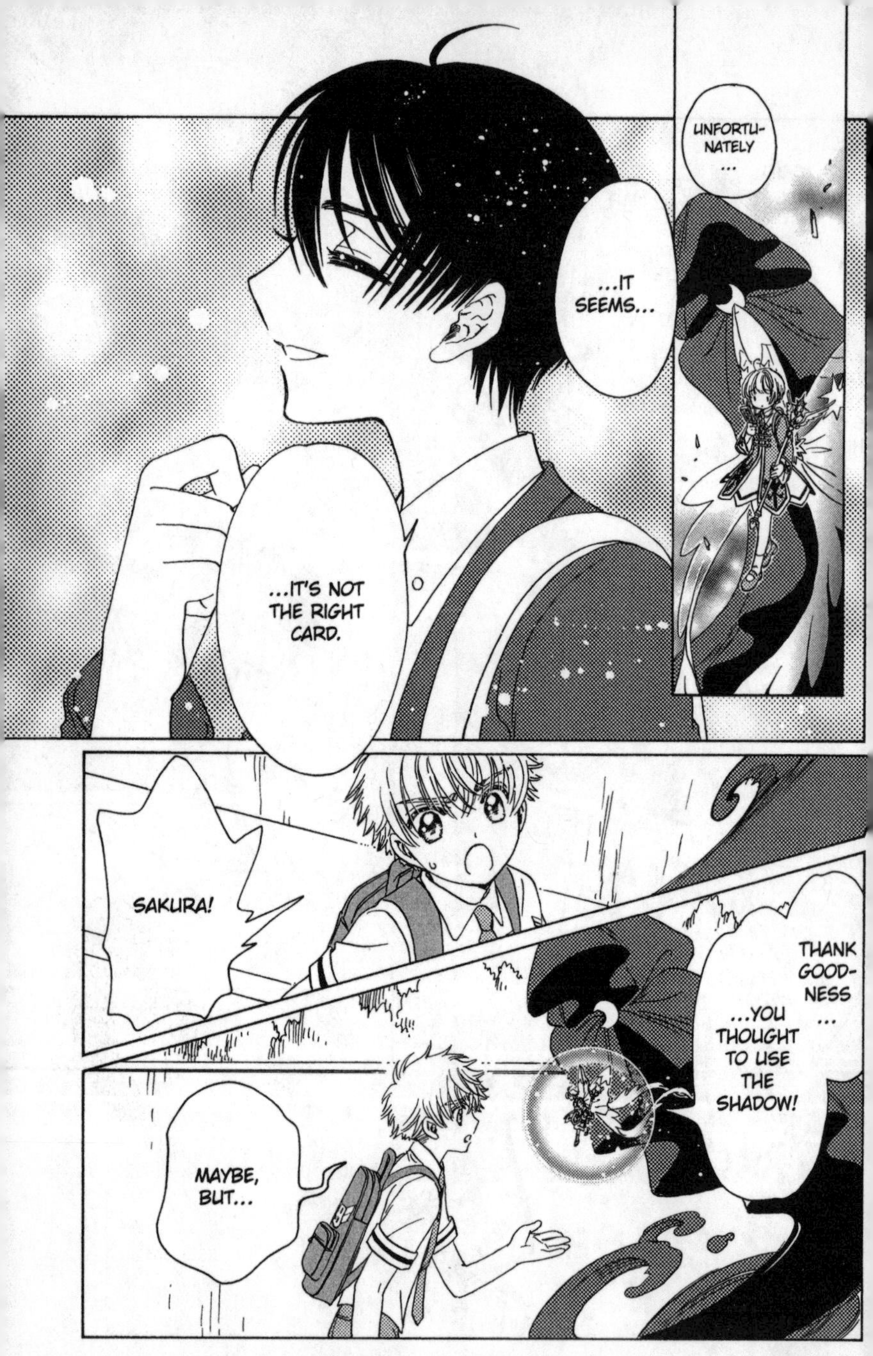
UNFORTU-NATELY ...
...IT SEEMS...
...IT'S NOT THE RIGHT CARD.
SAKURA!
THANK GOOD-NESS ...
...YOU THOUGHT TO USE THE SHADOW!
MAYBE, BUT...

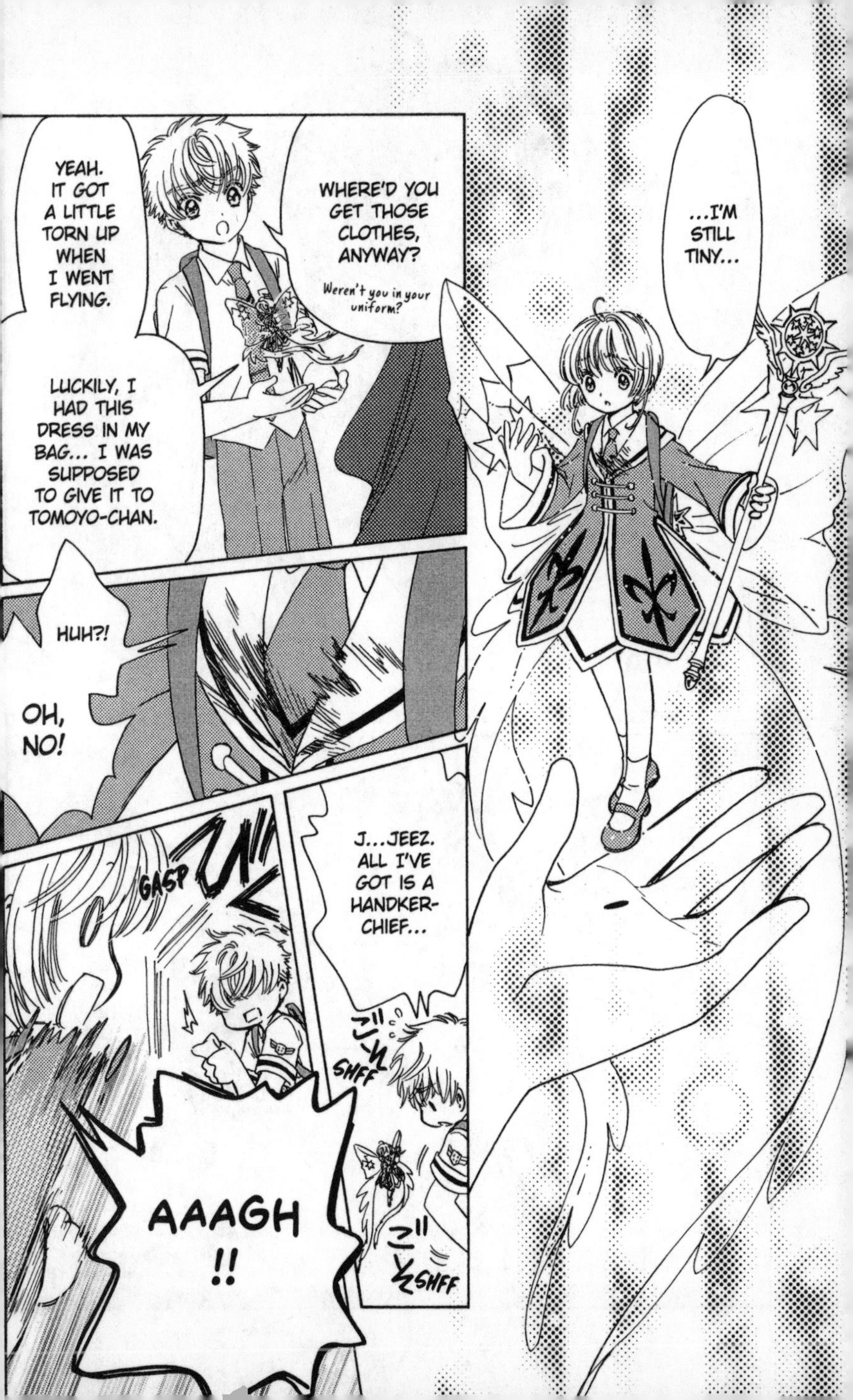
...I'M STILL TINY...
WHERE'D YOU GET THOSE CLOTHES, ANYWAY?
Weren't you in your uniform?
YEAH. IT GOT A LITTLE TORN UP WHEN I WENT FLYING.
LUCKILY, I HAD THIS DRESS IN MY BAG... I WAS SUPPOSED TO GIVE IT TO TOMOYO-CHAN.
HUH?!
OH, NO!
J...JEEZ. ALL I'VE GOT IS A HANDKERCHIEF...
SHFF
SHFF
GASP
AAAGH !!

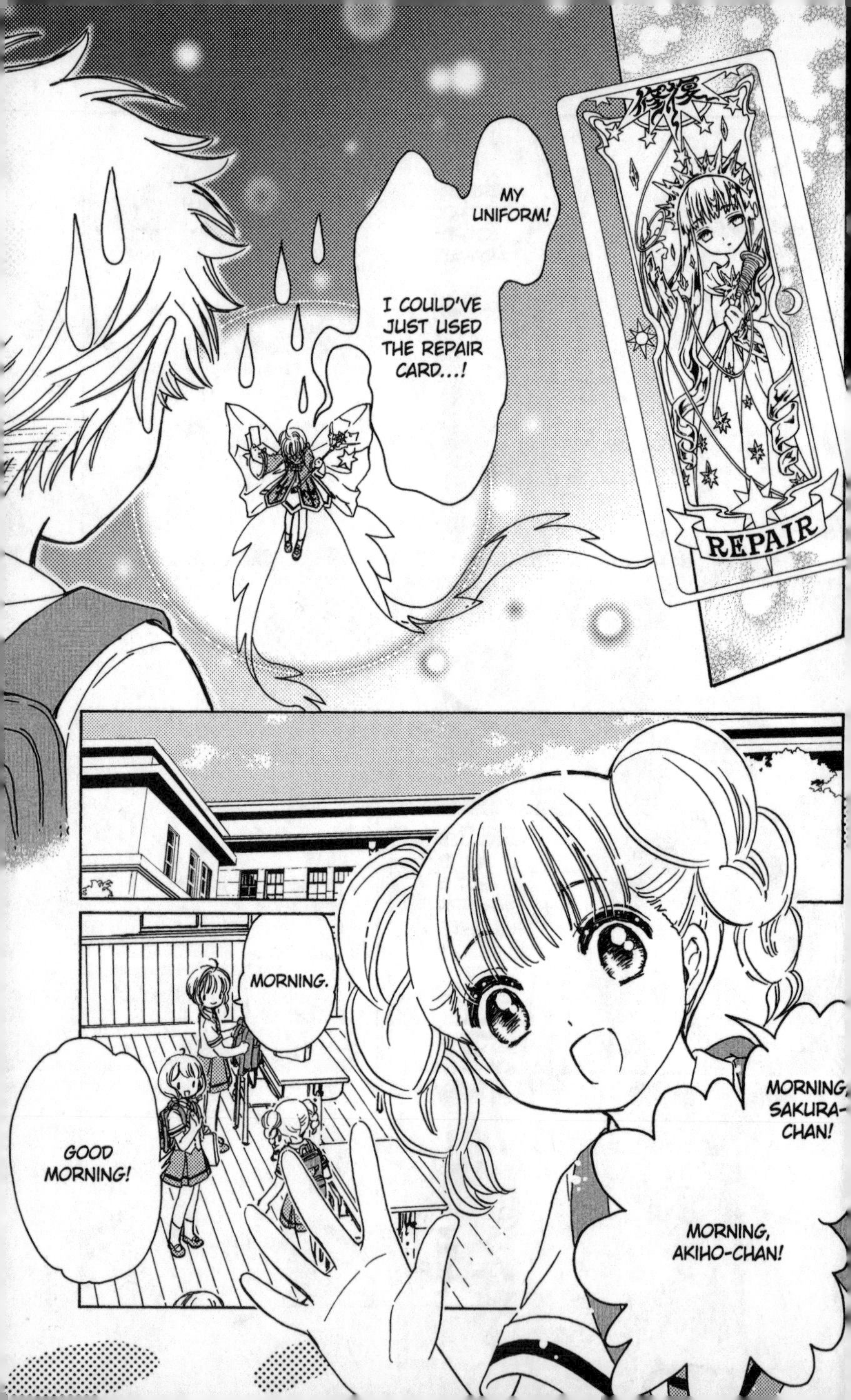
MY UNIFORM!
I COULD'VE JUST USED THE REPAIR CARD...!
REPAIR
MORNING, SAKURA-CHAN!
MORNING, AKIHO-CHAN!
MORNING.
GOOD MORNING!

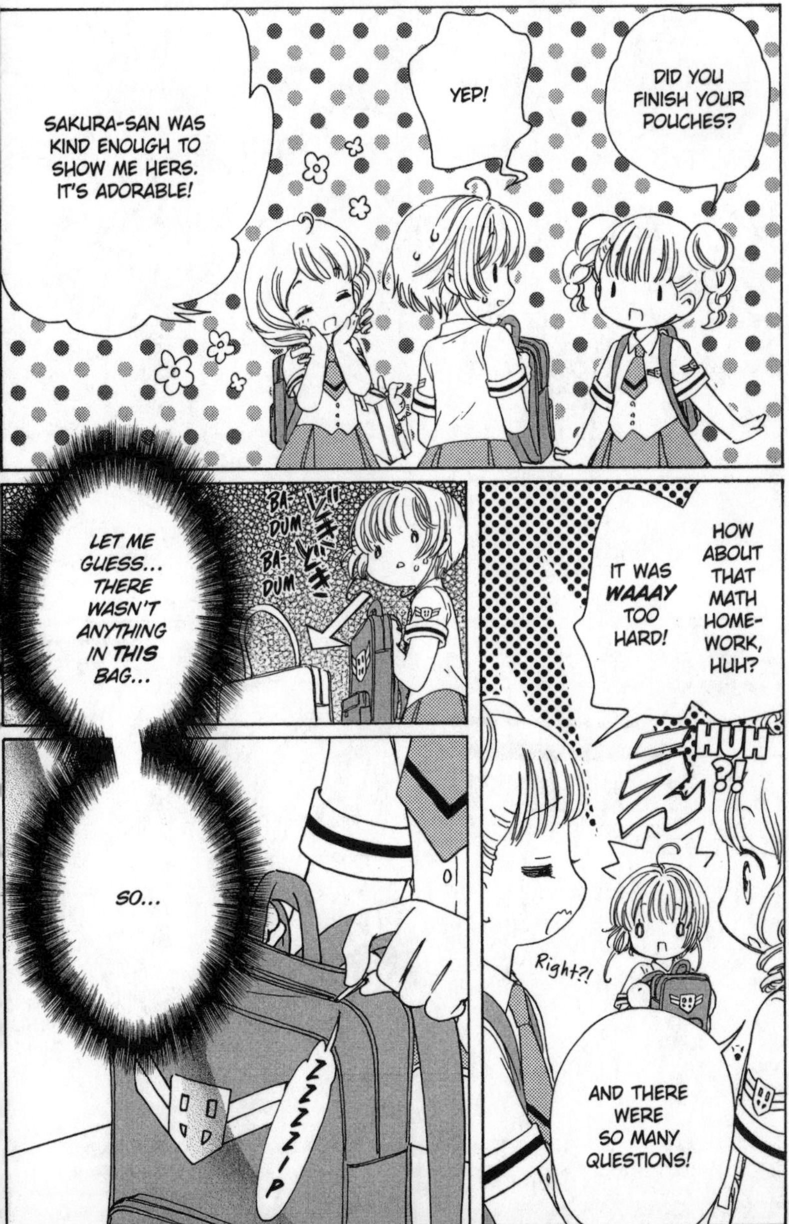
DID YOU FINISH YOUR POUCHES?
YEP!
SAKURA-SAN WAS KIND ENOUGH TO SHOW ME HERS. IT'S ADORABLE!
HOW ABOUT THAT MATH HOMEWORK, HUH?
IT WAS WAAAY TOO HARD!
HUH?!
Right?!
AND THERE WERE SO MANY QUESTIONS!
BA-DUM BA-DUM
LET ME GUESS... THERE WASN'T ANYTHING IN THIS BAG...
SO...
ZZZZIP

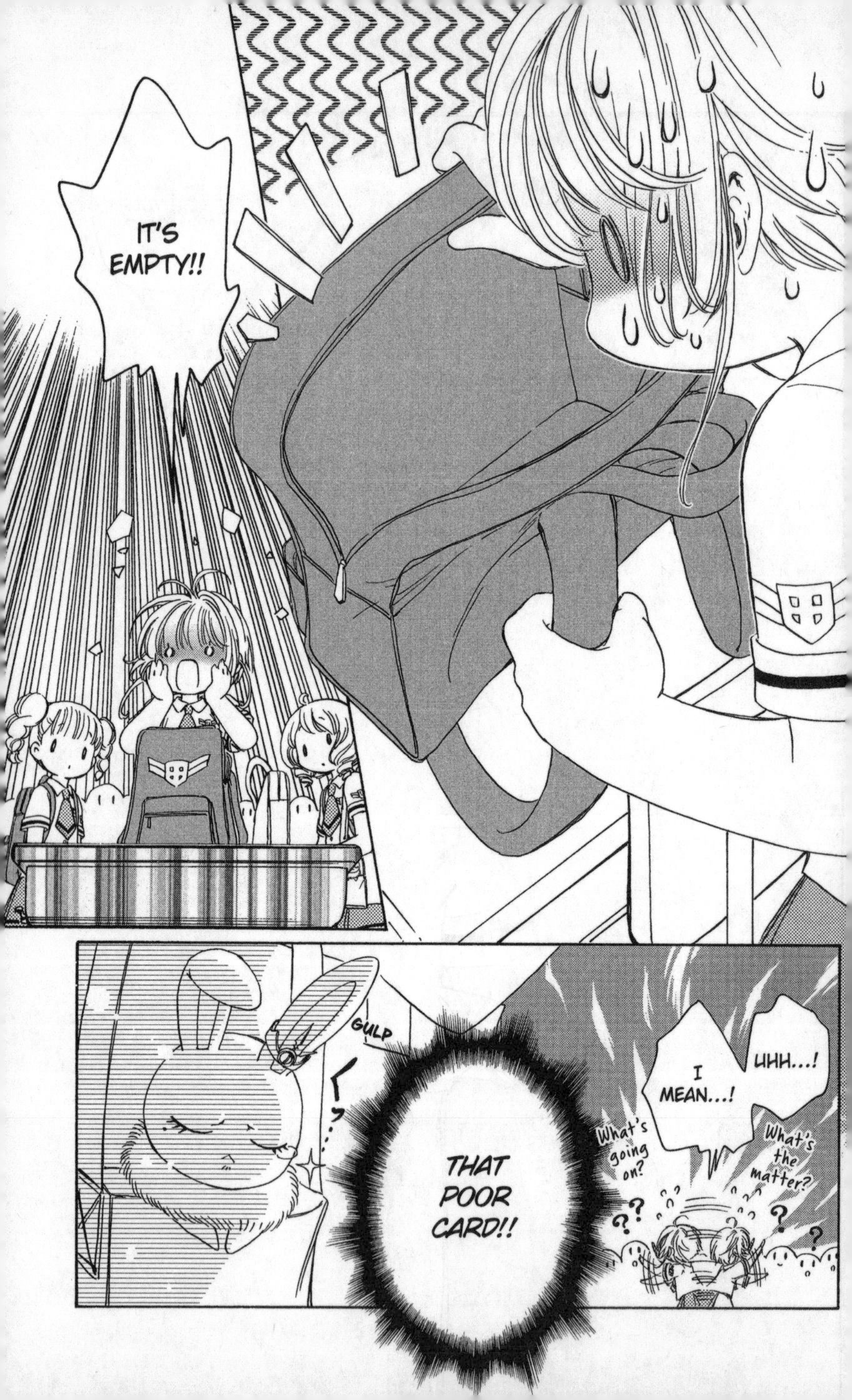
IT'S EMPTY!!
UHH...! I MEAN...!
What's the matter?
What's going on?
GULP
THAT POOR CARD!!

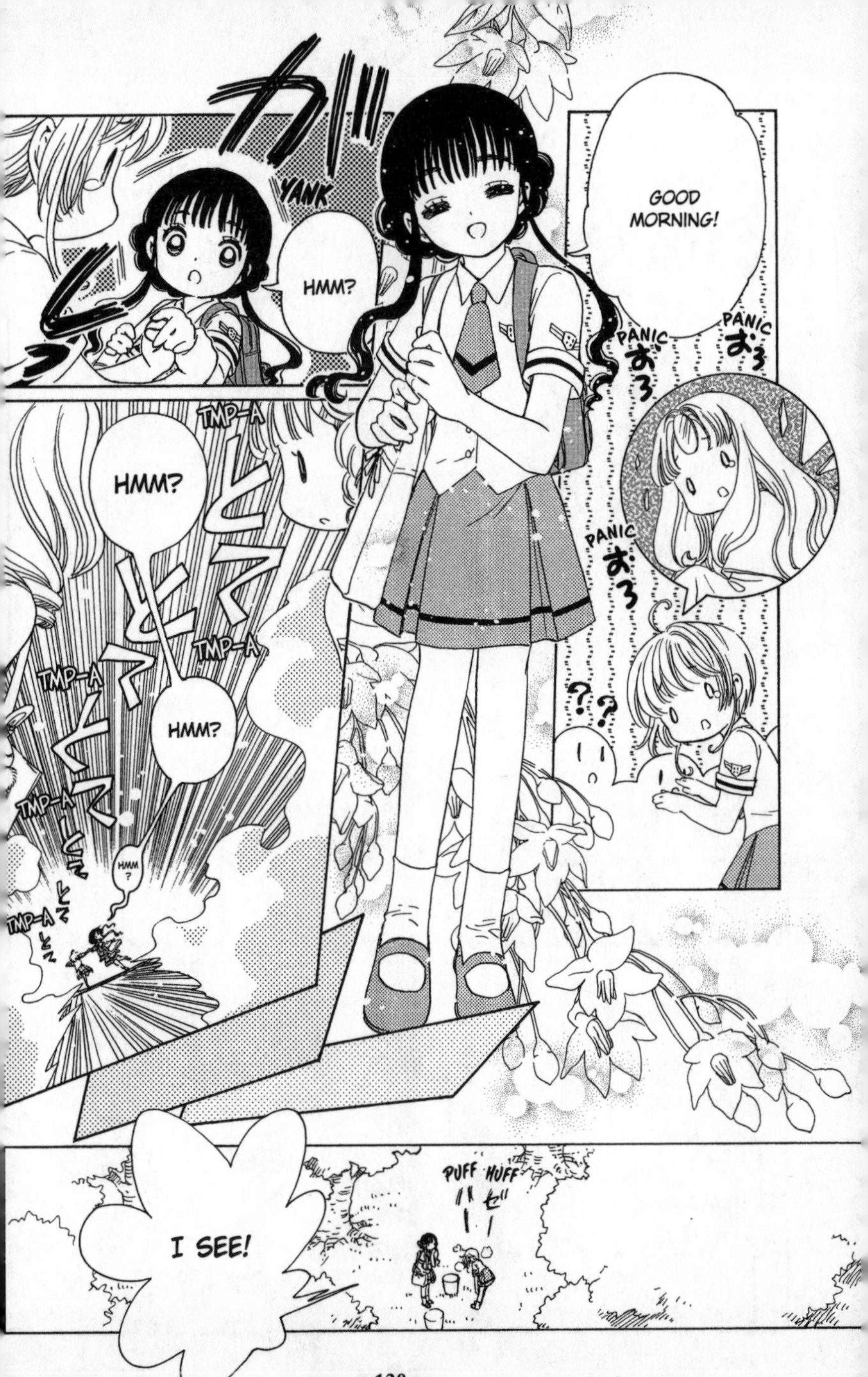
GOOD MORNING!
PANIC おろ
PANIC おろ
PANIC おろ
YANK
HMM?
TMP-A
HMM?
TMP-A
TMP-A
HMM?
TMP-A
HMM?
TMP-A
PUFF HUFF
I SEE!

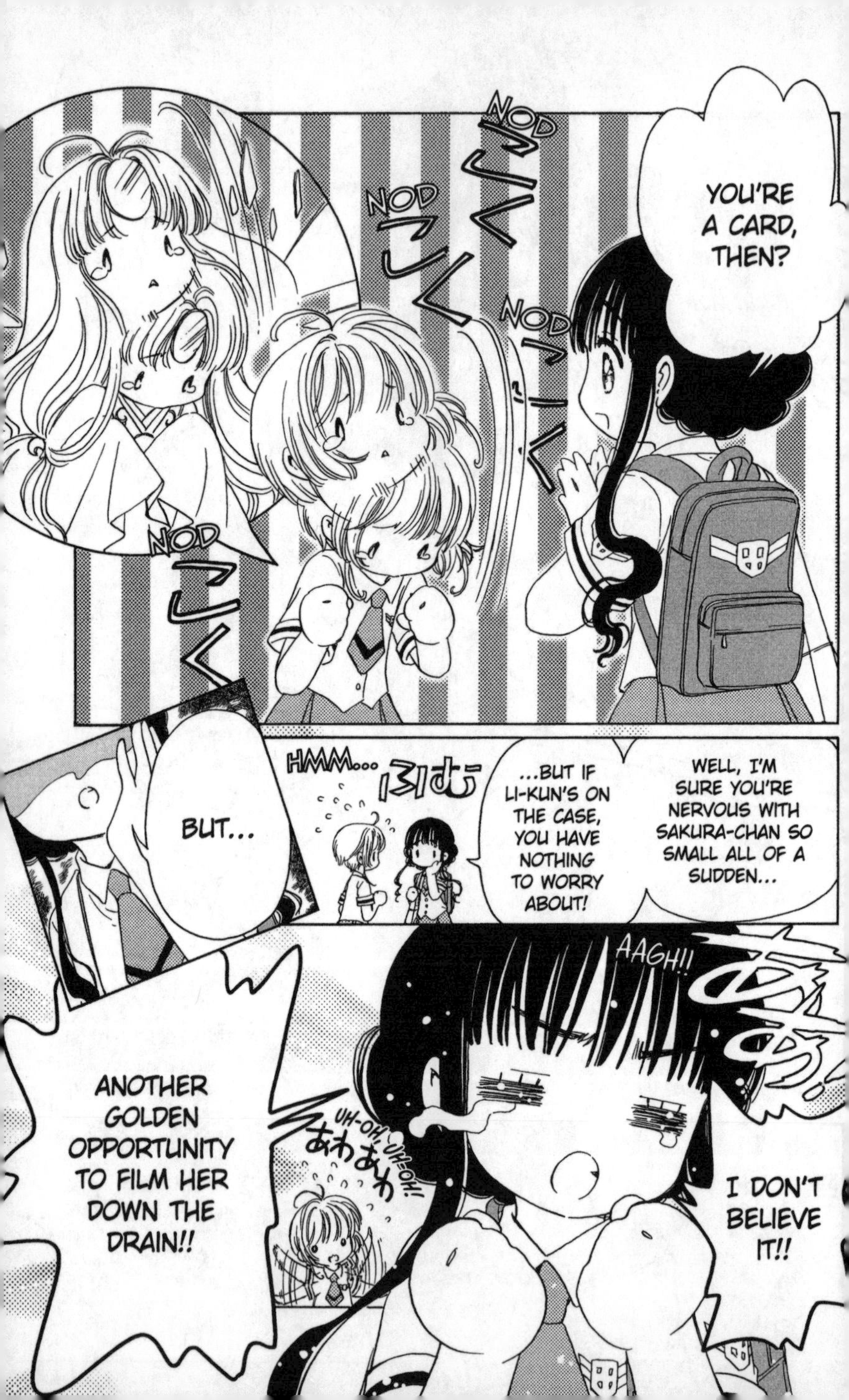
YOU'RE A CARD, THEN?
NOD
NOD
NOD
NOD
WELL, I'M SURE YOU'RE NERVOUS WITH SAKURA-CHAN SO SMALL ALL OF A SUDDEN...
...BUT IF LI-KUN'S ON THE CASE, YOU HAVE NOTHING TO WORRY ABOUT!
HMM... ふむ
BUT...
AAGH!!
I DON'T BELIEVE IT!!
UH-OH, UH-OH! あわあわ
ANOTHER GOLDEN OPPORTUNITY TO FILM HER DOWN THE DRAIN!!

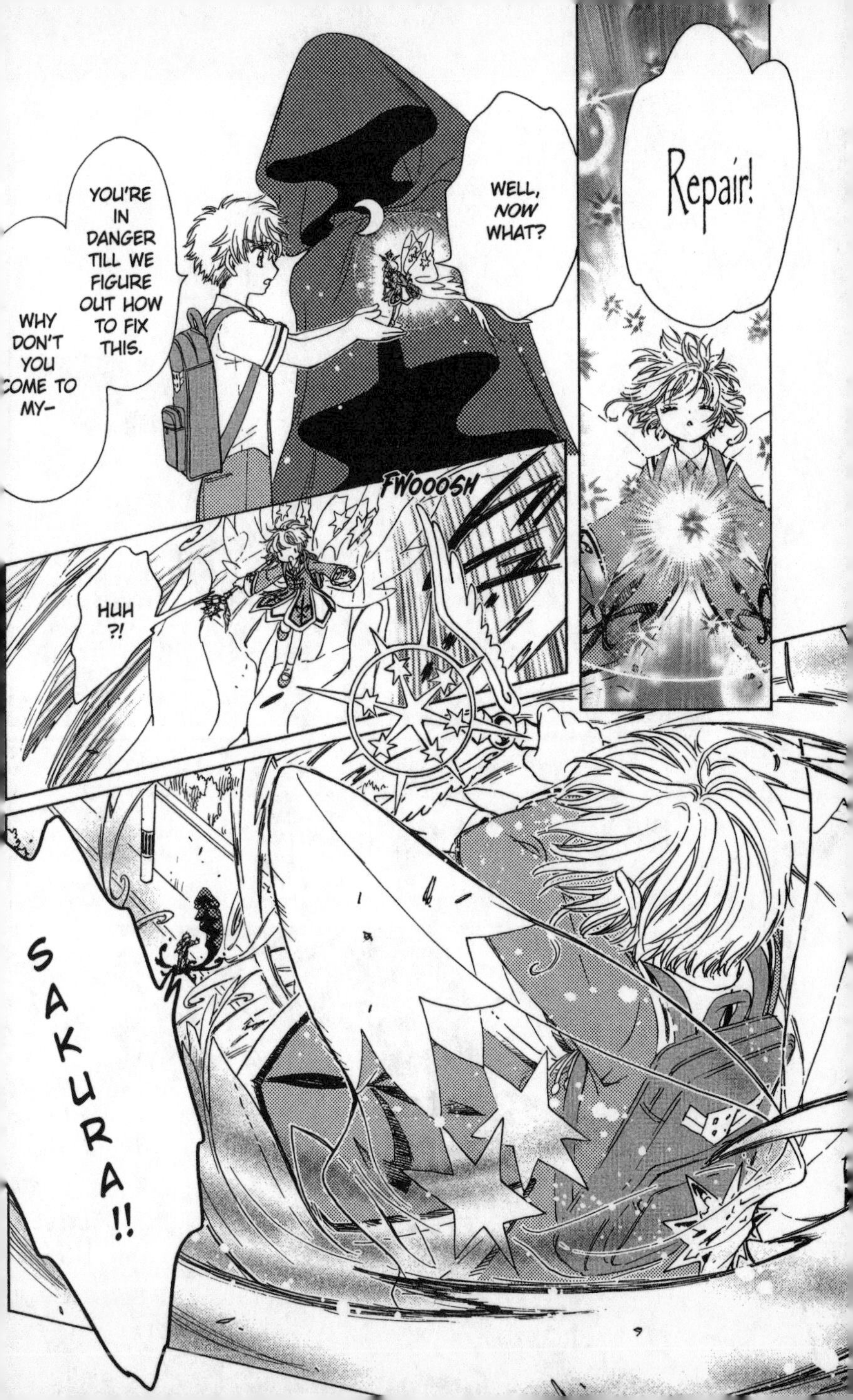

Repair!
WELL, NOW WHAT?
YOU'RE IN DANGER TILL WE FIGURE OUT HOW TO FIX THIS.
WHY DON'T YOU COME TO MY-
FWOOOSH
HUH ?!
SAKURA!!

Cardcaptor
Sakura
CLEAR CARD

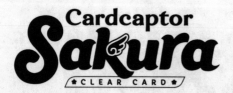

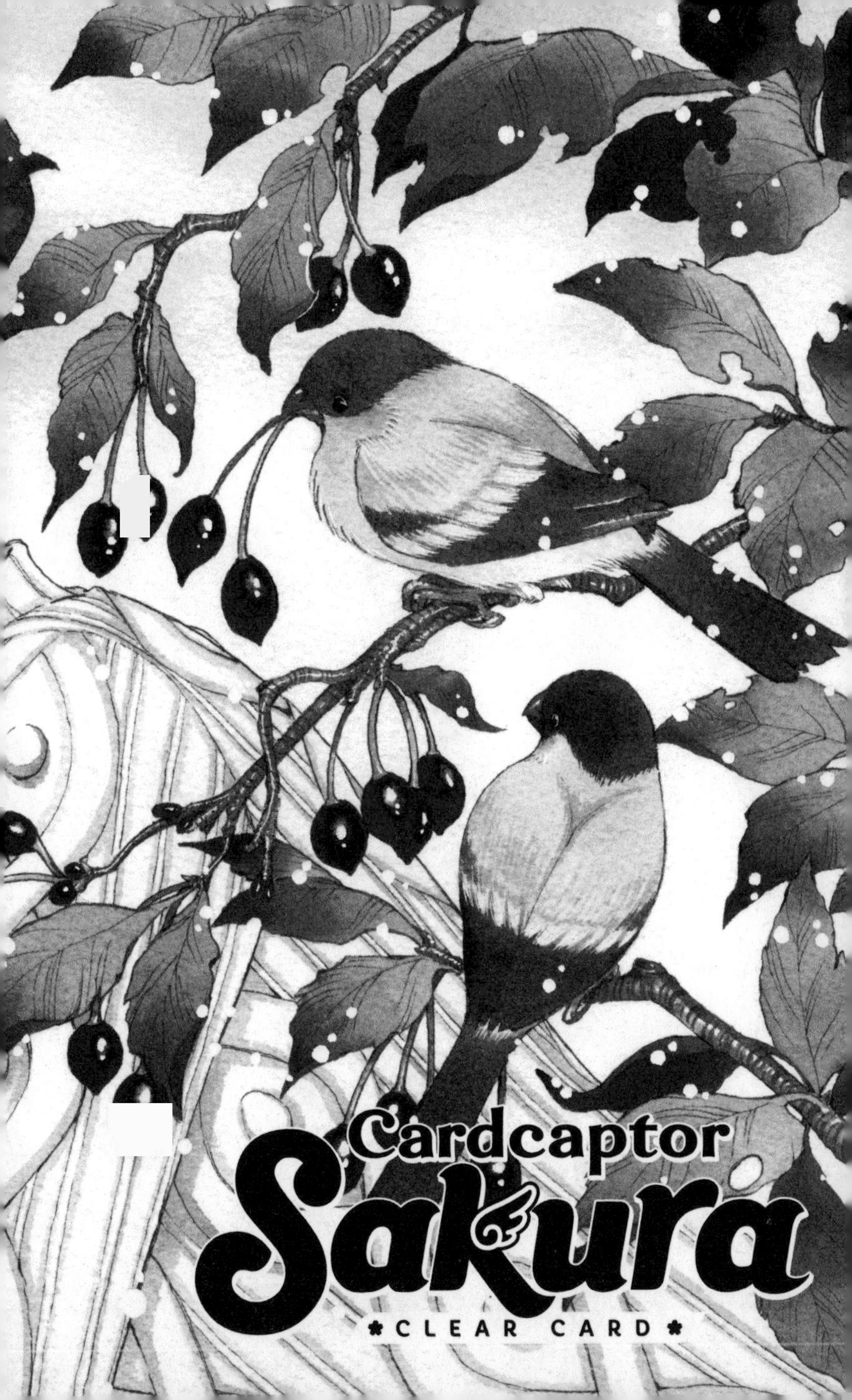
Cardcaptor
Sakura
CLEAR CARD

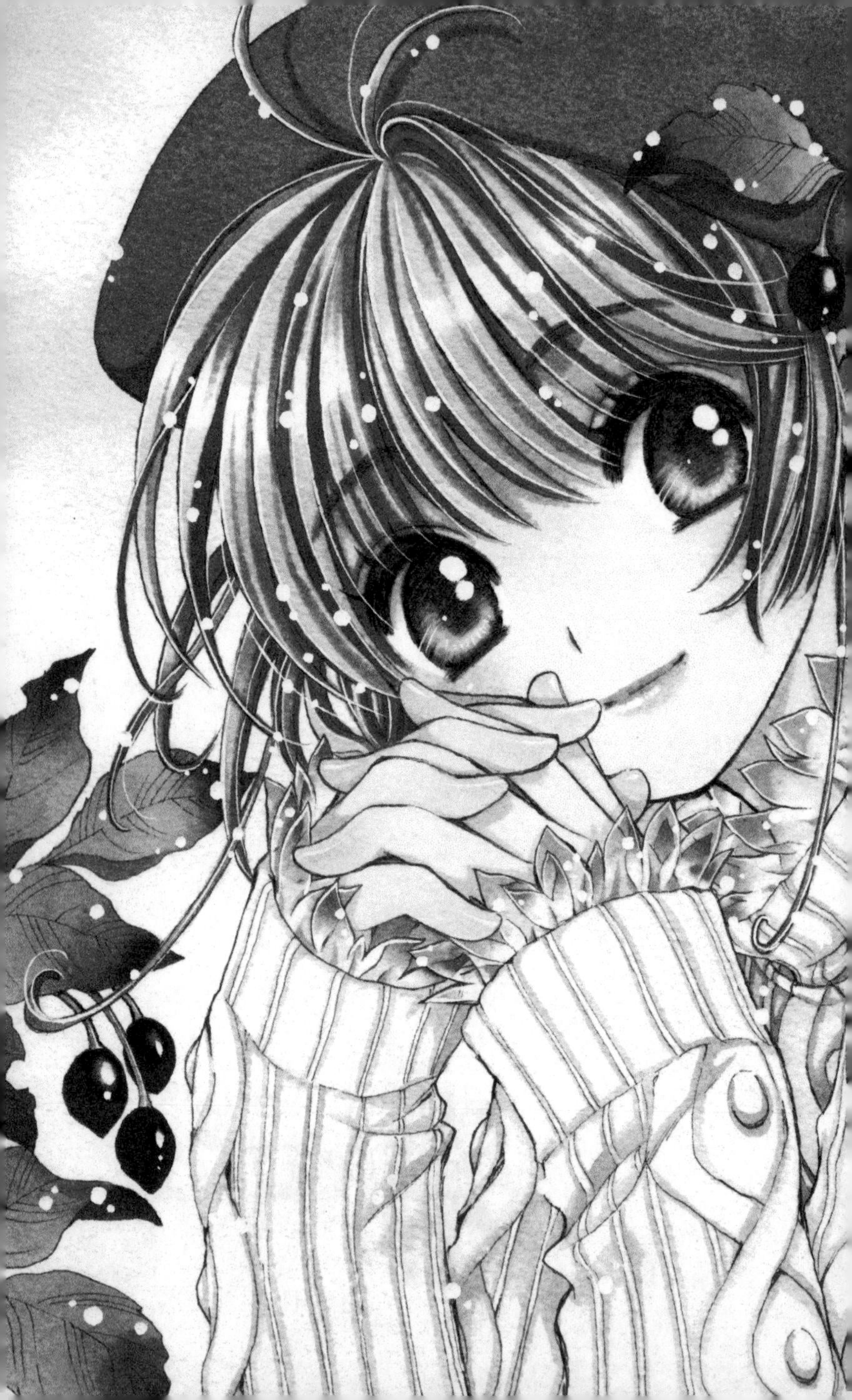

Cardcaptor
Sakura
CLEAR CARD

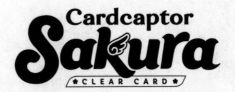

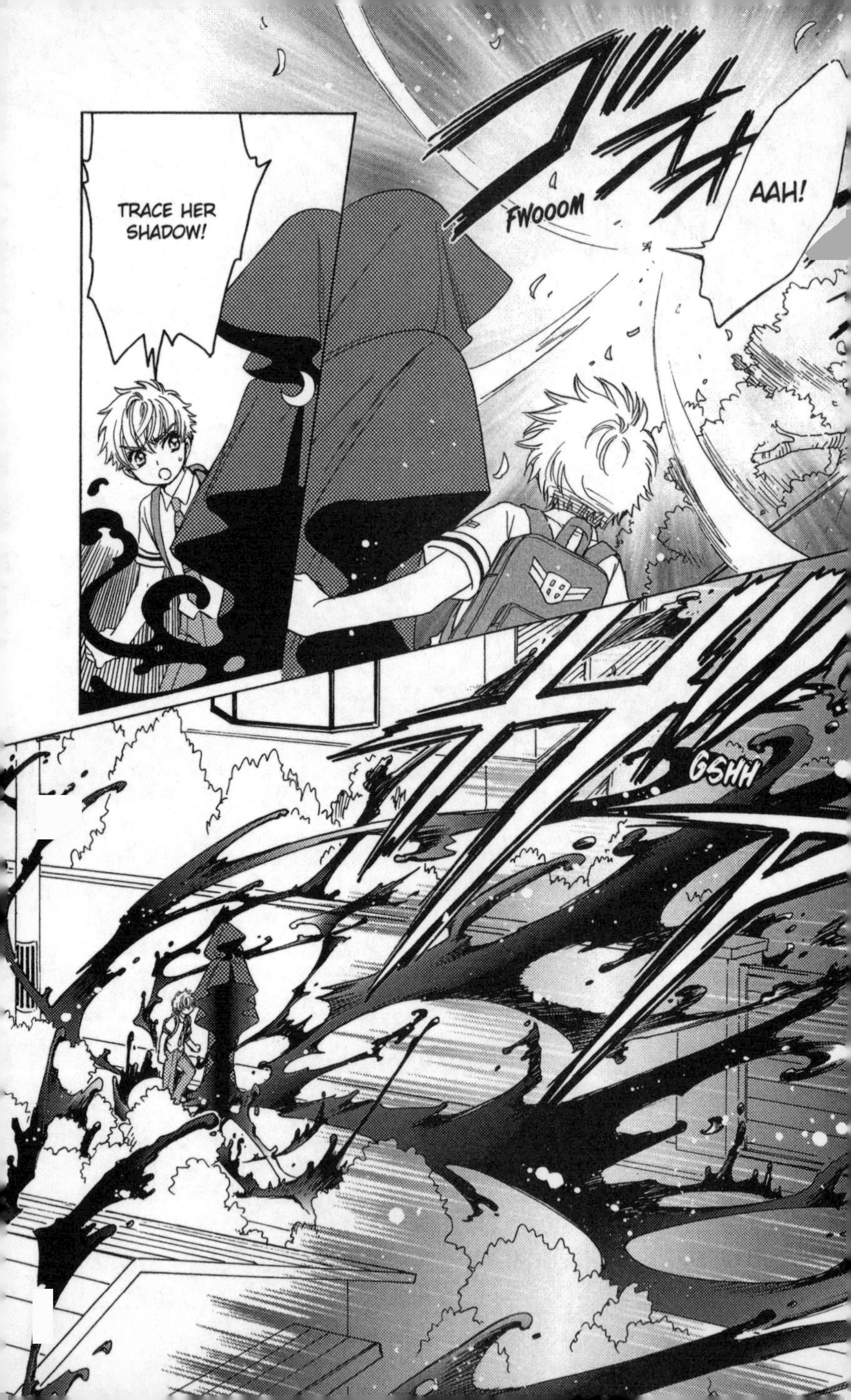
AAH!
FWOOOM
TRACE HER SHADOW!
GSHH

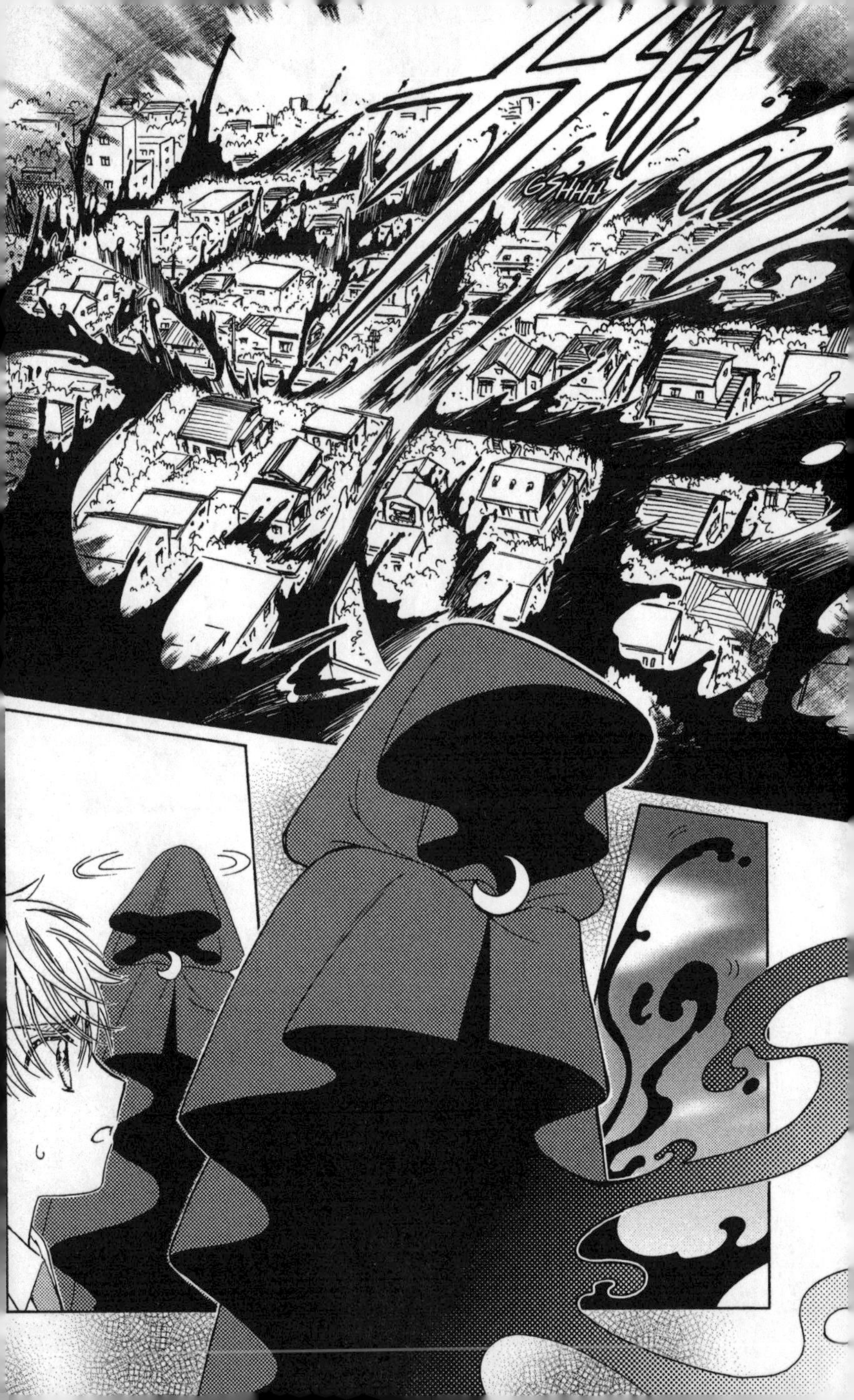
GSHHH

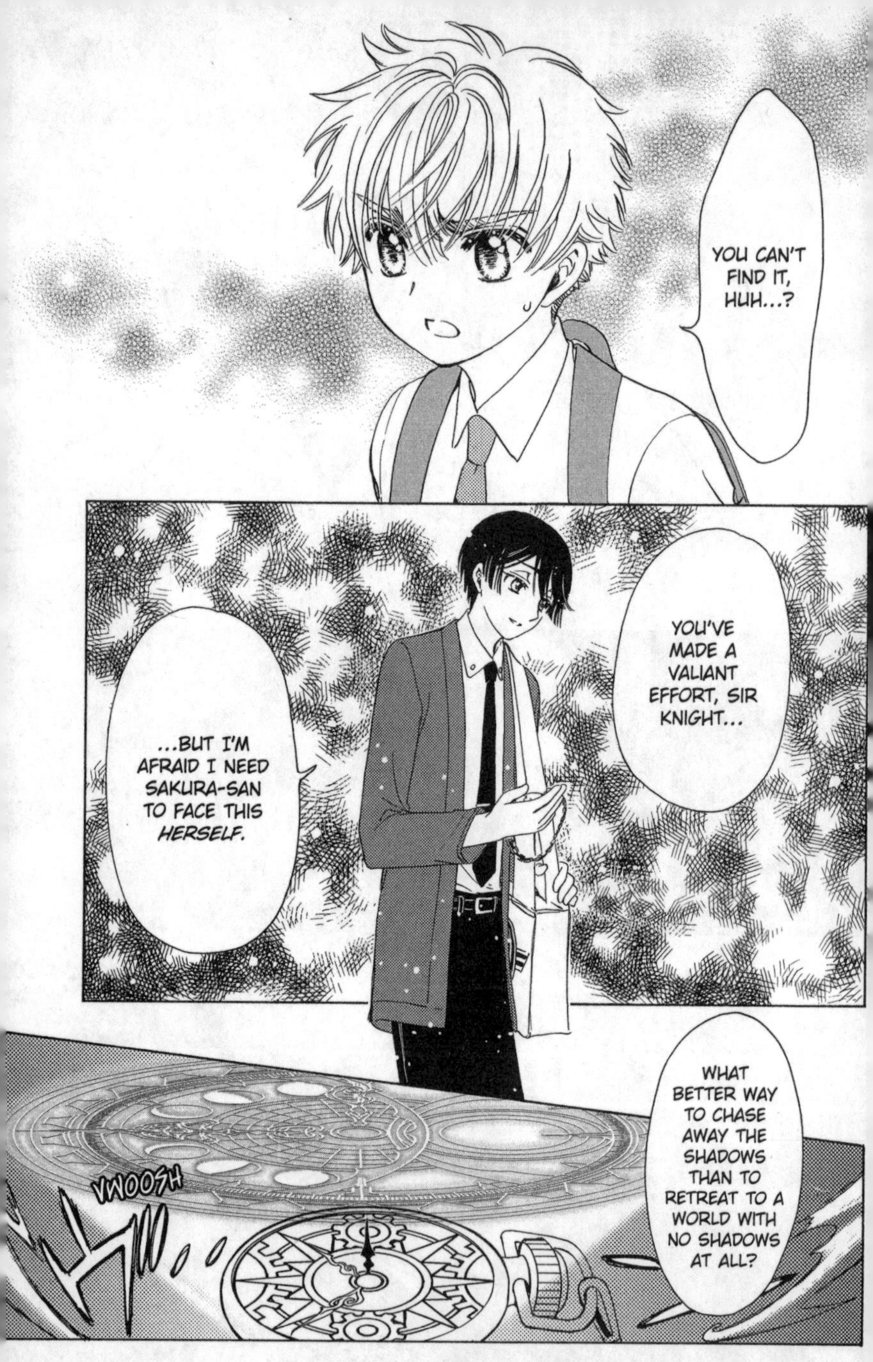
YOU CAN'T FIND IT, HUH...?
YOU'VE MADE A VALIANT EFFORT, SIR KNIGHT...
...BUT I'M AFRAID I NEED SAKURA-SAN TO FACE THIS *HERSELF.*
WHAT BETTER WAY TO CHASE AWAY THE SHADOWS THAN TO RETREAT TO A WORLD WITH NO SHADOWS AT ALL?
VWOOSH

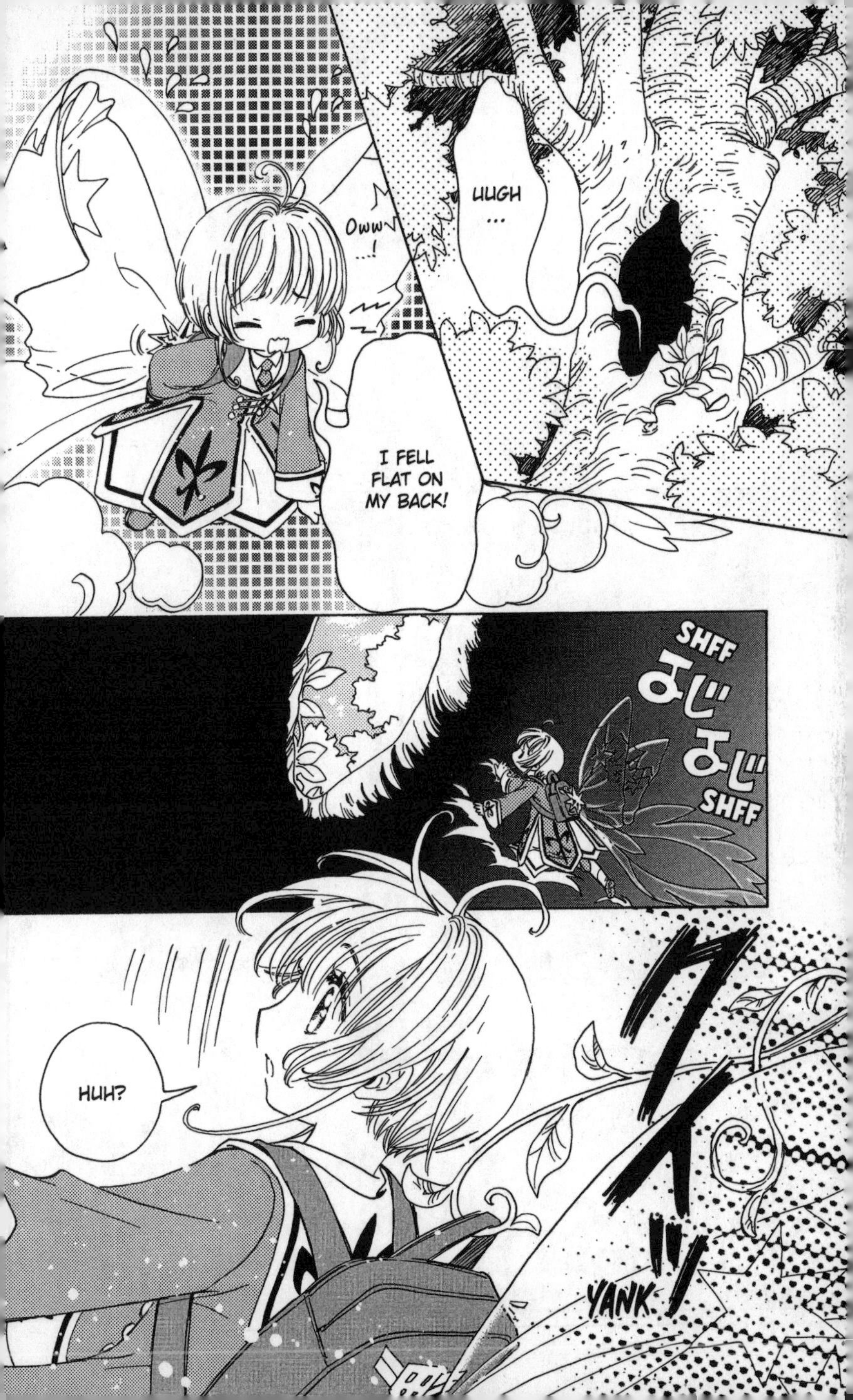
UGH
...
OWW
...!
I FELL FLAT ON MY BACK!
SHFF
よじよじ
SHFF
クイッ
YANK
HUH?

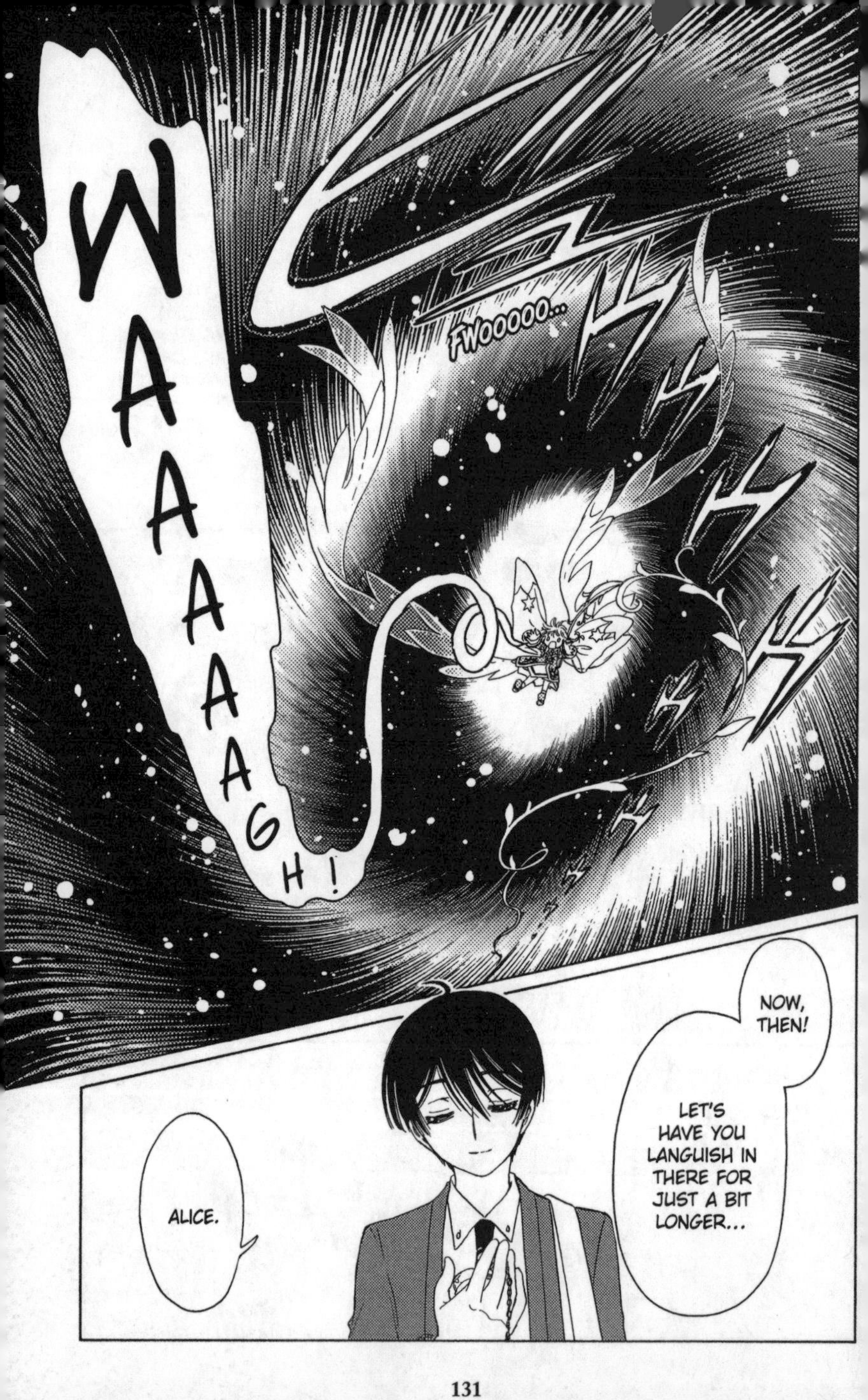
WAAAAAGH!
FWOOOOO...
NOW, THEN!
LET'S HAVE YOU LANGUISH IN THERE FOR JUST A BIT LONGER...
ALICE.

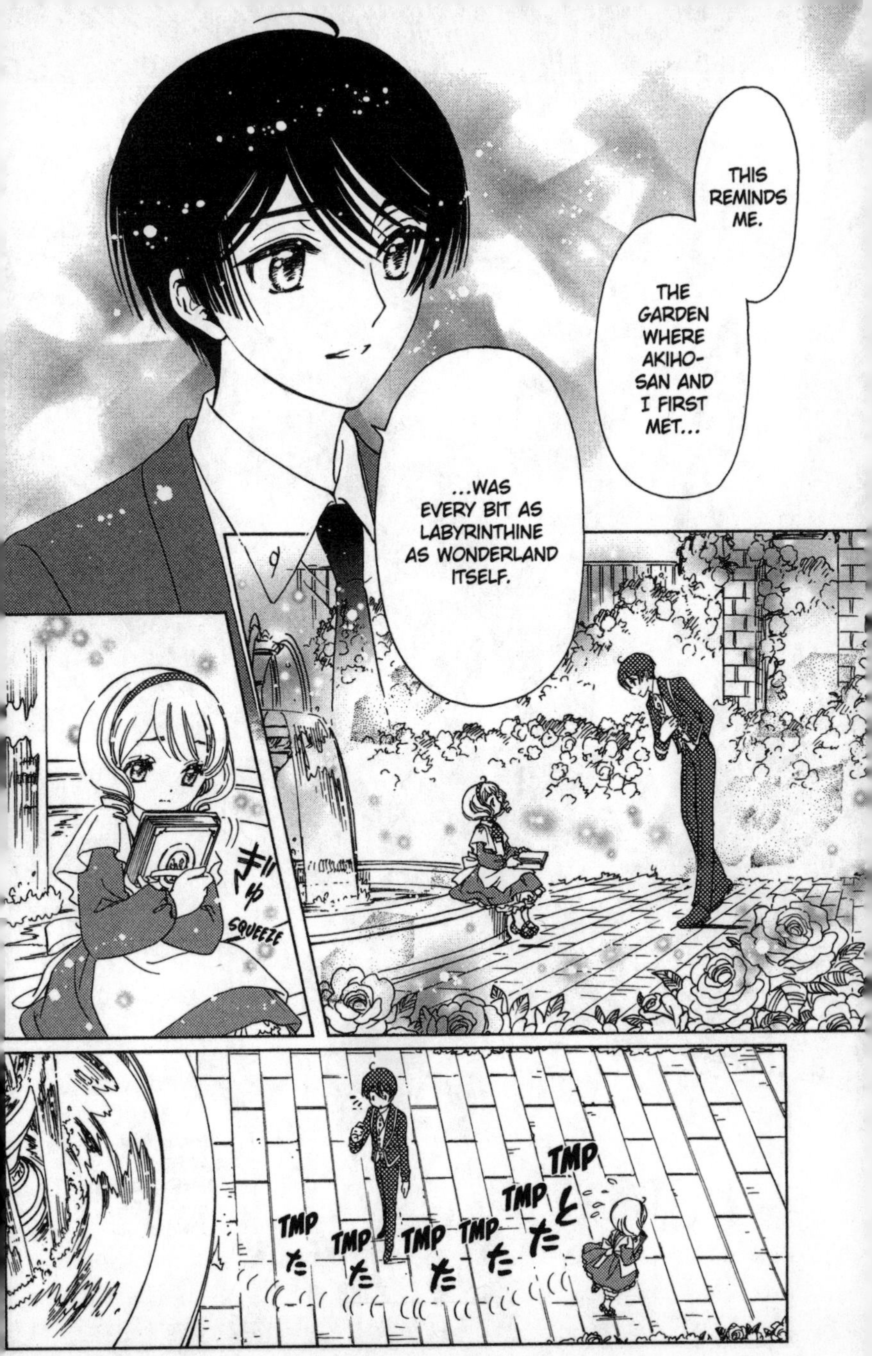
THIS REMINDS ME.
THE GARDEN WHERE AKIHO-SAN AND I FIRST MET...
...WAS EVERY BIT AS LABYRINTHINE AS WONDERLAND ITSELF.
ぎゅ
SQUEEZE
TMP と
TMP た
TMP た
TMP た
TMP た
TMP た

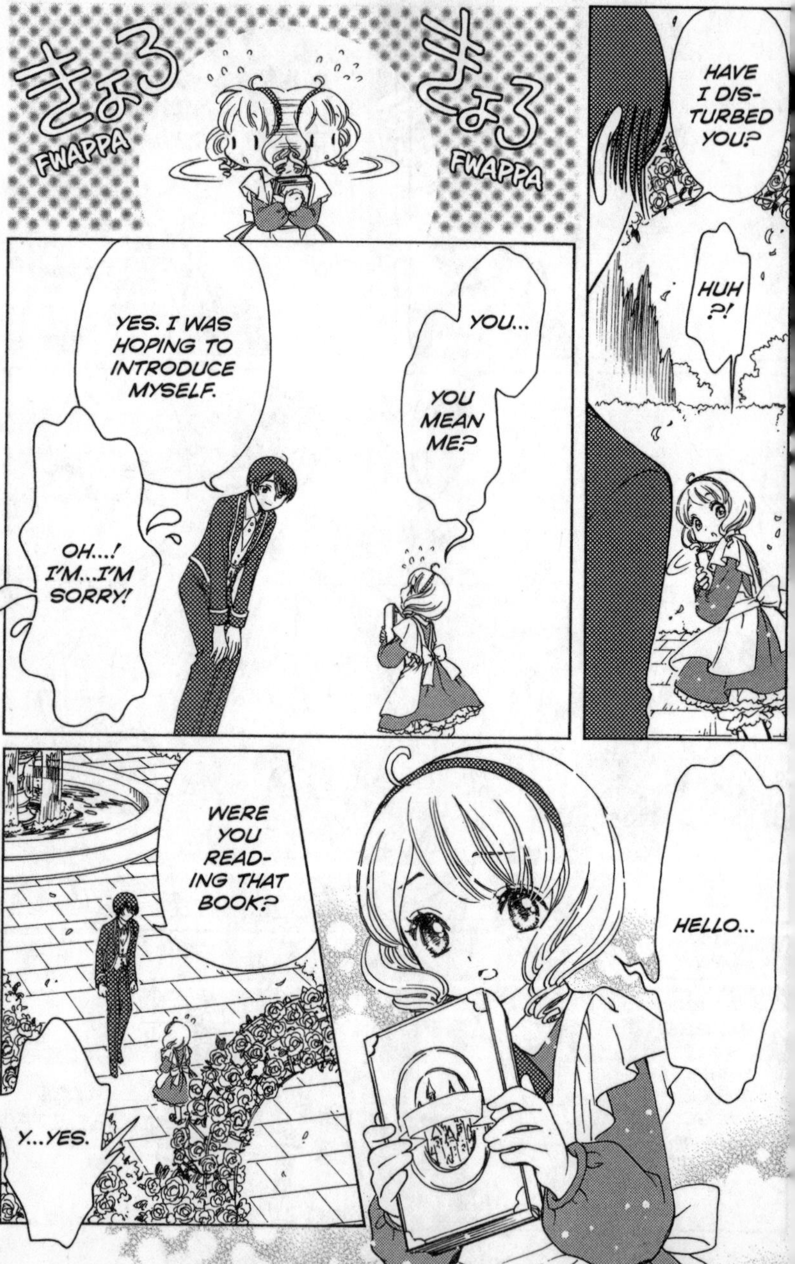
HAVE I DIS-TURBED YOU?
HUH ?!
きょろ
FWAPPA
きょろ
FWAPPA
YOU...
YOU MEAN ME?
YES. I WAS HOPING TO INTRODUCE MYSELF.
OH...! I'M...I'M SORRY!
HELLO...
WERE YOU READ-ING THAT BOOK?
Y...YES.

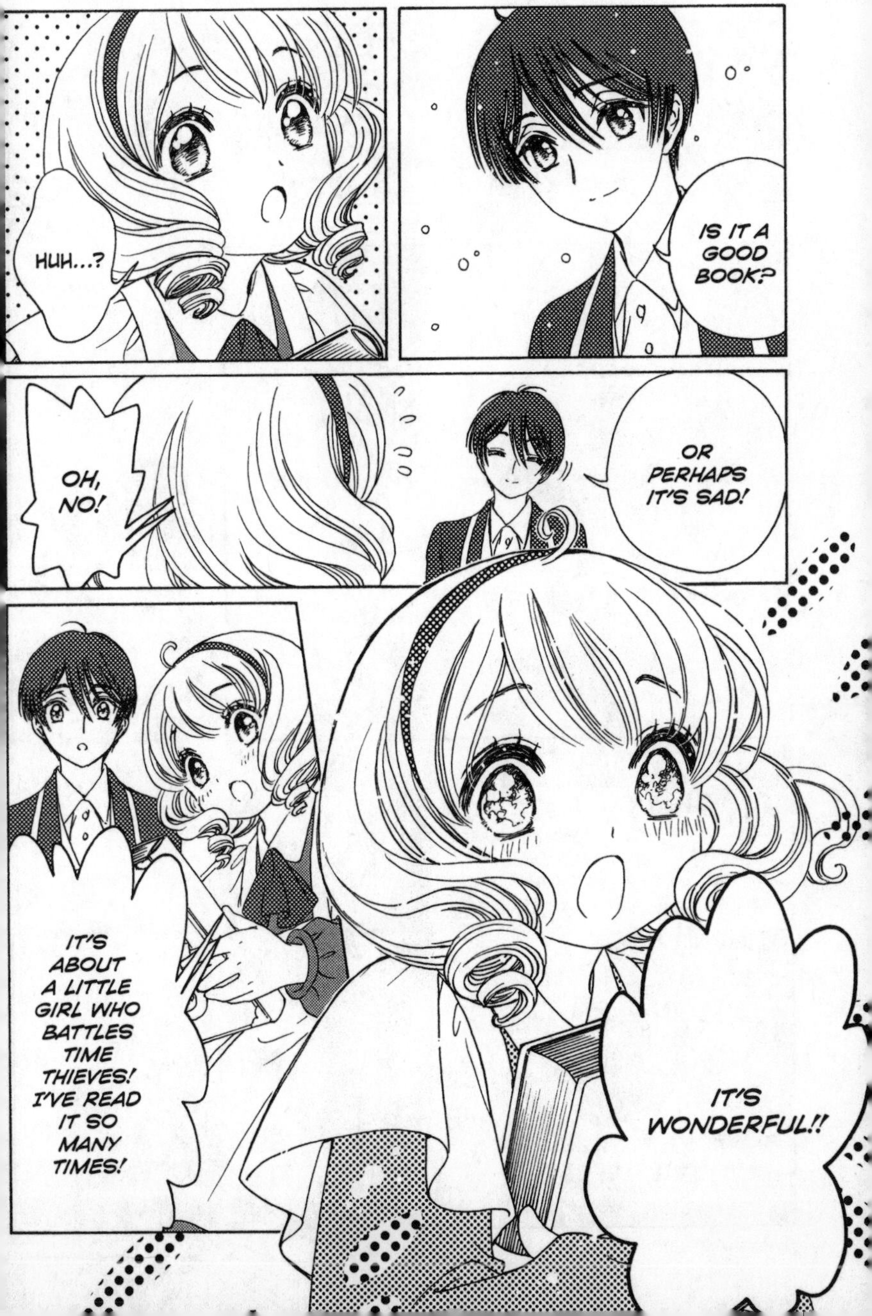
IS IT A GOOD BOOK?
HUH...?
OR PERHAPS IT'S SAD!
OH, NO!
IT'S WONDERFUL!!
IT'S ABOUT A LITTLE GIRL WHO BATTLES TIME THIEVES! I'VE READ IT SO MANY TIMES!

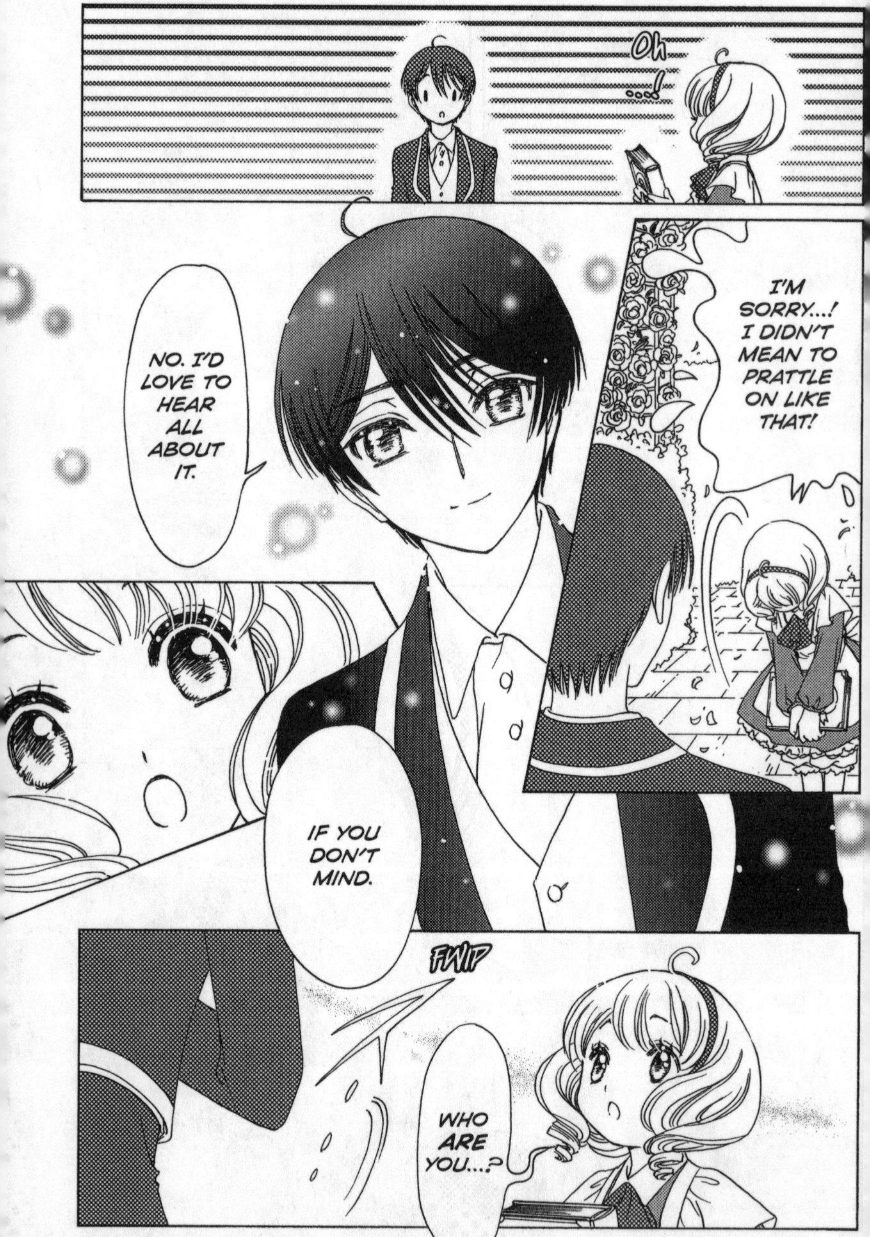
Oh...!
I'M SORRY...! I DIDN'T MEAN TO PRATTLE ON LIKE THAT!
NO. I'D LOVE TO HEAR ALL ABOUT IT.
IF YOU DON'T MIND.
FWIP
WHO ARE YOU...?

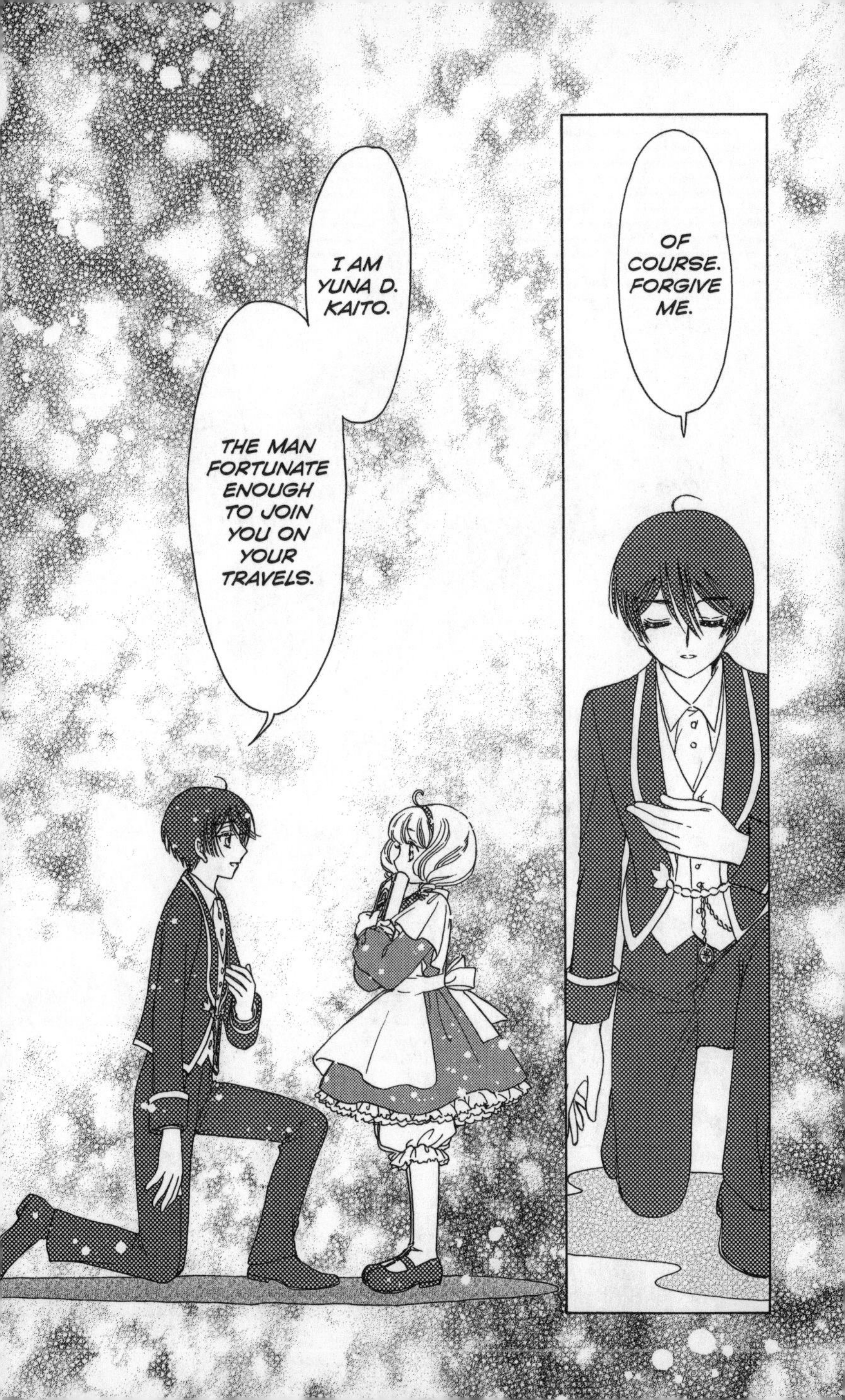
OF COURSE. FORGIVE ME.
I AM YUNA D. KAITO.
THE MAN FORTUNATE ENOUGH TO JOIN YOU ON YOUR TRAVELS.

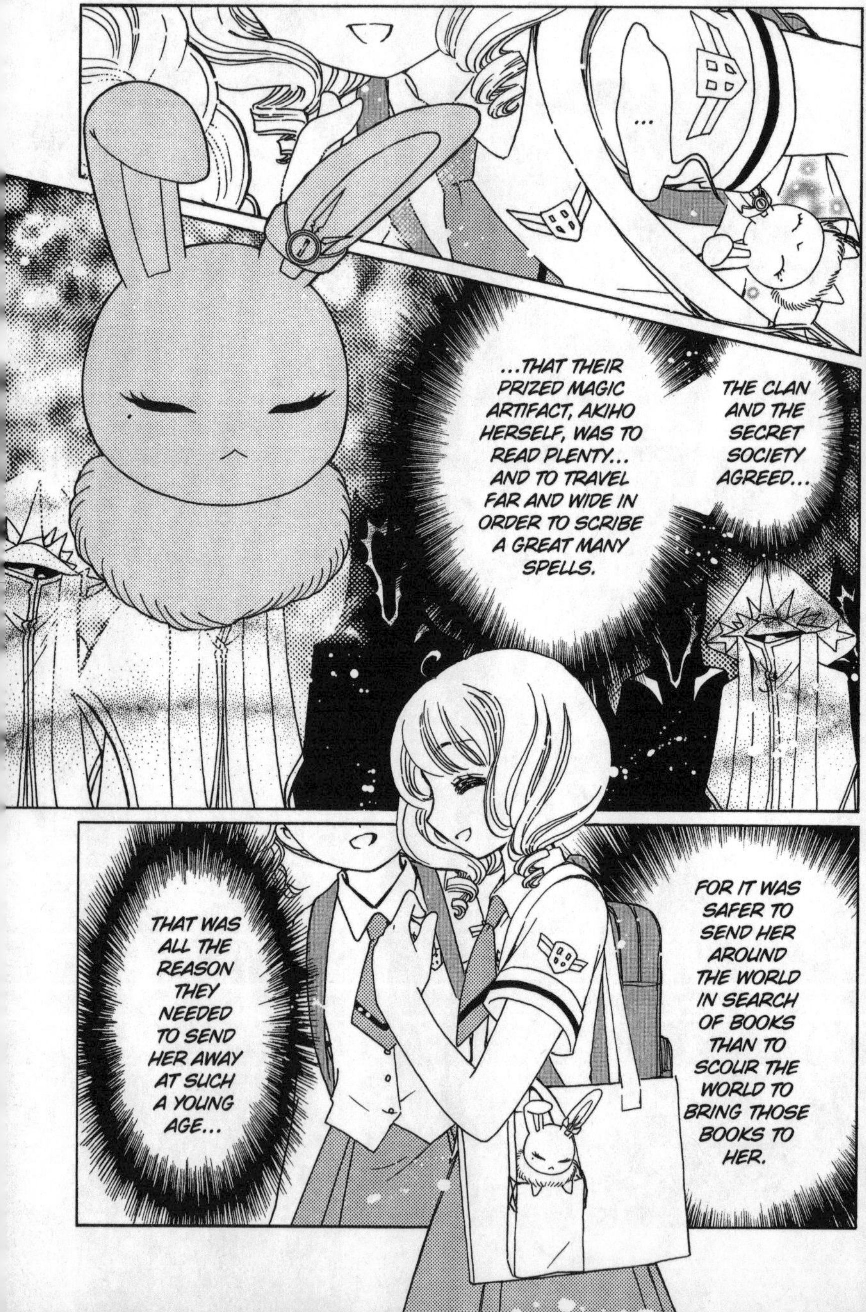
...
THE CLAN AND THE SECRET SOCIETY AGREED...
...THAT THEIR PRIZED MAGIC ARTIFACT, AKIHO HERSELF, WAS TO READ PLENTY... AND TO TRAVEL FAR AND WIDE IN ORDER TO SCRIBE A GREAT MANY SPELLS.
FOR IT WAS SAFER TO SEND HER AROUND THE WORLD IN SEARCH OF BOOKS THAN TO SCOUR THE WORLD TO BRING THOSE BOOKS TO HER.
THAT WAS ALL THE REASON THEY NEEDED TO SEND HER AWAY AT SUCH A YOUNG AGE...

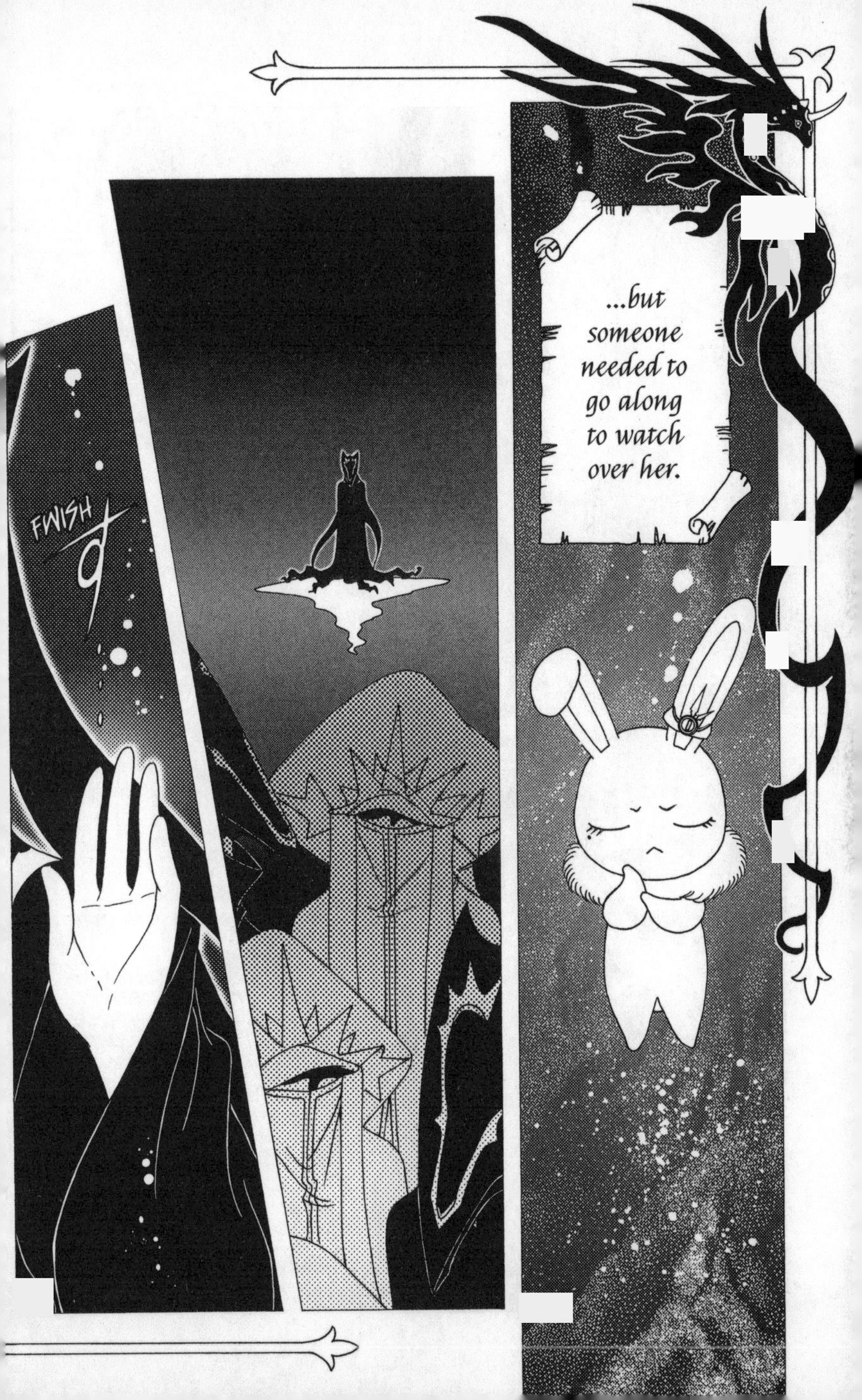
...but someone needed to go along to watch over her.
FWISH

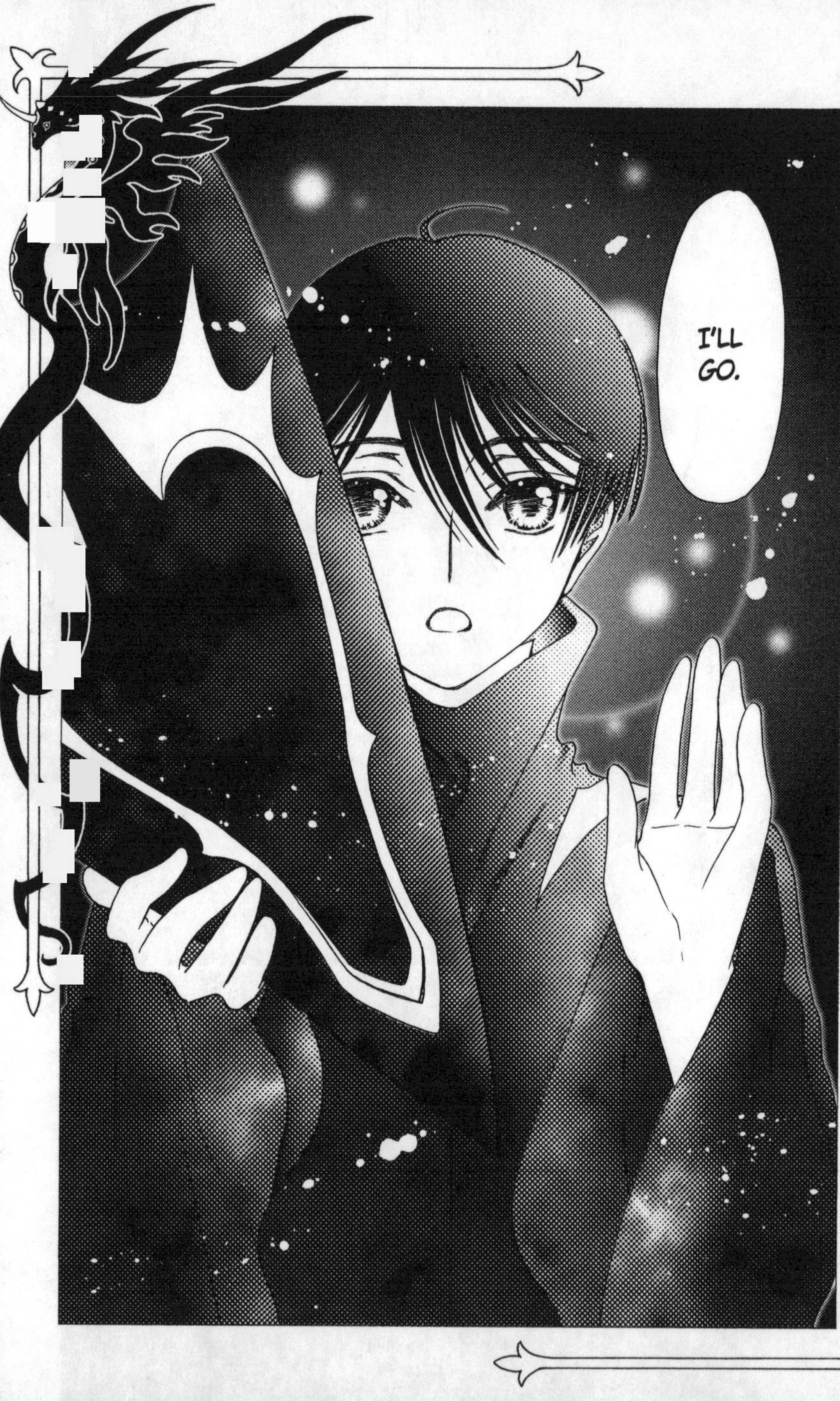
I'LL GO.

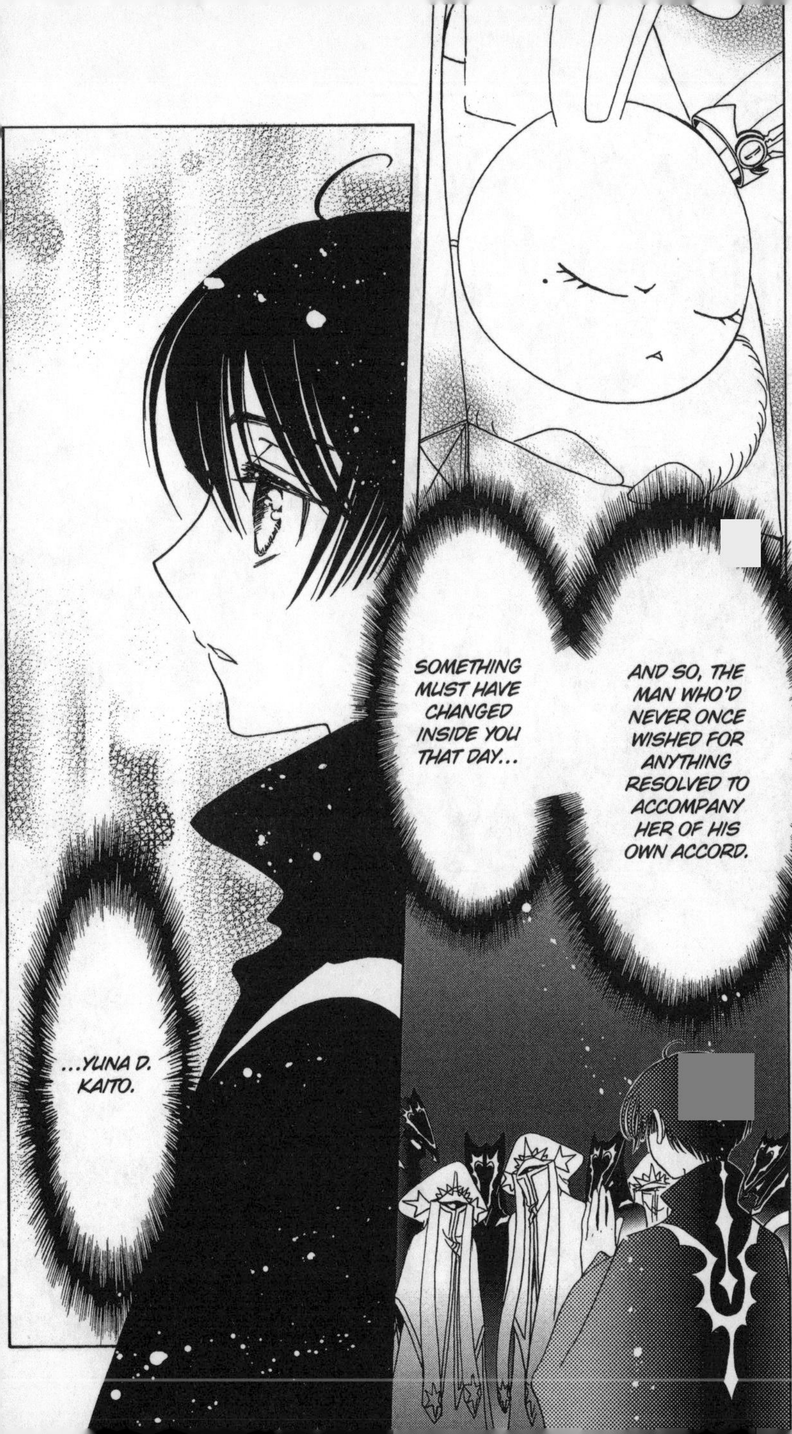
AND SO, THE MAN WHO'D NEVER ONCE WISHED FOR ANYTHING RESOLVED TO ACCOMPANY HER OF HIS OWN ACCORD.
SOMETHING MUST HAVE CHANGED INSIDE YOU THAT DAY...
...YUNA D. KAITO.

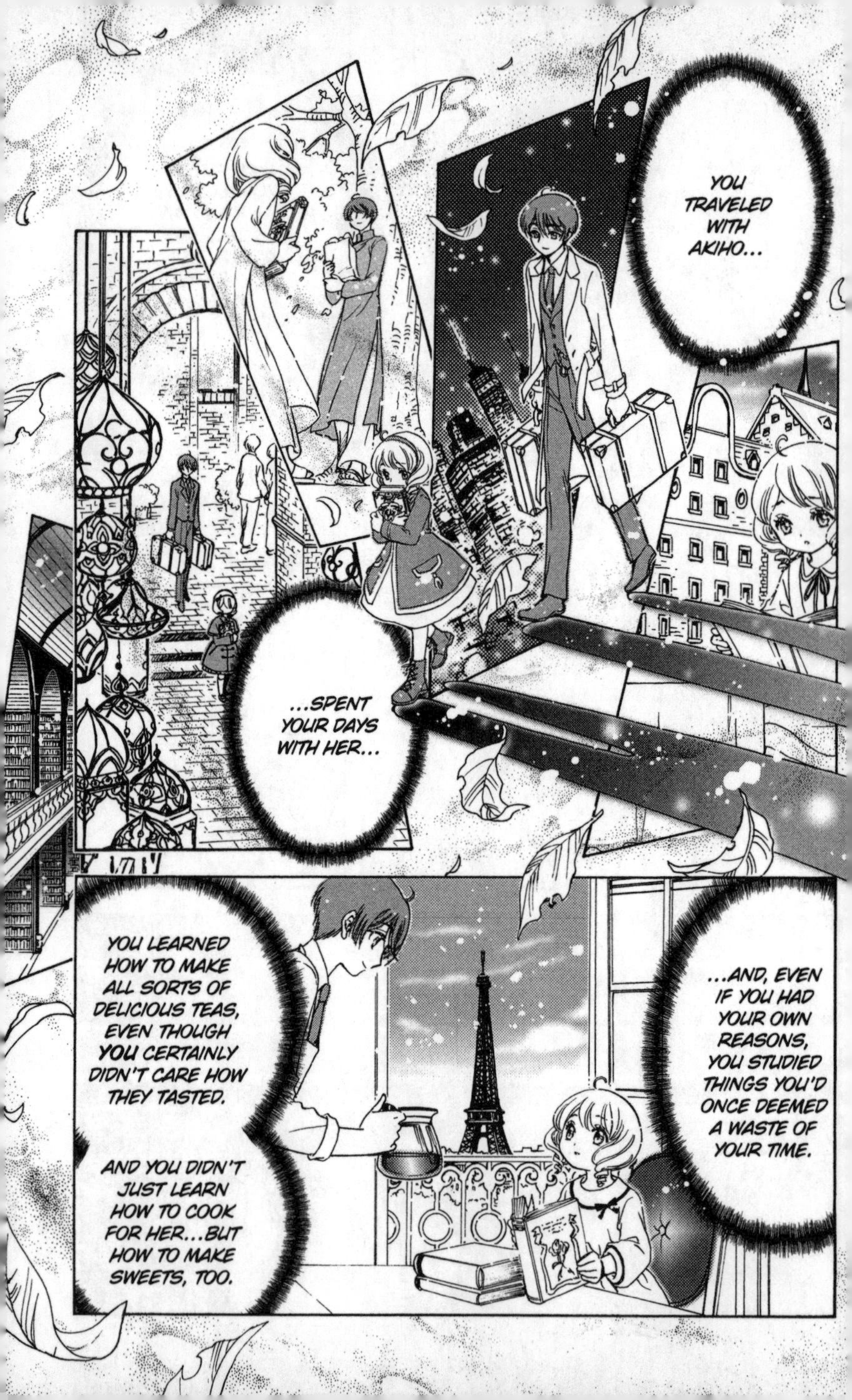
YOU TRAVELED WITH AKIHO...
...SPENT YOUR DAYS WITH HER...
...AND, EVEN IF YOU HAD YOUR OWN REASONS, YOU STUDIED THINGS YOU'D ONCE DEEMED A WASTE OF YOUR TIME.
YOU LEARNED HOW TO MAKE ALL SORTS OF DELICIOUS TEAS, EVEN THOUGH YOU CERTAINLY DIDN'T CARE HOW THEY TASTED.
AND YOU DIDN'T JUST LEARN HOW TO COOK FOR HER...BUT HOW TO MAKE SWEETS, TOO.

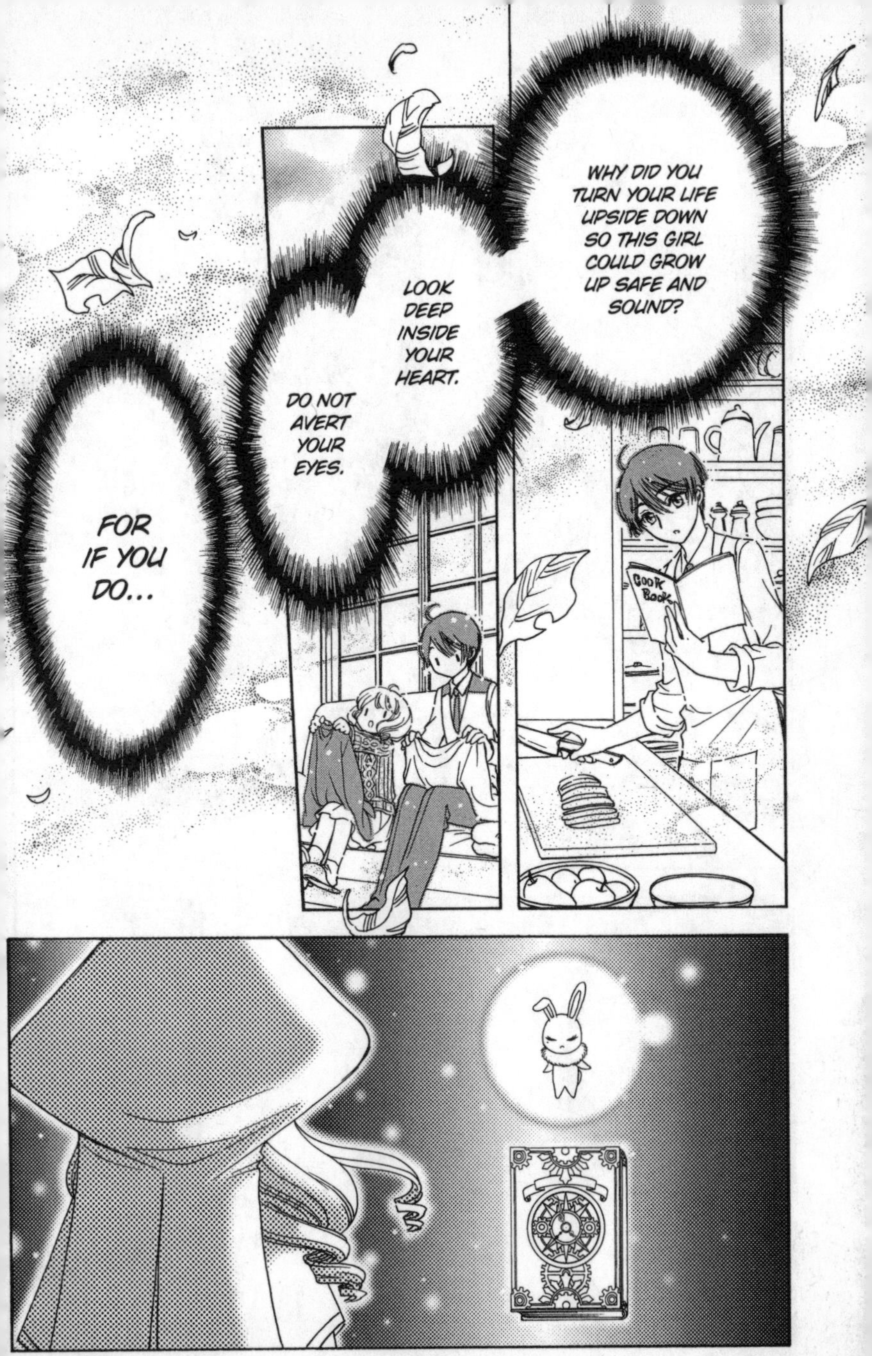
WHY DID YOU TURN YOUR LIFE UPSIDE DOWN SO THIS GIRL COULD GROW UP SAFE AND SOUND?
COOK Book
LOOK DEEP INSIDE YOUR HEART.
DO NOT AVERT YOUR EYES.
FOR IF YOU DO...

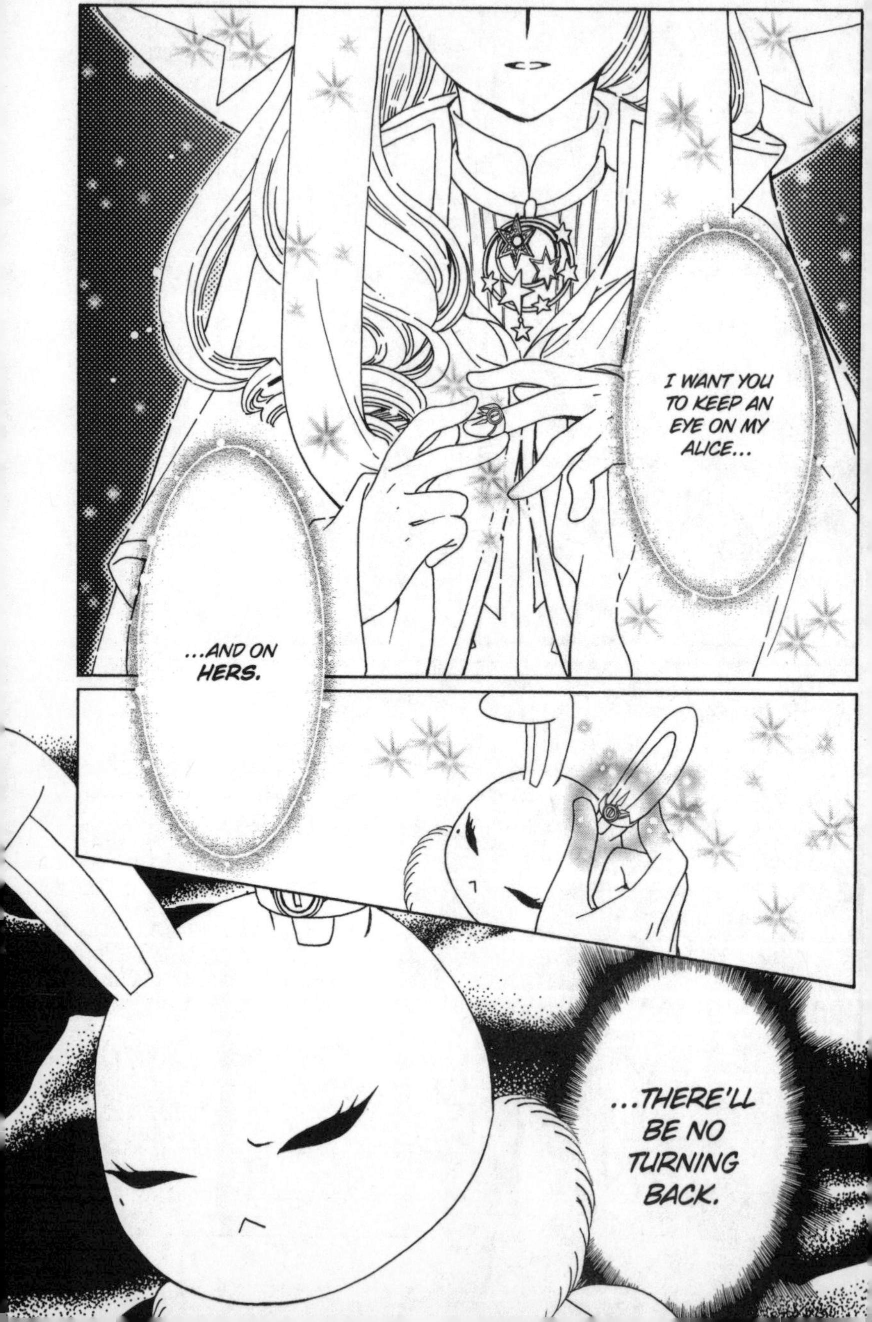
I WANT YOU TO KEEP AN EYE ON MY ALICE...
...AND ON HERS.
...THERE'LL BE NO TURNING BACK.

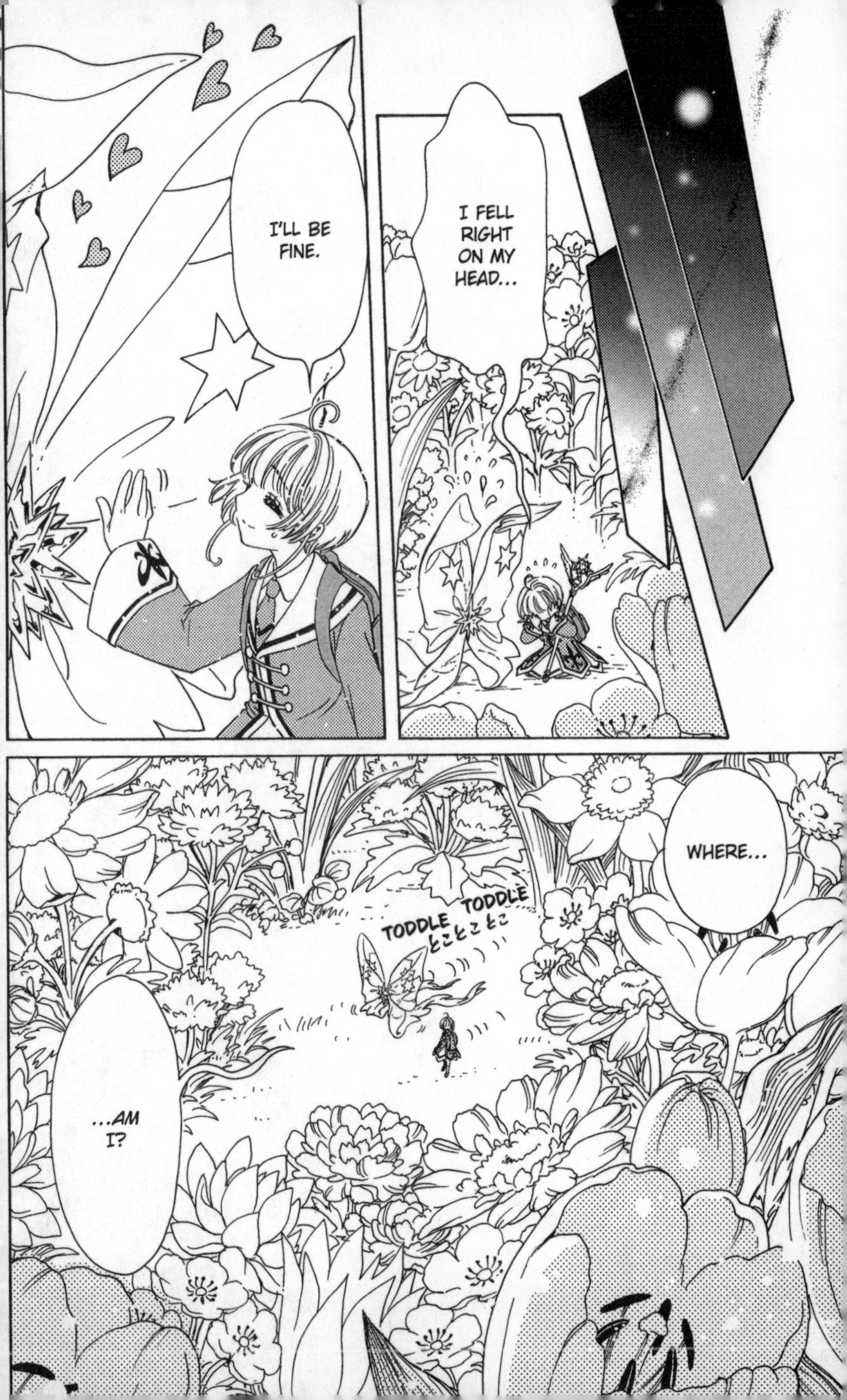
I FELL RIGHT ON MY HEAD...
I'LL BE FINE.
WHERE...
TODDLE TODDLE
とことことこ
...AM I?

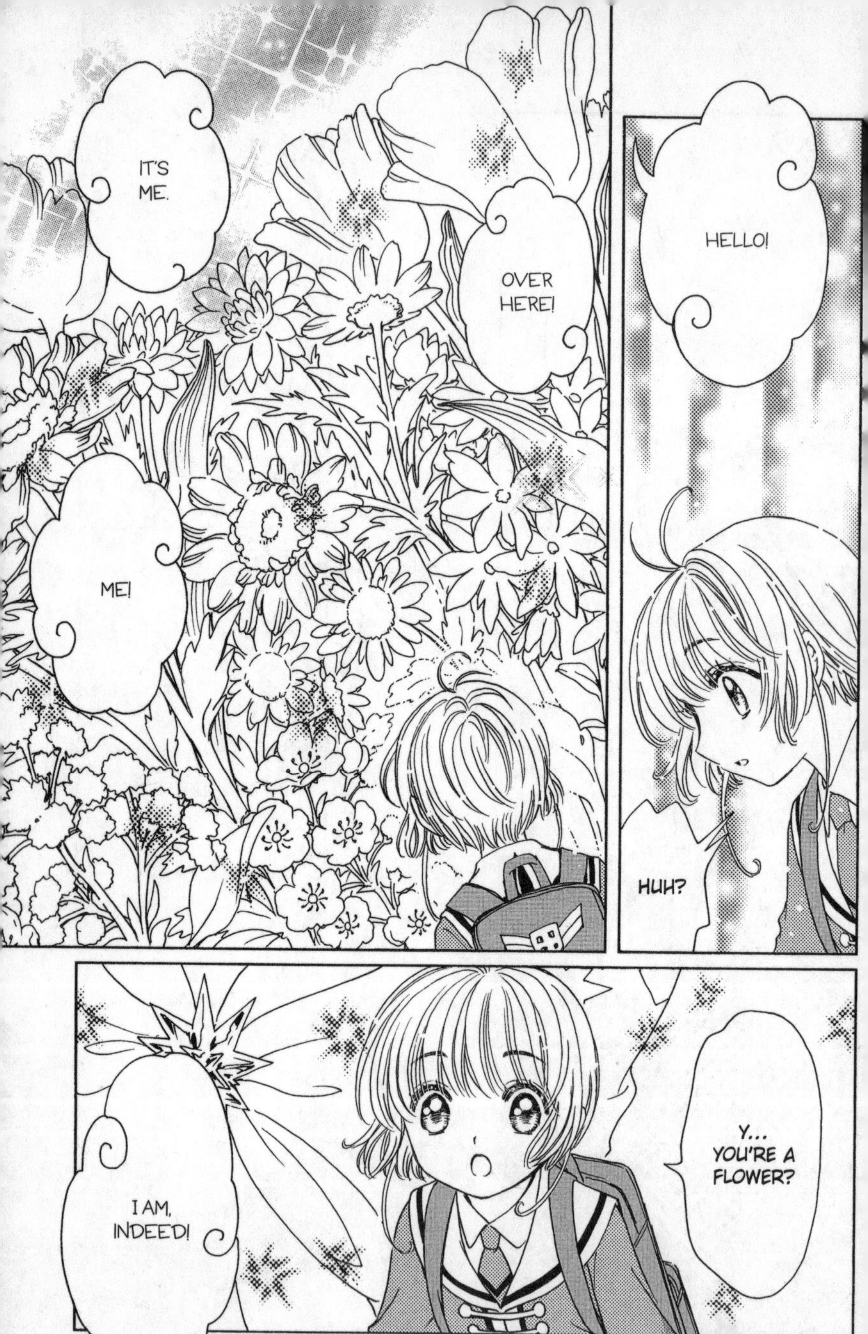
HELLO!
HUH?
OVER HERE!
IT'S ME.
ME!
Y... YOU'RE A FLOWER?
I AM, INDEED!

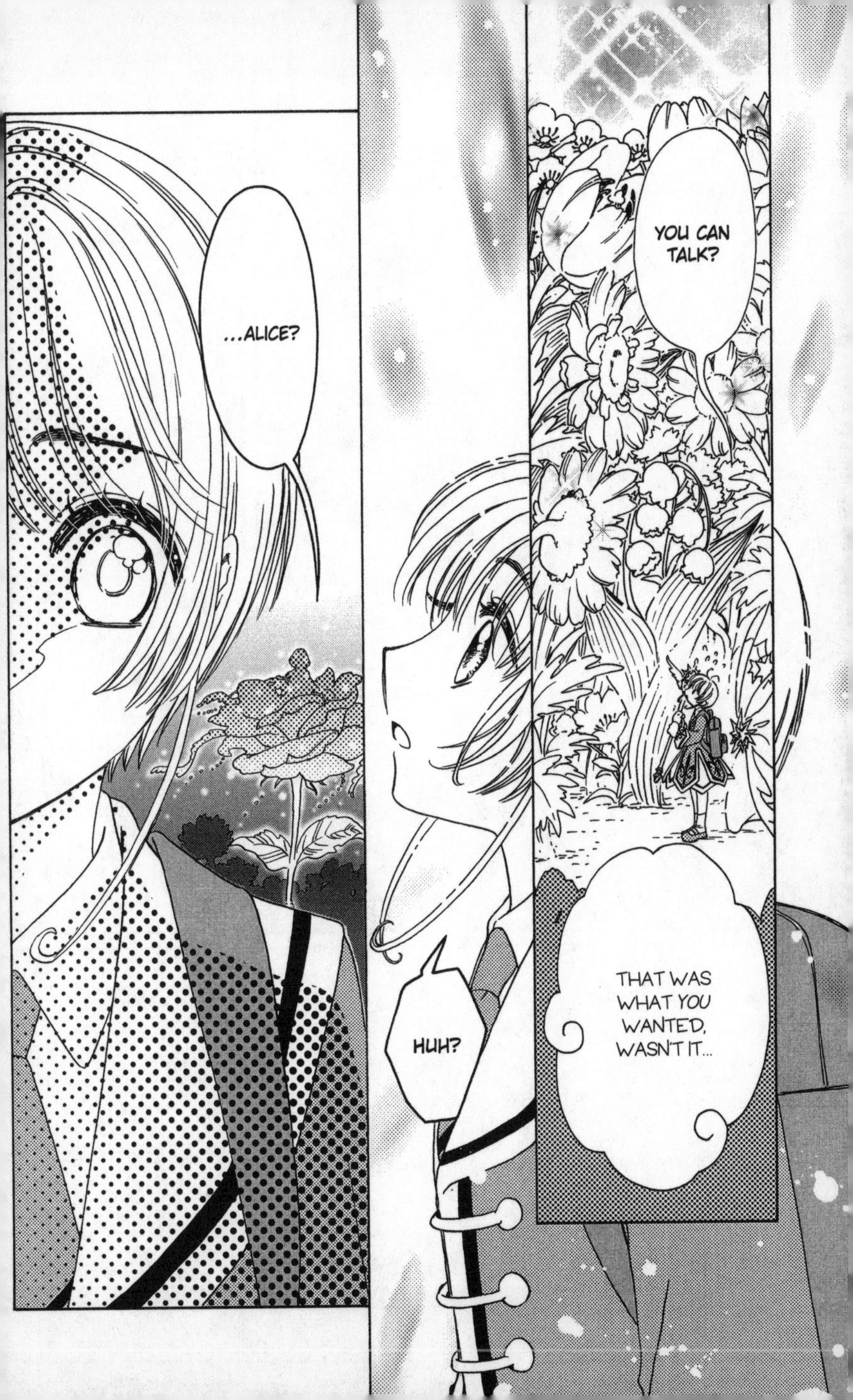
YOU CAN TALK?
THAT WAS WHAT YOU WANTED, WASN'T IT...
HUH?
...ALICE?

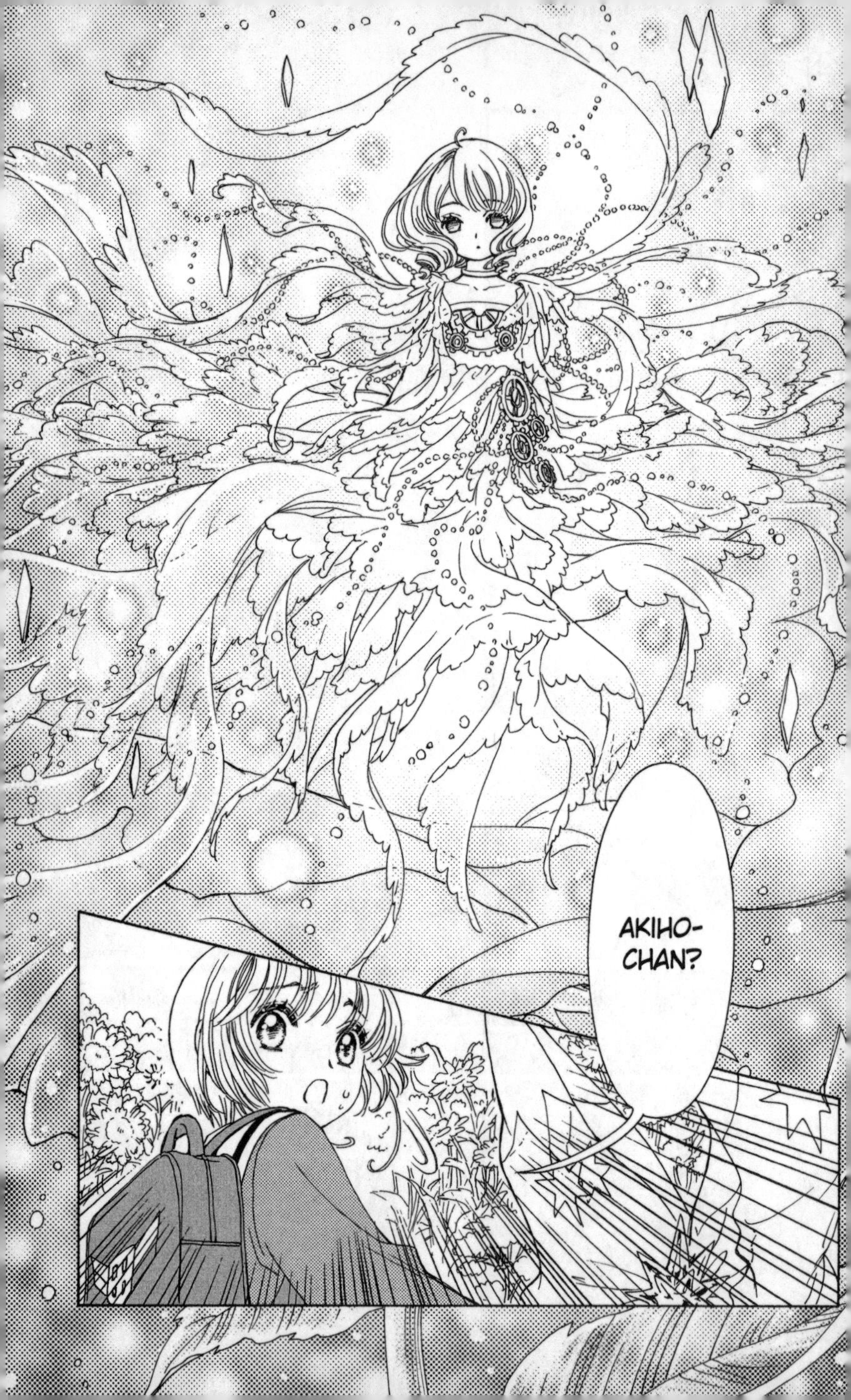
AKIHO-CHAN?

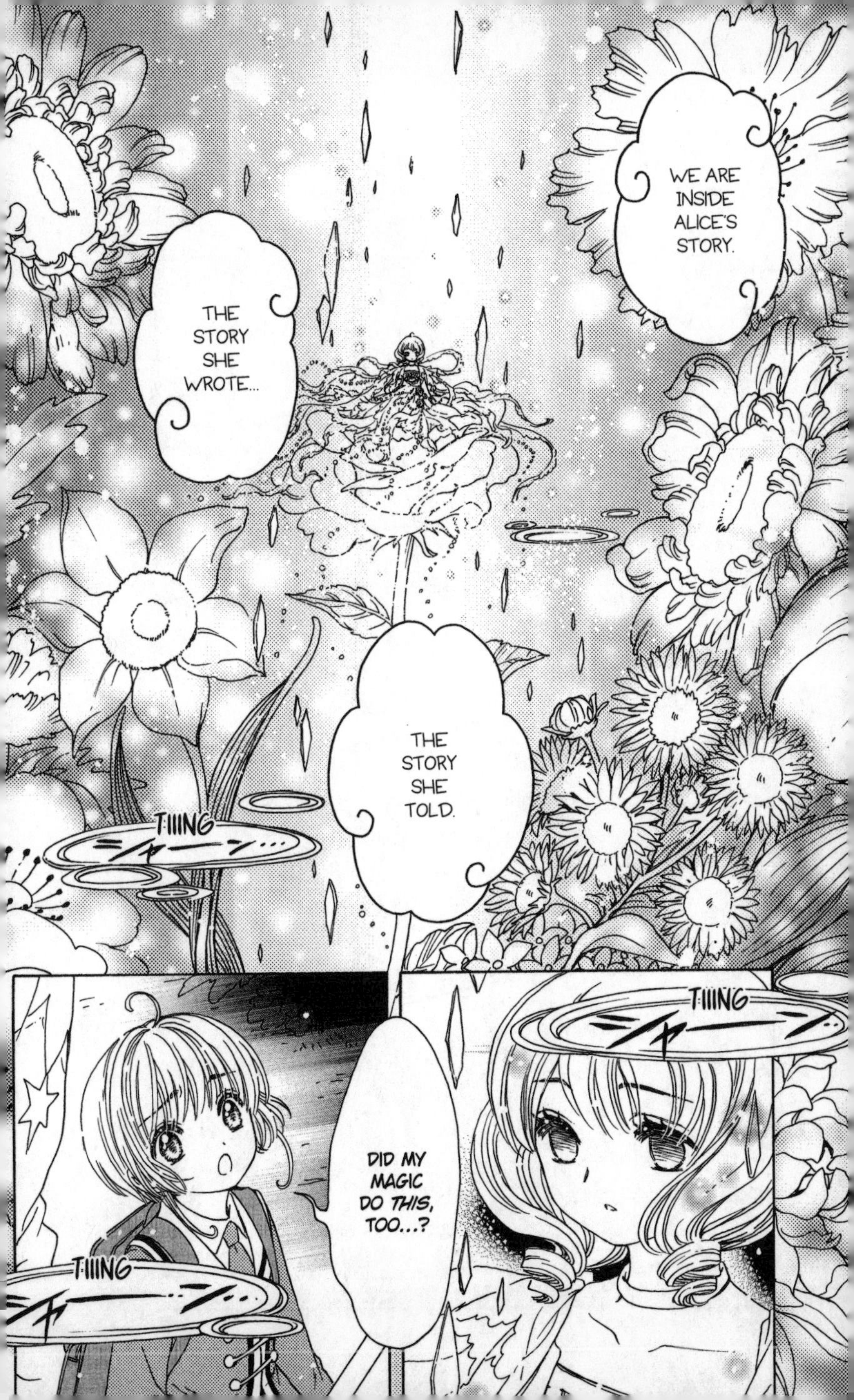
WE ARE INSIDE ALICE'S STORY.
THE STORY SHE WROTE...
THE STORY SHE TOLD.
TIIING
TIIING
DID MY MAGIC DO THIS, TOO...?
TIIING

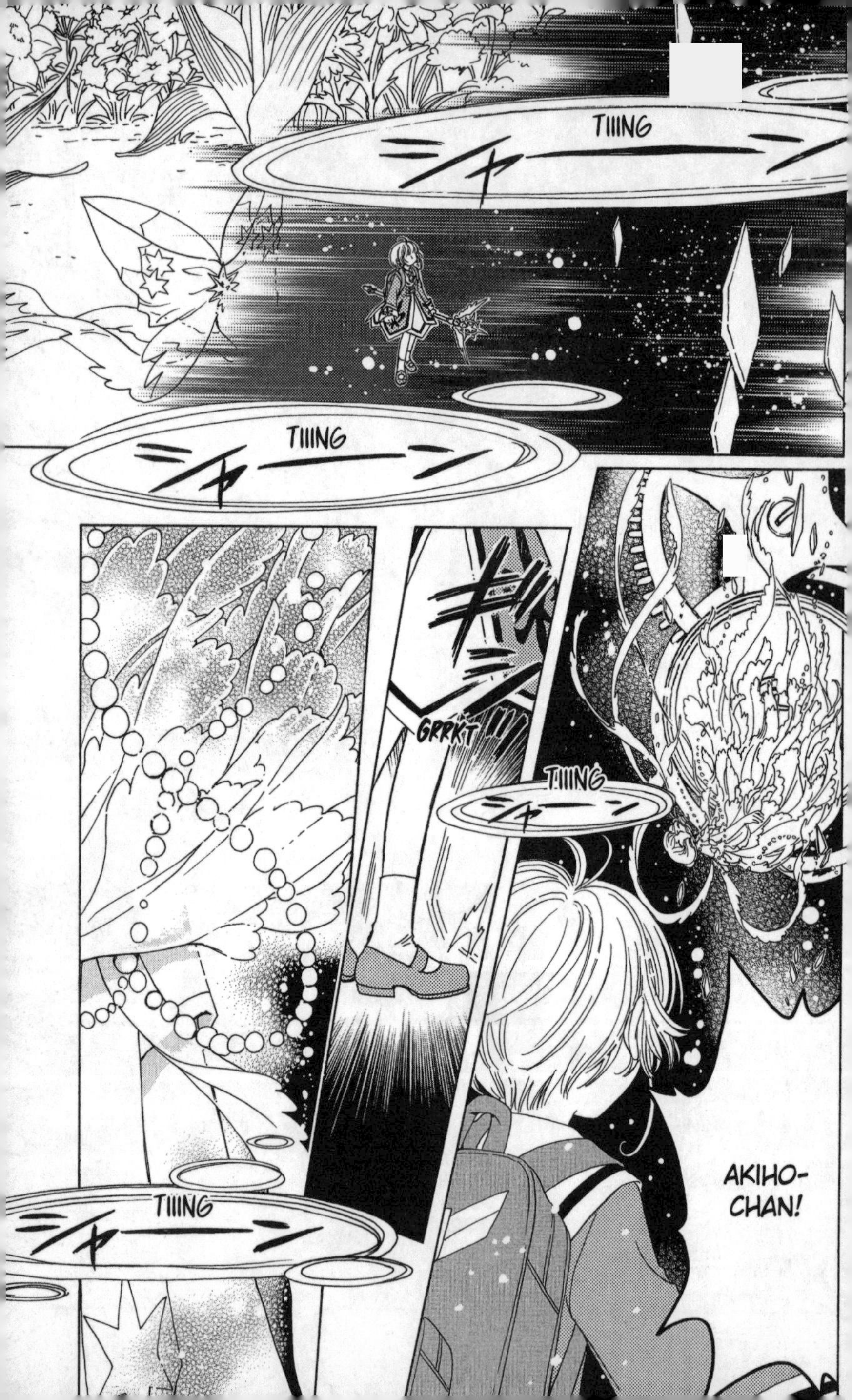
TIIING
TIIING
TIIING
AKIHO-CHAN!
GRRKT
TIIING

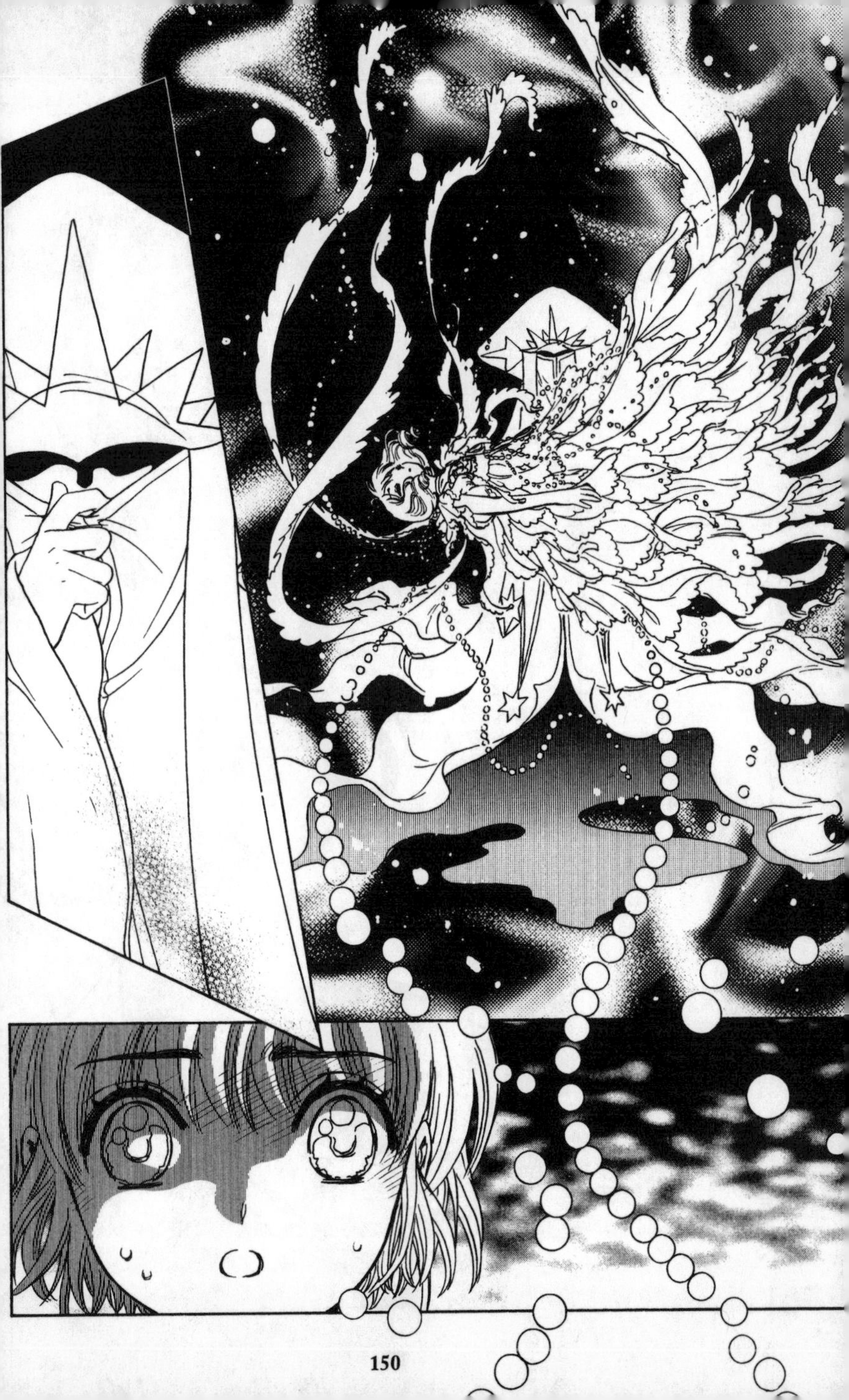

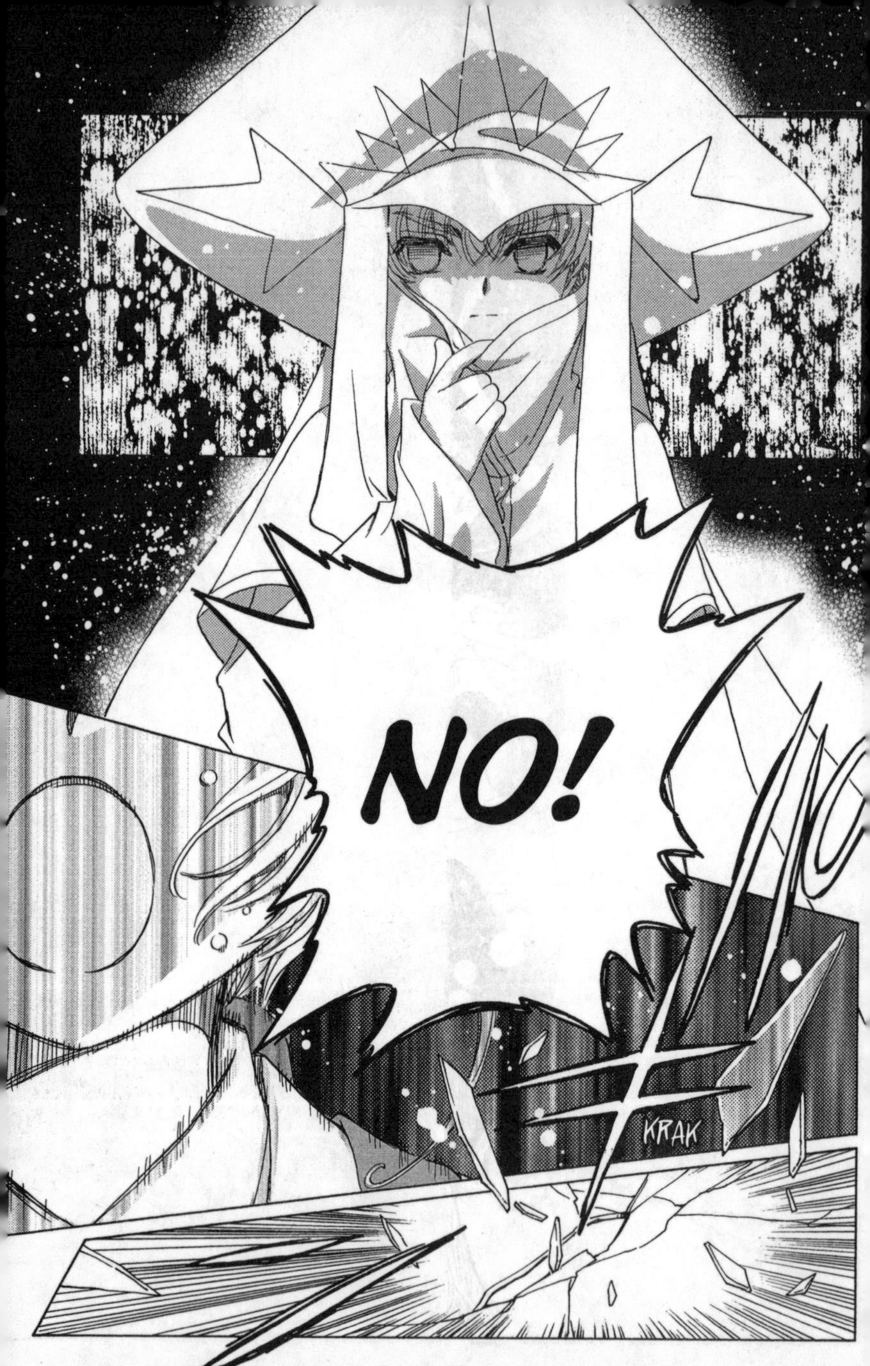
NO!
KRAK

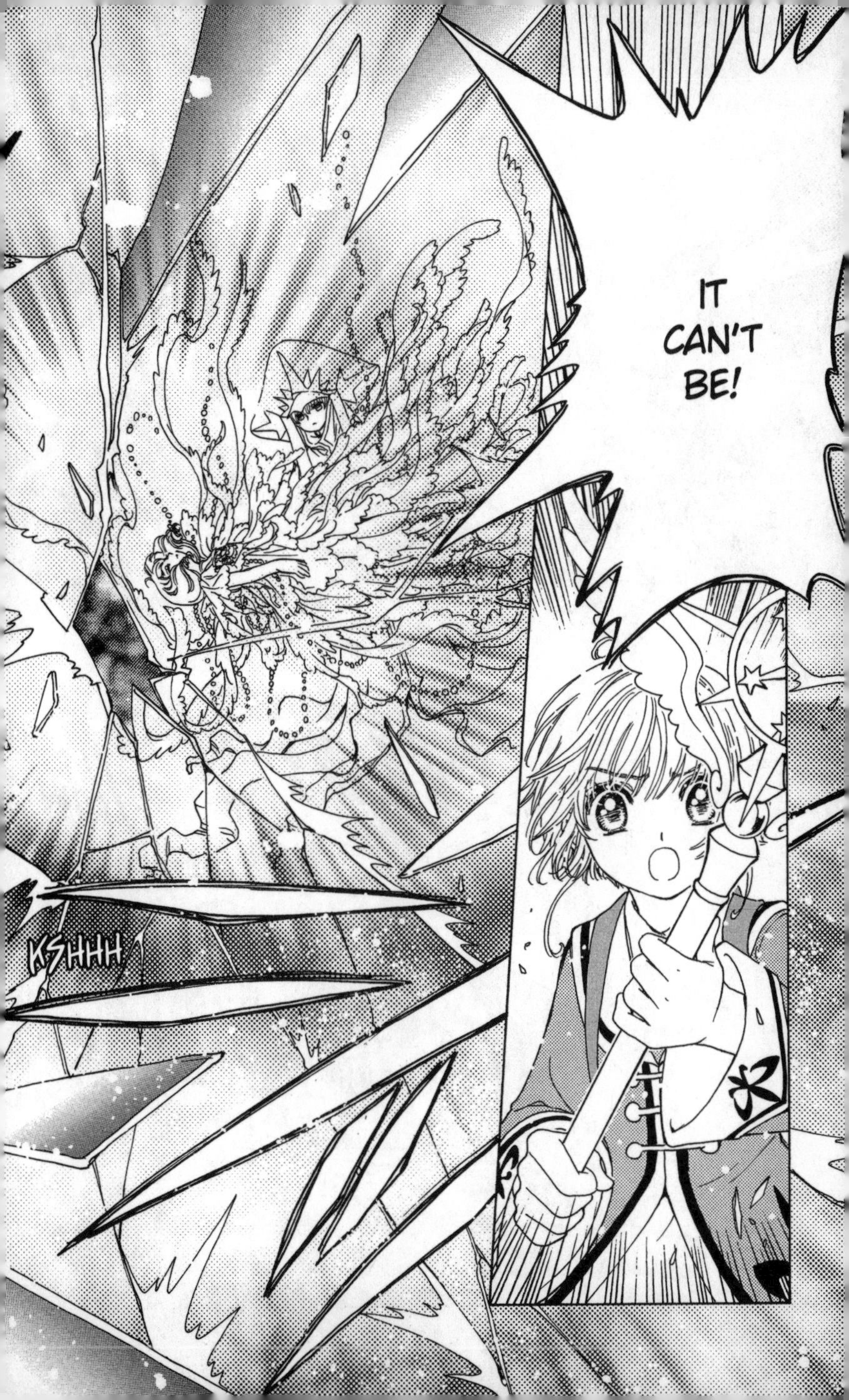

IT CAN'T BE!
KSHHH

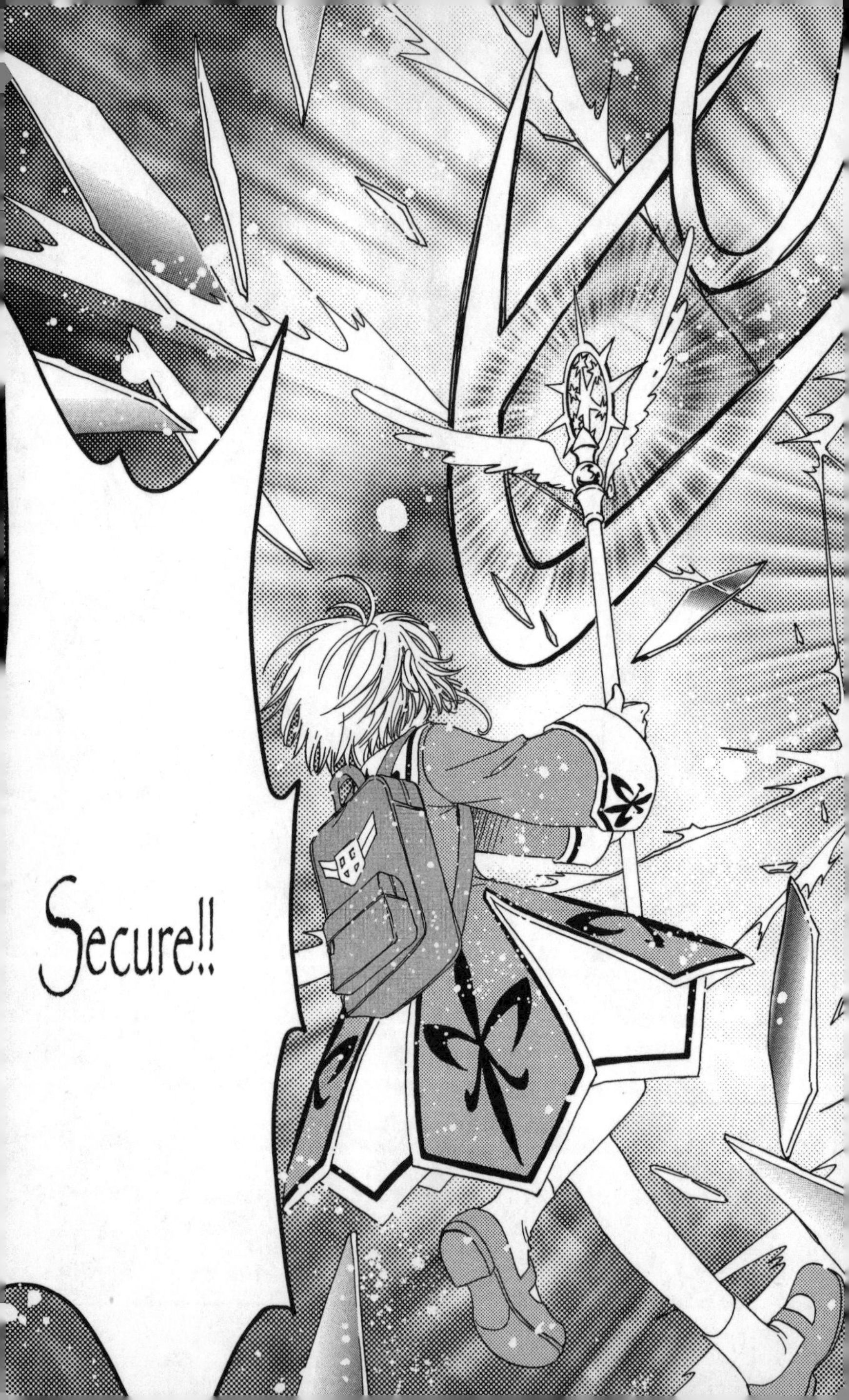
Secure!!

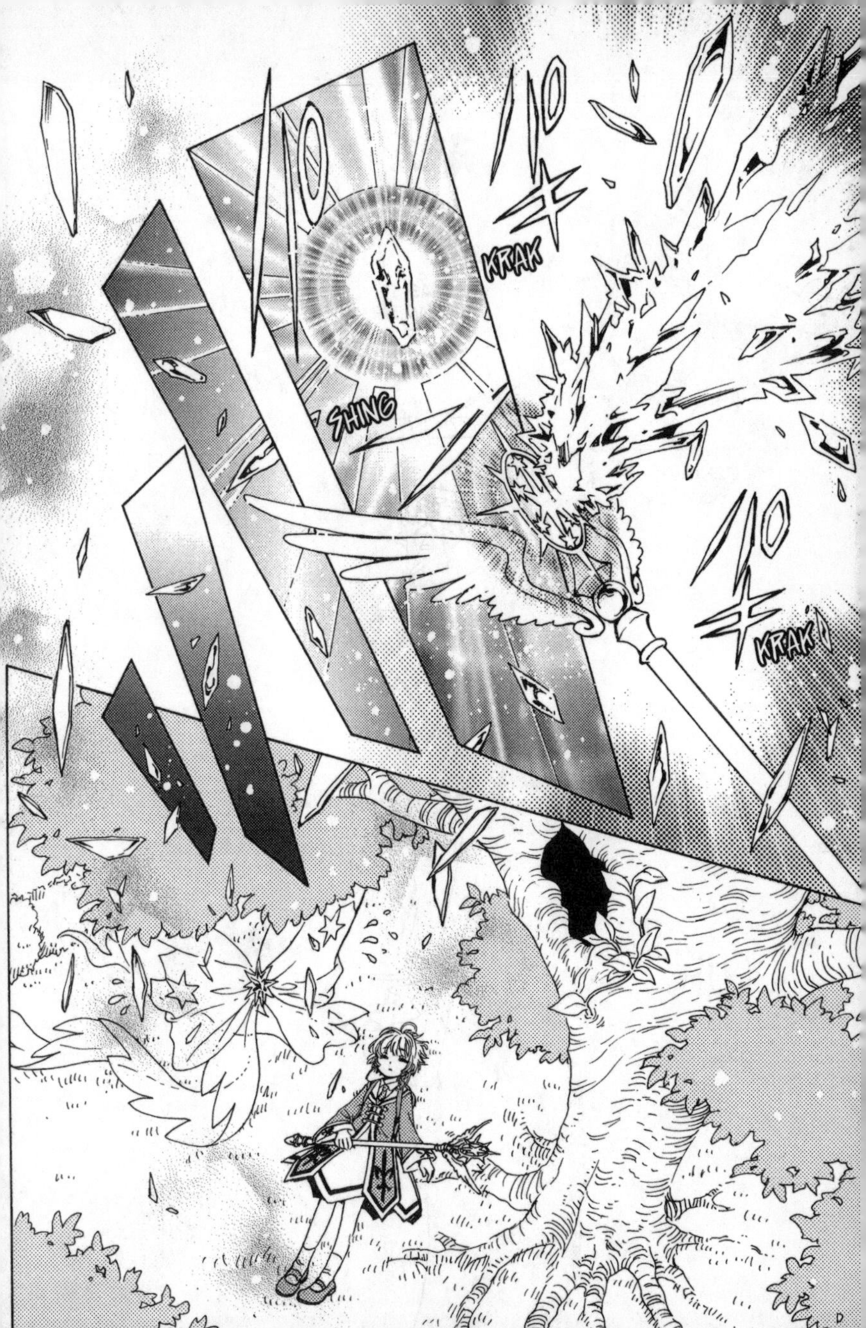
KRAK
SHING
KRAK

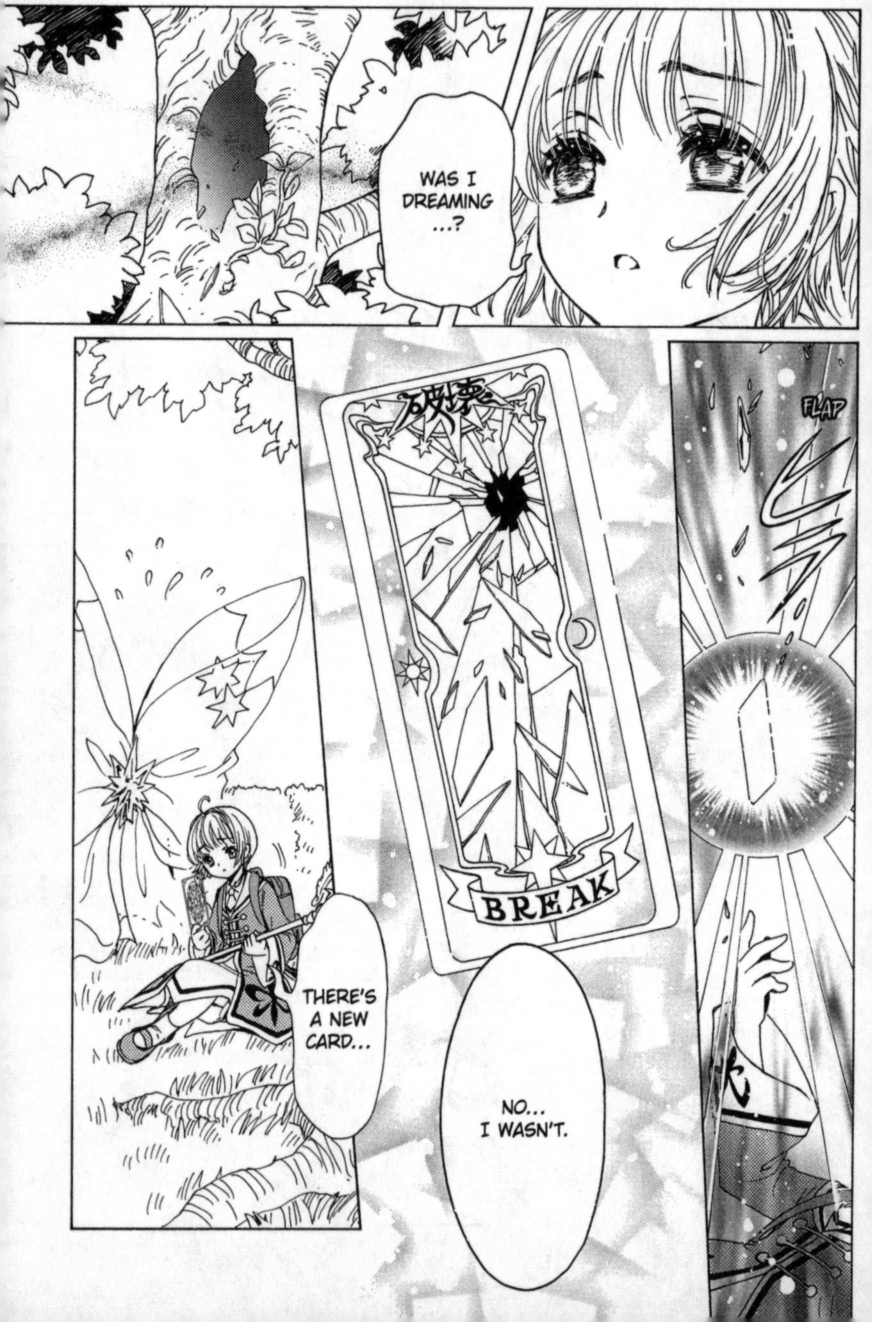
WAS I DREAMING...?
FLAP
破壊
BREAK
NO... I WASN'T.
THERE'S A NEW CARD...

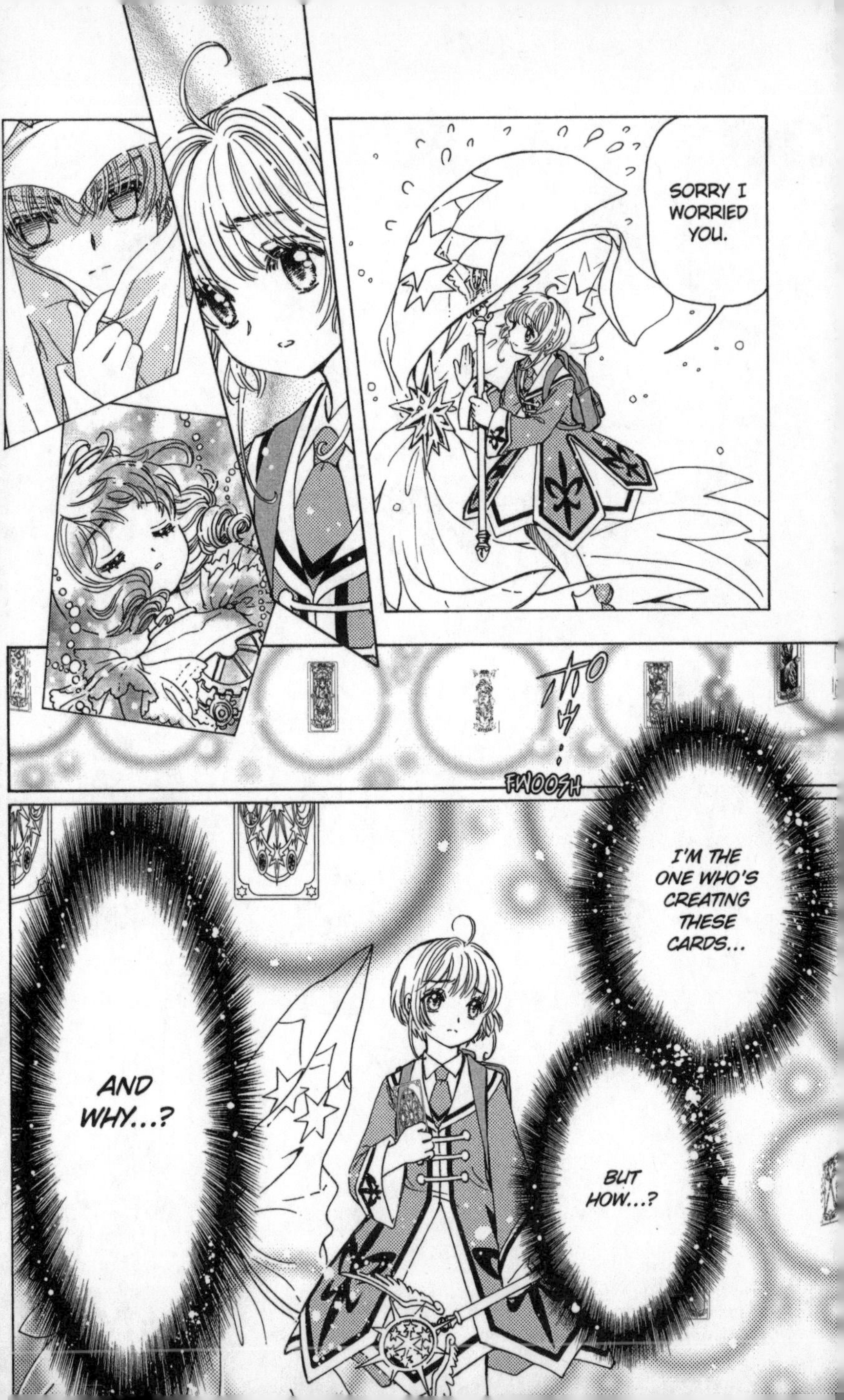
SORRY I WORRIED YOU.
FWOOSH
I'M THE ONE WHO'S CREATING THESE CARDS...
BUT HOW...?
AND WHY...?

🍀 Continued in Volume 9 🍀

THE MAGICAL GIRL CLASSIC THAT BROUGHT A GENERATION OF READERS TO MANGA, NOW BACK IN A DEFINITIVE, HARDCOVER COLLECTOR'S EDITION!

CARDCAPTOR SAKURA
COLLECTOR'S EDITION
C L A M P

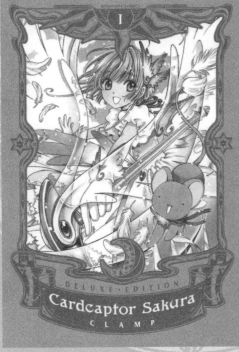

Ten-year-old Sakura Kinomoto lives a pretty normal life with her older brother, Tōya, and widowed father, Fujitaka—until the day she discovers a strange book in her father's library, and her life takes a magical turn...

- A deluxe large-format hardcover edition of CLAMP's shojo manga classic
- All-new foil-stamped cover art on each volume
- Comes with exclusive collectible art card

KC
KODANSHA
COMICS

One of CLAMP's biggest hits returns in this definitive, premium, hardcover 20th anniversary collector's edition!

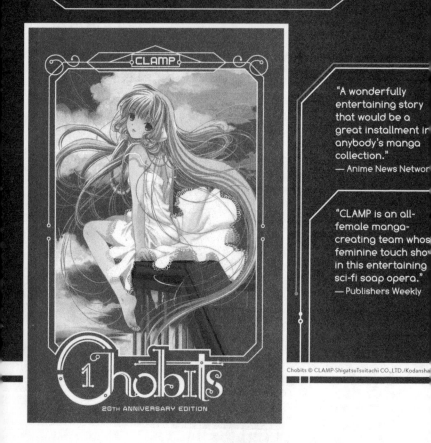

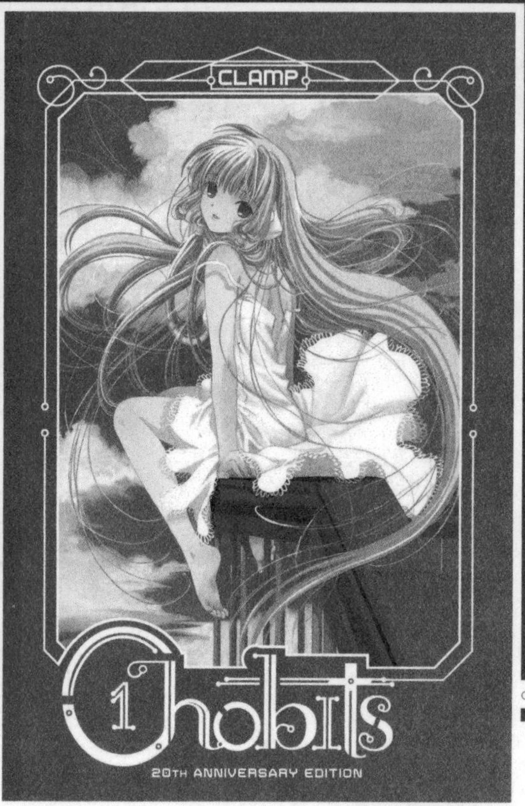
CLAMP
1 Chobits
20TH ANNIVERSARY EDITION

"A wonderfully entertaining story that would be a great installment ir anybody's manga collection."
— Anime News Networ

"CLAMP is an all-female manga-creating team whos feminine touch sho in this entertaining sci-fi soap opera."
— Publishers Weekly

Poor college student Hideki is down on his luck. All he wants is a good job, a girlfriend, and his very own "persocom"—the latest and greatest in humanoid computer technology. Hideki's luck changes one night when he finds Chi—a persocom thrown out in a pile of trash. But Hideki soon discovers that there's much more to his cute new persocom than meets the eye.

KC KODANSHA COMICS

Cardcaptor Sakura: Clear Card volume 8 is a w
places, and incidents are the products o
or are used fictitiously. Any resemblance
persons, living or dead, is entirely coinc

A Kodansha Comics Trade Paperback Original
Cardcaptor Sakura: Clear Card volume 8

Published in the United States by Kodansha Comics, an imprint of
Kodansha USA Publishing, LLC, New York.

Publication rights for this English edition arranged through Kodansha Ltd., Tokyo.

First published in Japan in 2020 by Kodansha Ltd., Tokyo, as
Kaadokyaputaa Sakura Kuriakaado Hen volume 8.

ISBN 978-1-63236-906-2

Printed in the United States of America.

www.kodanshacomics.com

9 8 7 6 5 4 3 2 1
Translation: Erin Procter
Lettering: Erika Terriquez
Editing: Tiff Ferentini and Alexandra Swanson
Kodansha Comics edition cover design: Phil Balsman

KODANSHA COMICS

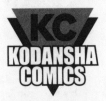

Publisher: Kiichiro Sugawara

Director of publishing services: Ben Applegate
Associate director of operations: Stephen Pakula
Publishing services managing editor: Noelle Webster
Assistant production managers: Emi Lotto, Angela Zurlo